Language Use and School Performance

Language Use and School Performance

Aaron V. Cicourel
UNIVERSITY OF CALIFORNIA, SAN DIEGO

Kenneth H. Jennings
UNIVERSITY OF CALIFORNIA, SAN DIEGO

Sybillyn H. M. Jennings
UNIVERSITY OF CALIFORNIA, SAN DIEGO

Kenneth C. W. Leiter
RICE UNIVERSITY

Robert MacKay
UNIVERSITY OF TORONTO

Hugh Mehan
UNIVERSITY OF CALIFORNIA, SAN DIEGO

David R. Roth
UNIVERSITY OF TEXAS, AUSTIN

Academic Press, Inc.

NEW YORK   SAN FRANCISCO   LONDON

A Subsidiary of Harcourt Brace Jovanovich, Publishers

ACADEMIC PRESS, INC.
111 Fifth Avenue, New York, New York 10003

United Kingdom Edition published by
ACADEMIC PRESS, INC. (LONDON) LTD.
24/28 Oval Road, London NW1

LIBRARY OF CONGRESS CATALOG CARD NUMBER: 74-19998

ISBN 0–12–174950–9

PRINTED IN THE UNITED STATES OF AMERICA

To Marvine, Nancy, and Suzanne

CONTENTS

ACKNOWLEDGMENTS

The study undertaken during 1969-1970 was made possible by a grant from the Ford Foundation's Division of Public Education. We are grateful to Marjorie Martus for her encouragement and advice during all stages of this study. Obviously, the study could not have been done without the help of the schools in Districts A and B, and we thank the administrators, teachers, and their parents for their receptiveness to our research. They have requested that they remain anonymous.

The children were the most cooperative and their flexibility allowed us to learn just about everything from them.

We are pleased to thank John Nelson for his help in gaining access to different schools. We want to thank Ishmael de la Rocha, Carla Haley, Yolanda Lopez, Ruth Roth, and Valerie Shaw for their outstanding research assistance. Debbie Dunkin and Philip Kuykendal helped by carefully transcribing tapes. We are grateful to Sybillyn Jennings and Hugh Mehan for their excellent assistance in preparing the manuscript for publication. Ken Jennings was especially helpful with advice and actual video-taping in one school, and provided constructive criticism throughout the study. Mrs. Colleen Carpenter was especially accurate and efficient in typing an earlier draft.

Our acknowledgments are brief, but their brevity should not detract from the fact that we received exceptionally cooperative assistance from many warm and generous people. We hope they all feel it was worth it.

Chapter 1
INTRODUCTION

Aaron V. Cicourel
University of California, San Diego

A basic theme of this report is that early school experience is probably the most important stage in a child's educational career. By the time a child has completed the first grade and is promoted (or pushed) into the second grade (roughly moving from infant school to junior school in Great Britain) a rather rigid bureaucratic tracking system is set into motion. Children may escape from this tracking (or streaming) system, but our experiences tell us that existing educational practices are likely to prevail that sustain the initial tracking. The child's ability to read and write becomes more and more of a necessity as he enters the second and third grades. The educational material employed presupposes reading and writing skills, while verbal instructions incorporate language constructions that presume knowledge gained from having read textual material. A child who cannot read and write at a level commensurate with classroom instructional materials in the first grade is unlikely to receive remedial help in the higher grades that will overcome his lack of skills. Schools are not financially endowed enough nor do they have personnel adequately trained to deal with children who enter the second grade with deficient reading and writing abilities. These skills are tied to a knowledge or proficiency with standardized language understanding and use. This study describes research on the acquisition and use of language at home and in the primary school. We seek to clarify everyday school decisions made by school personnel based on the child's performances in particular classroom and testing situations that influence the child's educational career early in life.

1

A central question addressed in our work includes how the child's world comes to be formulated and re-formulated by adults in educational settings by utilizing often uncorrelated data based on routine class-room lessons, educational testing, promotion inter-views, and teacher-administrative meetings.

We examined the school personnel's formulations of the child's abilities, progress, and potential by studying a number of elementary school educational settings and language systems. The educational set-tings included classroom lessions, psycholinguistic, reading, and intelligence testing sessions, and in-formal variations of formal tests presented in class and at home. We seek to show how basic research issues in sociolinguistics and cognitive sociology can clarify questions about language and social inter-action in everyday life that can be used to describe and understand serious problems in the education of the child.

While present educational philosophies recognize differences in the backgrounds of different children, they seldom acknowledge the necessity of developing a different curriculum and hiring teachers with more sophisticated skills. Because primary school edu-cational philosophy and programs are often unaware of recent advances in the study of language and cognitive development, it is difficult to absorb these findings into their curricula. Teachers are not being trained to handle children whose background requires a deeper knowledge of the relation between language and thought and a need for innovative shifts in teaching and evalu-ative procedures.

The above questions will be elaborated and ad-dressed in various ways in the following chapters. In this introduction I want to stress that many of the issues we examine are not new, but our approach is different in that we locate school problems and the education of teachers within a context that addresses basic questions and issues in everyday school life. We seek to learn about the child's experiences and his conceptions of a lived-in world through his oral

and non-oral expressions. Teaching programs do not
stress basic issues in language socialization such
as how the child attributes meanings in daily interaction with others or when attending to a text or a
written test. Our study of actual school settings
enabled us to address both basic research issues and
applied problems involving teaching philosophies, curriculum implementation, and the evaluation of children
as 'failing' or 'successful.'

The setting for our research was two school districts in the same area of southern California. The
population for the area in the 1970 census was approximately 130,000. The population of one school (School
A) was 50% white and 50% Chicano, and was situated in
a lower income area of the city. The population of
the other school (School B) was more evenly mixed
between Anglo, Black, and Chicano children, and was
located in an upper middle area but within walking
distance of lower middle and very low income areas
of the city. We were able to study two first-grade
classrooms in the two districts. We also were able to
spend considerable time in the kindergarten classes
of one district where we were especially fortunate
with the reception of our research. The actual research sometimes required daily participation in the
classroom where we observed, and often audio or videotaped, educational testing being done with children
from the first grades. We also selected a number of
Anglo, Black, and Chicano children from these classrooms and received permission from their parents to
observe and test them at home.

A few words about the type of study we did are
in order. We sought to make use of audio and video
equipment throughout the study to approximate a kind
of quasi-experimental control in the field setting
of the school. A central consideration was our interest
in maximizing the ways in which we could study an activity like a classroom lesson or a testing session.
This meant showing ourselves and the reader how a
lesson developed by the teacher or a test given to a
particular school population could be examined by

3

recognizing that different kinds of information are available in a lesson on spatial concepts in which the use of locatives would be employed (*under* the tree, *above* the line) prior to the teacher's presentation of the lesson to the class (see Mehan, Chapter 3). Then by observing and videotaping the presentation, we were able to interrogate the children afterwards about their understanding of the lesson. After several days, the teacher was interviewed about the lesson once again. She was first asked to reconstruct the lesson, its purposes and goals. Then she was shown a videotape of the lesson and was asked to describe aspects of the lesson, the children's performance during it, and her reactions toward it.

This research strategy has been called "indefinite triangulation" (Cicourel, 1973: 124 ff) because it provides details on how various interpretations of "what happened" are assembled from different physical, temporal, and biographically provided perspectives of a situation. Comparing the teacher's accounts of the lesson before and after it was presented, and comparing the teacher's version with those of the children produced different accounts of the "same" scene. It was sometimes difficult to recognize that the children and the teacher witnessed the same event. The children's responses during the lesson provided different conceptions of correct and incorrect answers which contrasted with the teacher's expectations stated prior to and subsequent to the lesson. The children seemed to receive and organize the lesson in terms of their own orientations at the time of the event, and these conceptions do not always match the teacher's account of the lesson's purpose and conduct.

In our analysis of testing situations (MacKay, Chapter 5,; Roth, Chapter 4; Mehan, 1971) we created a contrast between the official version of the meaning of test materials and the child's interpretation of these materials. The test is supposed to reveal the child's innate competence. The test assumes that other factors which might influence results are attributable to random errors or systematic biases that can be corrected. Hence the conditions which permit the adult to make sense of the test or lesson, and the knowledge required of the child to receive and recognize information relevant for taking the test or learning the lesson, are not made explicit to the child, nor are teachers and testers always aware of the importance of these features.

After standardized reading, intelligence, and language development tests were given to the first grade children in both schools, a small group of children were asked to explain their answers and to provide the reasons why they answered as they did. The children's accounts were then compared to the official versions provided by testing protocol. As in the classroom lesson situation, the children were not always attending to testing material in the way expected by the test protocol. Often this differential perception led the child to a wrong answer, which in turn led to a low test score. However, MacKay (Chapter 5), Mehan (1971), and Roth (Chapter 4) challenge the conclusion usually drawn from incorrect test scores: that the child being examined lacked particular abilities. Instead they suggest that it is necessary to examine the structure of the child's accounting practices and reasoning processes in order to draw valid inferences about his competence.

Our observation of teacher, tester, and children's performances in testing and classroom situations suggest that children do not always share the teacher's or tester's idea of what the lesson or test is about. Although both the adult and the child's conception of what is happening in a test or lesson is based on their background or experience, and prior strategies for dealing with such events, they do not draw the same substantive conclusion from the available materials. Hence, the informational context of lessons and tests influence both the child's performance and the teacher's, tester's, and researcher's inferences about the child's underlying competence.

Our research shows that what could be called 'errors' in responding to standardized curricula and tests may be the result of misunderstandings on the part of teachers, testers, and children, which are created by the inter- actional activities they are engaged in. Problems of attention, memory, dialect difference, incorrect guesses, and the like, emerge in educational interaction, but are not addressed as central ingredients of learning and evaluation that take place in the classroom. Treat- ing errors and misunderstandings as natural aspects of educational encounters would enable participants to have access to them and become less preoccupied with a rigid notion of what is right and what is wrong. Our materials show that the problem of what is right and wrong cannot be resolved by some absolute notion of a correct answer.

The implication of this observation may be better appreciated when it is recognized that the descriptions of what we claim to observe are always conducted from the particular vantage point and perspectives from which we receive, think about, and use information and lan- guage to describe what we claim to perceive. As re- searchers, lay-men or teachers, we make thousands of decisions each week based on many observations; but we rely on selective particulars of the situations we ob- serve which do not clearly document or justify courses of action. Our usual way of perceiving and arriving at decisions and courses of action, therefore, are central processes that must be understood if the practical aspects of our research on teaching activities are to be understood.

This means that the teacher, for example, must understand the children's learning problems in a context that includes classroom dynamics of noise, interruptions, absences, special dialects, bilingualism and the like. Correlational measures based on tra- ditional 'objective' tests are not adequate to handle these problems; most of these conditions are contextually based and seldom enter into the analysis of question- naires or psychological tests. New techniques using audio- and videotaped information are needed to capture the dynamics of interactional competence and interactional settings. In this study we provide a beginning in that direction.

6

SOME RESEARCH TROUBLES

Specific details describing the research setting will be supplied in each chapter to clarify for the reader the manner in which our research strategy was realized and the research conducted. Here I merely want to indicate some of the obstacles we encountered in attempting to do our study, as well as some of the difficulties that this type of research creates for the individuals whose help we needed. All field research is difficult and time-consuming. More time is often spent developing the appropriate conditions for carrying out the research and maintaining relationships for its continuation, than actually gathering research data. In one (District A) school district I developed and sustained contacts over a 2-year period during the tenure of two principals in the elementary school studied. Developing the appropriate contacts was made easier initially by one person in the Superintendent's office, the first principal, and two of the teachers in kindergarten and first grade. Considerable interest in the project was expressed at all times by those who agreed to participate. While most of the school was not interested in the study, personnel at various levels in this first district sustained a continuing interest in our research.

The second (District B) school district was something of a contrast. Making contacts proved difficult at all times except through one person in the Superintendent's office. I spoke to the principals but did not find many of them very encouraging. All agreed that the project was important and should be done, but many were concerned about the possibility of parental complaints, about taking children away from their classwork, and the feasibility of the study. After many months of discussions with a large number of personnel at different levels in the school district permission was finally granted.

Several months passed before interested doctoral students were included in the final research team. During this lapse of time, just a few weeks before we were to begin our field observations, I accidentally

7

met the new assistant superintendent. He made it clear that permission would have to be negotiated again. Another long series of negotiations was initiated. Finally, with the help of an assistant to the superintendent, I was allowed to give a lecture on the project to the first grade teachers of several elementary schools in District B. I hoped to convince them to allow us to participate in one of their classrooms. Although many teachers expressed an interest in the project and said it should be carried out, all of those present refused to become involved. They asked if participation was to be voluntary or if they were being 'told' to participate by the central office. When notified that the participation was voluntary, various excuses were offered. In the end, we gained entrance to a classroom because a teacher who had not attended the meeting but had only heard about it from a colleague agreed to participate. Many of the teachers told me after the meeting that the study would make them 'nervous' about what we might find. These teachers were concerned about being subjected to close observation on a day-to-day basis.

The teacher from District B proved to be exceptionally helpful, but her principal was worried that we might exceed what she felt were the the limitations outlined by the assistant superintendent. This concern on the part of the principal proved troublesome when we wanted to pursue the kindergarten aspect of the study. The kindergarten teachers were very cooperative, but the principal would not allow us to spend time in their classroom on a regular basis. Much of the work with the kindergarten teachers had to be done carefully so as not to appear to be overstepping the unclear bounds of the principal's conception of the study.

The point is that the kind of research we have done is acknowledged by administrators and teachers as *important*, yet there is little enthusiasm for our activities because the day-to-day workings of the classroom and administration may become exposed in ways that could be construed as damaging to the teacher and administration. Our efforts to understand educational

processes and evaluation procedures used by the school
necessitate the intimate cooperation of teachers and
school administrators. The fact that cooperation is
often not forthcoming makes (continual) research into
these important matters difficult. There is limited
enthusiasm among many teachers and administrators because the demands of research teams are not trivial.
The teachers must put up with the observations of the
researchers and this can bother many who are unsure
of themselves or feel they have a particulary "difficult" class. The administrators and teachers also
fear that the results of the study might damage their
reputation or bring about some kind of reprisals from
other administrators or parental groups in the community.

A central point that must be stressed here is that
the fears and concerns of teachers and administrators
are not conducive to the creation of a research atmosphere which can be beneficial to researchers, teaching,
and administrative personnel. If we are to minimize
these fears and concerns so that they do not become obstacles to improving school curricula, different testing instruments, and helping children, then the school
setting must become a laboratory wherein teaching
activities and research are integrated. Researchers
require the continual inputs of teachers and administrators if theoretical ideas are to be translated into
identifiable practical consequences that become tests
of the theories. New curricula cannot be created unless teachers, administrators, and researchers can
communicate their concerns and make these separate
interests part of the school's daily routine. The
creation of a laboratory atmosphere is necessary if
the usual suspicions that researchers arouse in the
cooperating group over the course of field work are
to be minimized so that 'mistakes' can be examined
openly as both data and sources of change. This goal
cannot occur unless teachers and administrators become part of the research process. Favorable research
conditions are essential for the research to proceed
and for the integration of findings into the

improvement of educational practices.

In one of the schools studied, the teacher became sufficiently integrated into the research setting so that she could be aware of some of her problems in the classroom, sort out which ones were inevitable, and with our help attempt some changes.

A problem in doing field studies is that they are not often funded by government agencies who give money for research in education. A strong educational psychology bias demands that only certain research strategies be used to ensure presumed "rigorous" controls, sampling conditions, and "objective" measurements of the activities studied. Most of these "rigorous" studies miss their intended goal because they are so inflexible vis-a-vis what is to be called data and how these data are to be collected. The present study was turned down for funds by the U. S. Office of Education because of objections to our "sampling" and the absence of questionnaire type measurement techniques considered to be "objective." We were told that the ideas were very interesting and imaginative, but that changes in the research design were necessary. Our response is that the measurement techniques asked for merely mask the dynamics of interaction which we believe are central to the study of classroom and testing performance.

We think that the large gap between teachers' practices and researchers' findings is for the most part due to the teachers' inability to see the relevance of these so-called traditional "objective" measures for understanding daily problems in the classroom. The teacher seldom knows how to evaluate the simple correlational relationships presented, nor can the teacher understand how test scores are related to the child's performance in class on tasks that are embedded in interactional settings the testing situations eliminate or ignore. We shall see in later chapters that the interactional contexts are an important source of information about the child's reasoning and social abilities.

THE USE OF AUDIO-VISUAL MATERIALS IN FIELD RESEARCH

In the chapters that follow we present materials derived from transcripts of classroom and testing interaction or interviews. The transcripts were created from the soundtracks of audio- or videotapes recorded in classrooms, homes, and meetings. The brief remarks that follow outline a few points to clarify the procedures used and the troubles encountered in video-taping, assembling transcripts, and analyzing materials. A more detailed account is given in Mehan's Chapter 3.

Our interest in using video tapes stemmed from a desire to make explicit some of the conditions that are masked in traditional sociological and educational psychological research where surveys, tests, and field and interview notes are the basis for presenting findings. We feel that the audio-visual materials help clarify the basis for many of the measurement decisions routinely made in social and behavioral science research.

We used a tripod-mounted Sony camera (AV 3200) with a wide-angle lens connected to a Sony half-inch video-recorder (AV 3600). The T. V. monitor used in the recording also enabled us to allow children to view themselves after their participation. Teachers and testers could be interviewed about the lessons and tests they gave (as outlined previously in describing the indefinite triangulation procedure). The camera was set up in full view of the participants so that its presence was explicit and could be routinized as part of the daily activities. Having the video equipment in full view of the participants meant that we were limited in how much of a setting we could capture, depending on the lesson of the day or the kinds of activities that different groups performed. Locating the recipient of a teacher's or child's remarks often required difficult camera moves, while individual voices were often unidentified if the camera was focused on one part of the room.

The use of video equipment did not eliminate the

usual problems of field research whereby the selective attention of the researcher's observations and notes truncate severely the interactional settings available for study. But the equipment enabled us to focus on many details of interaction that are missed in participant observer studies and simultaneously made us aware of the enormous problems of describing what appeared as routine classroom and testing activities. Even with several researchers available and necessary for video recording and independent observations and field notes, it became obvious to us that traditional field studies cannot capture the subleties of emergent social interaction. It is difficult to monitor how accounts are created by participants during and after some episode.

All of us became acutely aware of the difficulties of assembling a transcript from the video tapes because of the disjuncture that exists between what can be seen and what is heard. Having the audio part of the video tape copied for transcription with a heavy-duty tape recorder makes it easier to actually assemble a transcript but this procedure can distort the meaning of the materials depending on how one decides to analyze the transcript. Paying close attention to the video activities means that a linguistic or conversational data base will ignore many of the important features of the picture that are necessary for understanding the structure of the interactional scene. Having observed the video-recorded scene means that the observer will continually add information from his memory of the setting to enhance or alter the impression possible from the transcript. But we were all selective in the kinds of materials we included or excluded from the analysis of some setting, and, of course, this general problem turns out to be the central issue in how a study is to be described for a reader. It is difficult to show how the selective nature of our research accounts simplifies the phenomena addressed while simultaneously providing the impression of 'completeness' because of the global nature of the language used.

The use of audio-visual materials provides the
reader with a basis for evaluating the researcher's
procedures and claims to knowledge if the assembly
of a data base and its analysis become a problematic
feature of the findings reported. In this study we
have tried to provide the reader with information
about these problems while trying to underline the
fact that the substantive problem facing the teacher
and tester involves a similar set of issues. The
classroom lesson is too diffuse and the testing situation is too reified for making inferences about the
child's abilities and performances. This report
attempts to highlight these methodological issues
while addressing the substantive problems in a setting
that preserves the contextual quality of routine classroom and testing activities.

OVERVIEW AND CONCLUDING REMARKS

In Chapter 2 Leiter notes how the school's screening practices for grouping kindergarten children relies
on testing procedures and decisions that are situationally organized, yet the teachers' reports of these
judgments are described as context free. School officials do not view the contingencies of the child's
performance as constitutive of the judgments made
about underlying competence. The background characteristics of the child are seen as negative evidence for
supporting the deficiencies noted in the placement
interview with the child.

The teachers are not trained to make assessments
of linguistic and cognitive performance, hence their
attributions of comptence depend on their experiences
with other children of a similar age. The evaluations
are difficult to describe and do not readily articulate
with principles of child development and growth. The
teachers are often forced to rely on common social
stereotypes for categorizing children into ability
groups.

Mehan in Chapter 3 shows how the teacher and child
can arrive at different interpretations of a classroom

lesson because of the complexity of the interactional situation. The child's conception of location is seen to have a variable quality that the simple designation of a correct or incorrect response does not capture. Mehan shows how the features of the interaction scene contribute to judgments of 'correct' and 'incorrect' answers in the lesson.

The material examined by Roth in Chapter 4 demonstrates that the reasoning abilities of the child who receives a low test score can be seen as similar to the child who obtains a high test score. But responses to test items do not permit judgments about the child's reasoning ability. Roth's analysis of audio and video materials shows that all of the children could produce elaborate cross-referenced interactions, regardless of test scores. Hence, all children had abstract understandings of the items far in excess of those indicated by their test score.

The test does not allow teachers or testers to make independent judgments about reasoning ability, because only a numerical tabulation representing the child's answers is available. The child's answers may be based on different cultural experiences, but the test can never reveal such differences. An understanding of the child's competence requires that we at least recognize the complexity of the interactional setting which produces test results.

In Chapter 5 MacKay further documents the observations made by Mehan and Roth by examining a group-administered reading test employed by school districts throughout the state of California. He demonstrates the test fails on its own terms. The group test is even more likely to mask the child's reasoning ability than the individualized test or classroom lesson. The materials that MacKay discusses reveal the contingent character of the test for the child. The test does not reflect the child's classroom learning experiences. The child's reasoning strategies for decoding the meaning and intent of the task he is asked to do are hidden from review by the teacher and tester.

Jennings and Jennings in Chapter 6 are concerned

with how our methods for describing what children know can be attributed to differences in what they call target and frame abilities. They describe methodological problems encountered in attempting to study the child's comprehension of active and passive sentences. Each sentence was read to two subjects (a boy and a girl) by the experimenter. The children were to act out the sentences according to the instructions contained in the sentence. Jennings and Jennings show how the experiment fails to reveal observations and reasoning by the child that occur during the experimental session. These data normally do not become part of the researcher's data. Similar problems emerged when seven cards were presented to a 4½ year-old child to study her pictorial representation of action sequences and their verbal description. Jennings and Jennings underline the significance of the experiment and school testing as social occasions, despite the great care given to controlling what is done with the child.

Cicourel in Chapter 7 examines the issue of language use in classroom and testing situations as a complex information-processing system in which the child and the teacher or tester must deal with various kinds of materials and tasks. He points out that understanding the child's awareness of visual or nonverbal acoustical information, his conceptions of what is happening in tests or lessions, the side games he indulges in with classmates, his differential attentiveness to different settings, requires a notion of interactional competence (Cicourel, 1973; Mehan, 1972) that incorporates principles from theories of language acquisition, cognitive processing, and social interaction. Especially important for comprehending the role of interactional competence in classroom and testing situations is the child's and adult's cross-modal integration of information within a socially emergent setting. The child and teacher must reflexively recognize and use multiple sources of information including body movement, nonverbal acoustical materials, as they interact with their language abilities in these socially organized settings.

Our studies stress that changes in the classroom

and in testing situations cannot come about unless we
are willing to recognize the poverty of existing theories
of education and the bureaucratic expediency of classroom and testing procedures. We are still training
teachers and using psychological tests based on verbal
learning theories that have not incorporated recent work
on language acquisition, cognitive processes, and interactional competence. The evaluative procedures now used
in schools naively presume that adequate 'objective'
instruments exist for making judgments about the child's
performance and his underlying competence. These claims
of objective conditions are achieved by ignoring or
minimizing the significance of the child's information
processing activities in complex social settings, and
the situationally relevant features that emerge in the
classroom and in testing activities. Objectivity is
claimed in standardized testing conditions by holding
constant or eliminating cultural background conditions
and socially relevant features. These so-called objective measures do not recognize that each child's
performance is a product of each child's conception of
his own language abilities and social understanding as
they interface with the natural intrusions and contributions of the learning or testing setting as socially
defined by adults.

Chapter 2
AD HOCING IN THE SCHOOLS:
A STUDY OF PLACEMENT PRACTICES IN THE KINDERGARTENS
OF TWO SCHOOLS

Kenneth C. W. Leiter
Rice University

OVERVIEW

In this Chapter I am concerned with the placement
of students in particular classes. I will examine the
practices teachers use to assign students to classes
having particular characteristics, to place them in
ability groups within classes, and to promote them to
the next grade. I investigated these practices in two
kindergarten classes in two southern California school
districts. In Chapter 6, Jennings and Jennings raise
two issues which set the stage for this examination of
placement practices. They are: (1) An essential
feature of psycholinguistic research is that the researcher imposes adult models of reasoning and interactional comptence on the child; and, (2) educators
subscribe to the idea that the teacher's direct experiences with the student in the classroom are both
insufficient and misleading when used to evaluate the
student's abilities. These issues form a context for
the present study of placement practices because I am,
in effect, addressing the question, *"What are the
assessment practices used by teachers which organize
their daily experiences with the student?"* The
examination of these practices leads me to deal with
the adult models used by the teacher to accomplish
and sustain the factual properties of the students as
social objects.

The student in the elementary school is not simply
a student. He or she is a mature or immature student,
a bright average, or slow student. These *"facts"*
about students are of considerable import to teachers.
They help determine the student's school career. In

17

contrast to conventional sociology which takes such facts about students (usually in the form of statistics showing how many *"kinds"* of students go to college or high school) as the starting point of a discussion of the relation of the school system to the social system, I will employ the ethnomethodological perspective in this paper. From this point of view I will consider "the objective reality of social facts as an ongoing accomplishment of the concerted activities of everyday life" (Garfinkel, 1967: vii). Accordingly, both tracking systems as well as the kinds of students in the schools will be conceived of as the products of socially organized activities of school personnel.

During the last few years a continuing debate has been taking place among educators to determine whether classes should be organized heterogeneously or homogeneously. The arguments have concerned the practice of ability grouping (Ekstrom, 1959; Olson, 1967) and the "best" learning environment for bright, average and slow students. "This practice ability grouping rests on the assumption that bright children learn more when they are separated from their slower peers and grouped for instructional purposes with other bright children (Olson, 1967: 201)."

I do not intend to enter this debate in this chapter. Instead, I intend to ask how schools place students given they have decided to follow one or the other form of classroom organization. The question will not be whether or not the students are being placed correctly or whether one form of organization is better. Instead the question will be: *How* are students placed? I choose to address this question rather than enter the debate because, while the arguments on both sides seem to be equally convincing, neither side talks about the manner in which students are placed into groups in either system.

I do not mean to imply that there have not been other studies done in the area of tracking and teacher evaluation of students. Parsons (1969), in a paper describing the classroom as a social system, makes the point that the evaluations of students' performance

18

made by the teachers are crucial in determining the future status of the students. Rosenthal and Jacobson (1968) propose that teachers' expectations of students performances affect the students' achievement on IQ tests. Coleman (1958) argues that the tracking systems or ability groupings in the schools are designed to counteract the values of the adolescent subculture which interferes with students' performance and achievement. However, none of these studies examine the interaction between teachers (and other school officials) and children to see how placement decisions are made. Only one study even attempts to describe the evaluation activity and placement practices to see how they create student careers—*Educational Decision-Makers* (Cicourel and Kitsuse, 1963).

There are two respects in which this study of placement practices differs from those mentioned above. First, although the studies by Parsons (1969), Coleman (1968) and Rosenthal and Jacobson (1968) are ostensibly concerned with the school and raise the issue of the teachers' evaluations of their students, none of them study classroom processes. Neither Parsons nor Rosenthal and Jacobson describe the form of teacher expectations or how they are used to interpret the behavior of students. Coleman's data on adolescent subculture consists of answers to questionnaire items, not analysis of classroom interaction. The present study, on the other hand, is based on observation of classroom interaction as well as teachers' accounts of their students. Second, while the study by Circourel and Kitsuse (1963) comes the closest to the approach taken here because they attempted to study the evaluation process itself, they did not have access to the counseling sessions between the high school counselors and their students. In this study I not only obtained accounts by the teachers evaluating their students, I also recorded screening interviews between kindergarten teachers and incoming kindergarten students which formed the basis for placing students into one of two homogeneous kindergarten classes at one of the schools studied.

19

After an ethnographic description of the two kindergartens, this study of placement practices is divided into two parts. First, I describe those specific settings in which the kindergarten teachers are either actively placing students or gathering information used for that purpose. The placement settings at School A discussed in this part are the screening interviews used for separating incoming students into 'mature' and 'immature' classes, and how students are placed into first grade classes. In this subsection I will discuss the elicitation practices used by the teacher to negotiate the screening interviews and the role of these practices in the placement of students, the situated character of the screening results, the accomplished facticity of the interviews and the negotiation of placement of kindergarten students into first grade by the principal and the two kindergarten teachers.

The placement settings at School B I will discuss are the formation of ability groups through the use of routine activities of the classroom as a scheme of interpretation and the promotion of students into the first and junior first grades. Topics discussed in this subsection include: the continual use of informal testing, and the use of social types and practical circumstances in placing students.

The second part of the study describes the placement practices and their features or properties. By 'placement practices' I mean members' methods of inquiry used to assign students to classes and ability groups. These are socially organized activities through which students are identified and placed at various levels of the school or classroom. In this section I will discuss three placement practices: the use of social types to identify and interpret student's behavior; the Ability Group Track; and the Personality Track. We shall see that the use of social types forms the basis for the other two practices which are specific to each school. The use of social types as a placement practice will be examined within the context of these school-specific (and hence situated) placement practices.

20

The study begins with a description of the two schools
and their kindergartens.[1]

THE SETTING
School A

School A is an elementary school with grades
kindergarten through six and a student body of 420
students. Of this number 47.6% are 'minority group'
students. There are two kindergarten classes at this
school, both meeting in the morning from 8:30 to 11:45.
There are 31 and 33 students in each class and the
percentage of 'minority group' students in each class
is 54.8% and 51.5%, respectively. Both kindergartens
are taught by female teachers, one of whom has taught
for 25 years, while the other has taught for four years.
Most of the students at School A are predominantly from
'lower' or 'working-class' homes while some students
come from 'middle-class homes'. The two kindergarten
classrooms are set off from the rest of the school by
a fenced-in playground although one of the kindergartens
opens onto the main playground of the school.

The students at School A are differentiated into
two homogeneous kindergarten classes: a 'mature'
class and an 'immature' class. The basis of this differentiation is the students' performance in an interview with one of the teachers. This interview is
essentially the administering of a developmental test
designed by Ilg and Ames (1964) of the Gesell Institute.
The students are screened in this manner either during

---

[1]
The reader should not construe the ethnographic
details which follow as variables that are going to
be correlated with each other. I am not looking at
how they are correlated but at how each type of tracking system is accomplished. The issue is not whether
these kinds of teachers are placing students correctly
or if a certain kind of teacher results in a different
kind of tracking system, but how the students are being
placed. Issues of correctness are suspended under the
procedural policy termed by Garfinkel and Sacks (1970)
as "ethnomethodological indifference."

21

the Spring or in the Fall when the parents bring their children to the school to register, and the interview is part of other tests which include a speech and hearing examination, a health examination and verification of the child's birthdate (in California a child must have turned 5 by December 2nd in order to enter kindergarten). At the end of the year a kindergarten student was either 'retained' in kindergarten for another year or he was placed in one of three first grades. One of these first grades served as an unofficial 'junior' first grade. All of the 'weak' students were placed there. The decision to 'retain' a student or send him on to first grade was made by the kindergarten teachers who then discussed their decisions with the principal so that he could deal with the student's parents regarding any question about the placement.

School B

Like School A, School B drew most of its students from a 'working class' neighborhood and over 50% of the students were either Chicano or Black. There were two kindergarten classes, one meeting in the morning and the other meeting in the afternoon. The classes had 32 and 28 students, respectively, and of these 66% and 64% were 'minority group' students.

At School B, I found a tracking system which was structurally different from that at School A. The two kindergarten classes were 'team taught' by two kindergarten teachers. The free teacher would come into her colleague's class to teach two of the four ability-groups during 'activity time'. The kindergartens were heterogeneous, but within each class there were four homogeneous ability-groups: reading, high readiness; average, and low readiness. Each group had its own curriculum and the tracking system was used both in forming the ability-groups and then perpetuating them through first grade placements. Students were not 'retained' in kindergarten at School B. At the end of the year a kindergarten student was either placed in one of the two 'regular' first grades or in the

22

"junior" first grade.

PLACEMENT SETTINGS IN THE TWO KINDERGARTENS
     In this section specific settings are examined
in which kindergarten tachers in both schools are
either actively engaged in placing students or
gathering information for that purpose. Kindergarten
'settings' is intended as an analytic notion, because,
in actual practices all of the activities within the
classroom inform placement decisions.

School A
     The placement settings discussed in the following
section are the screening interviews used for differ-
entiating incoming students into the 'mature' and
'immature' classes and placement of kindergarten
students into first grade. In the Spring, 18 students
were 'screened' at School A. The 'screening' consisted of administering a test in the form of an interview which was developed by Ilg and Ames (1964) of the
Gesell Institute. The screening interviews which I
recorded and observed were conducted in the auditorium
of the school in little partitioned offices which were
open at the ceiling. Next to one of the offices in
which these interviews were held the speech teacher
was giving students a speech and hearing examination;
on the other side, the nurse was having students jump
up and down as part of their physical examination.
     The screening interview itself consisted of three
parts: an initial interview, complete-a-man, and copy
forms. The initial interview consisted of the teacher
asking questions of the child about her age, her family,
and what she did during her last birthday party. In
the "complete-a-man" part of the interview, the teacher
presented the student with a pencil and a dittoed drawing of a half-completed man—the student was supposed
to fill in the missing parts and talk about the
drawing. In the "copy forms" part of the test, the
teacher presented the student with drawings of a
square, triangle, circle, and a divided rectangle and
asked the student to copy each one as it was presented

23

to him. For the first two parts of the screening interview, the teacher works from a dittoed face sheet (see Appendix). This sheet served as a script for the teacher with lines and spaces for her to write in the student's replies. This dramaturgical terminology is used so that the transcripts of the interview can be examined vis-a-vis the script to locate and demonstrate the situated character of the screening test.

The sheet as a script does not tell the teacher how she is to get the information from the child. It only provdes her with questions which do not specify what it is they call for. For example, the first line of the Initial Interview reads as follows:

How old are you? ___ Shows fingers; ___ Counts them ___. For every interview one of the teachers said the following:

TEACHER: *How old are you La?*
STUDENT: *Four.*
TEACHER: *Four?*
STUDENT: *Four now.*
TEACHER: *You're four now?*
STUDENT: *I already had my birthday.*
TEACHER: *I see. Can you show me on your fingers how much is four? How many fingers are four? (Student holds up hand showing four fingers by tucking her thumb towards her palm.) That's right. Can you count them?*
STUDENT: *Yeah.*
TEACHER: *Let me hear you.*
STUDENT: *One, two, three, four.*

Her colleague handled the same part of the initial interview in the following manner:

TEACHER 2: *Okay Pe, how old are you?*
STUDENT: *Five years old.*
TEACHER 2: *Five, good. Do you know when your birthday is?*

24

STUDENT: *No.*

At this point Teacher 2 moved on to the next question on the script, *"Did you have a birthday party"* which she rewords as *Do you remember ever having a birthday party?*

The comparison between the two teachers treatment of the same section of the script suggests that the two differ in their reading of the script and its requirements. The first teacher interprets each entry of the script as instructing her to ask the child in order: (1) how old he is, (2) if he can show his age on his fingers, and (3) to count the fingers (or ask the child to count them). The second teacher on the other hand reads the same part of the script as saying: Ask the child how old he is, if he shows his fingers mark 'yes' in the slot, and if he counts them as well mark 'yes' in the slot. This comparison points to the 'open structure' of the script. The 'open structure' of the interview script results in the teachers' use of elicitation practices to manage the interview situation. These elicitation practices are not contained in the script but are used by the teacher to sustain the interview and to get information from the child.

Expanding Students' Talk. Both teachers expanded the remarks of the students they interviewed. Following are two examples from different teacher-student interviews as well as different sections of the screening interview. The first example comes from that part of the interview where the teacher asks about the occupation of the student's father. The second example is from the complete-a-man section of the interview.

(A)   TEACHER: *Do you know what kind of work he does?*
          STUDENT: *I'm not there.*
          TEACHER: *No you're not there so it's hard to tell sometimes isn't it humm?*
(B)   TEACHER: *How do you think he feels inside?*
          STUDENT: *Sad.*

25

TEACHER: *Do you think he's sad inside? Do you... How can you tell?*
STUDENT: *Cuz he mouth's sad.*
TEACHER: *Oh you made him a sad mouth did you. Oh I thought you were going to make him a happy mouth. You made him a sad mouth, that's how you can tell he's sad inside humm?*
STUDENT: *Umm humm.*

In both of these examples the teacher is expanding the child's answer to her questions by filling in what she presumes to be the intent or meaning behind it. The specific examples of this practice are:

TEACHER: *No you're not there so it's hard to tell sometimes isn't it humm?*

and

TEACHER: *Oh you made him a sad mouth did you. Oh I thought you were going to make him a happy mouth. You made him a sad mouth, that's how you can tell he's sad inside humm?*

Not only does the teacher go beyond the surface form of the student's answers, there is also an upward inflection and rise in intonation of the teacher's voice at the end of both of the expansions, which suggests that the teacher is using the expansions as a communications check. She seems to be saying in effect, "Is this what you mean?" The teachers' use of expansions in this manner parallels their use by parents as reported by Brown and Bellugi (1964) in their study of the child's acquisition of syntax.

Providing a Context. One of the teachers provided the students with a gestalt-like context in order to keep the interview going.

A. T_1: *What does that look like to you Ha?*

26

B. T_2: *Pe, I have here a picture of a man and the poor man doesn't have all of his parts. Look at him.... Now with this pencil, will you move your chair closer, and make the parts that the man needs?*

In the first example (A) the teacher not only leaves it up to the child to figure out what it is that's being presented to him, she asks him for his definition of it. In the second example, however, the other teacher provides the child with a context against which to compare the drawing when she says *I have here a picture of a man and the poor man doesn't have all of his parts....* With such a context the teacher is helping the student locate the missing parts and is also informing the student about the nature of the task.

A more dramatic example of the use of this practice occurred when the teacher presented pictures of a square, a circle, a cross, a triangle, and a divided rectangle which looked like ⊠ to one of the students.

TEACHER: *I see, good. Now I have to know how you came down (writes on student's paper). Now I have a picture of a window. Can you make that window?*

STUDENT: *Did it break?*

TEACHER: *Well it might. You make it way up there (student looks at the picture for a long time before she starts to draw but does it perfectly). Li that's very good. You did a nice job. You did a careful job. Observant. Now you've made me those nice pictures, and you've drawn a nice man for me; and you've told me all about the birthday party that you were going to have and the cake and ice cream and that you wanted some bellbottom pants for your birthday present. And now I'm going to staple this together and you just put the pencil here and sit down*

27

*in the chair. (At this point the
teacher reads to me her evaluation of
the child with the child right there.)*

This example shows both the teacher's use of the
practice of providing a gestault like context for the
student and it illustrates how the teacher's presentation of the question affects the results. When
the teacher says ...*Now I have a picture of a window.
Can you make that window?*, the object is made available and recognizable to the student. The student's
response is significant because it also demonstrates
that the object has indeed become recognizable through
the teacher's presentation:

> TEACHER: ...*Now I have a picture of a window.
> Can you make that window?*
> STUDENT: *Did it break?*

The child's statement strongly suggests that the
presentation of the object is indeed a variable of
the interview situation. The manner in which the
teacher presents objects to the child effects how the
child sees those objects.

Leading Questions. A third practice which was
used by both teachers was providing cues to the
students through the use of leading questions. This
practice was used mostly during the complete-a-man
section of the interview and was an effort on the part
of the teacher to help the student 'see more' in the
picture. The reader is invited to note not only the
leading questions but also the feed-back that the
teacher provides the student when he completes a part
of the *"man"* in the example below.

> TEACHER: *What does this look like to you Ha?*
> STUDENT: *It looks like a one-legged monkey.*
> TEACHER: *A one-legged monkey?*
> STUDENT: *Yeh an' one ear.*
> TEACHER: *A one-legged monkey with one ear huhh?*

STUDENT: *And one arm and no eyes.*
TEACHER: *No eyes. Why don't you give him what*
           he needs then, okay? Take that pencil
           and... all the things he needs.

At this point the teacher continues to question the
student about how the 'monkey' feels and then moves
on to the next part of the interview.

I want to point out several features of this exchange. Because of the student's 'strange' answer to
her initial question, during the first seven lines
the teacher has to decide whether or not the student
has recognized the task. The student convinces her
that he recognizes the task by being able to name the
parts that are missing from the drawing.

The teacher has to evaluate the student's answer
on the spot and has to decide whether or not the
student really knows what is going on. That decision
process involves the 'expansion' elicitation practice.
The expansion *Teacher: A one-legged monkey with one*
ear huhh? is formed by combining two previous utterances by the student, *It looks like a one-legged*
monkey and *Yeh an' one ear.* In addition, the teacher
temporarily suspends the fact that the student is
supplying missing parts to a 'monkey'. At a later
point in the interview she tries to get the student
to see the drawing as a 'man':

TEACHER: *Does a monkey wear clothes?*
STUDENT: *Yeah.*
TEACHER: *Okay does he still look like a monkey?*
STUDENT: *Umm humm... I like different kinds of*
           monkeys.
TEACHER: *What kinds of monkeys do you like?*
STUDENT: *The ones with clothes on.*
TEACHER: *Okay....*

The series of leading questions which the teacher
uses not only enable the student to 'see more' in the
drawing but also provide feedback for his actions and
statements because the teacher monitors and connects

them across the interview. Examples both of the use of leading questions and the teacher's monitoring of the student's replies are found in the following section:

> STUDENT: *Put a leg there and put a nose on here* (he draws).
> TEACHER: *Is that all he needs now look closely and see if he's missing anything.*
> STUDENT: *No.*
> TEACHER: *Now did you tell me he had one ear?*
> STUDENT: *Yeah right there.*
> TEACHER: *All right should he have one ear?*
> STUDENT: *No, no he needs another one.*
> TEACHER: *Oh he does (student draws) umm humm.*

Here the teacher first provides the student with a leading question, *Is that all he needs...,* and a command, *now look closely and see if he's missing anything,* in an effort to get the student to see additional missing parts. When the student indicates that the drawing is not *missing anything,* the teacher then retrieves a statement made by the student at the beginning of the exchange and confronts him with it — *Now did you tell me he had one ear?* The teacher is linking the student's utterances across the interview and connecting them with a leading question, *All right should he have one ear?,* which in turn relies on the assumption that the student possesses common knowledge or 'what everyone knows' (Cicourel, 1973; Garfinkel, 1967).

The Screening Interviews as a Situated Accomplishment. The situated accomplishment of the interviews consists of the teachers' use of these and other elicitation practices. That some of these practices cut across all of the interviews while others are teacher-specific and child-specific underscores rather than detracts from the accomplished nature of the screening interviews. They are necessarily accomplishments because there exists no set of instructions for

30

telling teachers how they are to obtain information.
To view these practices as being faulted versions of
how the teachers should have proceeded if they had
conducted the interviews 'scientifically', is to ignore
the fact that the ideals of science, like the script
used by the teacher, do not provide neither the teacher
nor the child with instructions for carrying them out.
(Cf. Mehan's discussion concerning teacher's instructions in this volume.) Therefore, the elicitation are
note to be regarded as faulted versions of how the
teachers should have proceeded; they couldn't have
proceeded in any other manner and still sustain the
interview as social interaction. Without their use,
the interviews would have degenerated into silence
occasionally broken by talk.

    <u>Reflexive Features</u>. It is important to note that
the teacher is involved in both deciding what is happening in the interview and simultaneously making it happen.
The "essential reflexivity" of the teachers' use of
elicitation practices lies in the fact that she evalu-
ates the information she receives from the student while
at the same time she produces that information through
her decision to 'probe' the student or by continuing on
with the next part of the interview. The teacher's use
of leading question to help the student 'see more' in
the complete-a-man section of the interview (see pages
23-25) is an excellent example of the interview's essential reflexivity: it is through the teacher's use
of leading questions that the student comes to *"see"*
that there are more parts to be added and which parts
are needed; while at the same time the teacher views
the parts added as the "results" of the test. Hence
through her use of the elicitation practices, she
decides what is happening as she makes it happen. In
this manner, the elicitation practices provide "continuous (reflexive) feedback" thus enabling her to
sustain the sense of "what's happening" (Cicourel, 1973).
In conclusion, then, the elicitation practices are
essential for the accomplishment of the screening interviews. They are essential in the sense that through

31

their "seen but unnoticed" use the teacher is able to sustain the sense of the interview as an ongoing interaction while at the same time producing its ongoing character.

   Indexical Features. The second aspect of the accomplished nature of the screening decisions which is illustrated by the teacher's discussion of Ka is the indexical nature of the screening results. A context must be created or in this case remembered to decide the specific sense of the results. An example of this property is found at the beginning of the section:

> TEACHER: *...And why she put that in there (a square inside of which is a circle with lines radiating out from it) I don't know if it's to represent a flat or something.*
>
> INT.: *No. I think that was the (draws on a piece of paper) thing. A couple of the kids did that...*
>
> TEACHER: *Oh that's right this was one of the....*

The comments of the teacher and the interviewer suggest that the recognition of the screening results depends on supplying a context. The teacher does not recognize the object drawn by the student even though it can be easily described. She recognizes it after the interviewer supplies her with a context consisting of his drawing the object and pointing out that several students represented it in the manner depicted by the student being discussed. The reader may say at this point, *"Well, the student did such a bad job that it was unrecognizable."* This is not the case for the teacher's comment; *"I don't know if its to represent a flag or something,"* suggests that the object is recognizable as a something. The object drawn by the student can be taken to be any number of things — it is potentially equivocal even though it can be described easily. Because of its potential

32

equivocality, labeling the object or deciding its specific sense is not an easy matter. Deciding the specific sense of the object requires that the member (teacher, researcher or anyone else reading the screening results) supply a context consisting of the setting, the occasion of the drawing, the person who drew the object, the intent of the person, etc. In fact the teacher's remark, *"I don't know if it's to represent a flag or something,"* suggests that she is attempting to assemble such a context to make the object sensible.

Scenic Features. In addition to the teacher's practice of *"filling-in"* missing information from the studen's answer, and the indexical nature of the screening results, another placement practice that was observed during the screening decisions meeting was the use of the student's age as an interpretive scheme for evaluating the student's performance. This practice is illustrated when the teacher makes the following comment about Ka:

> TEACHER: *...But for a child who will be that old it seemed to me that she should have been a little more outgoing....*

Here the student's age becomes in effect a scheme of interpretation for evaluating behavior and assigning the student a score on the screening test. This use of age is dramatically illustrated by the following comments made by the teacher about another student to her colleague:

> TEACHER 1: *I put the child down as a five-minus.*
> TEACHER 2: *Five minus, umm humm.*
> TEACHER 1: *And I think that's about right.*
> TEACHER 2: *Umm humm (Office secretary calls Teacher 2 out of the room).*
> TEACHER 1: *Maybe I ought to put her five plus because she does have a May birthday and she can do all this. I think I*

33

> *will: a five plus. She would be*
> *one of the more mature ones.*

Note that the decision is made on the spot and that the basis for the change is largely the child's age and what age stands for in the teacher's scheme.

Promoting Students. Another placement setting at School A was the promotion of students into the first grade and assigning them to specific first grade teachers. The ground rules for how the kindergarten students were to be placed into the first grade became apparent to me in a meeting with the new principal and the two kindergarten teachers. The meeting was scheduled to familiarize the principal with the techniques used to screen the incoming kindergarten students and to make the arrangements for the screening.

Once these arrangements had been made, the principal asked the teachers if they would like to help organize the first grade classes for the next year. He then placed on the table three large pieces of cardboard with strips of tape across each one and the name of a teacher at the top. He also placed on the table two envelopes from which he took pictures of the present kindergarten students. The teachers were to write on the back of each student's photograph two or three "descriptors" of the student and then place the picture on one of the pieces of cardboard. The instructions for placing the students with the teachers were as follows:

PRINCIPAL: *Here are these pictures of (Teacher*
1's). Now—
TEACHER 1: *No, mine were here first my friend.*
These are (Teacher 2's) — Wait a
minute those are mine.
PRINCIPAL: *Now what I want you to do is take*
each one of these and on the back with
a felt pen or something write two or
three descriptors. (Picks up a

picture.) What's outstanding about this child, Pa (___): sunny, cheer- ful, aggressive, retiring?

TEACHER 2: *Would you please write a long list that we could choose from, those are great (laughs).*

TEACHER 1: *No she's outgoing, an' strong aca- demically strong.*

PRINCIPAL: *Okay then that goes on the back here. Now recognizing that (jet overhead masks out talk). (First Grade Teacher A) is a different kind of person, what would be good for this child? Now does this child need somebody strongly oriented academical- ly? Does she need that kind of strong hand? Here's a warm mother (tapping First Grade Teacher b's card): I came into the auditorium and she had Li on her lap. Li had gotten money at lunch time but she didn't bring it quite by accident because the student teacher thought she'd brought money for her lunch and she had to take it back which just crush- ed her. And First Grade Teacher B instead of saying 'It's all right now you just get in line and go,' there she was sitting there with this child — you know it was beautiful.*

Now we're going to have some kids in here who are going to need a Momma-type. All right here's your Momma (tapping First Grade Teacher B's card). Here's a gal we want to protect (pointing to First Grade Teacher C's card which is actually going to be the new teacher's class). We don't want to give her really tough ones. I will not have her

35

picking up all the kids that are difficult.

TEACHER 1: *Hummm.*

PRINCIPAL: *People who have the experience, people who have the know-how pick up the tough ones because they know more and can protect against that kind of child. So these are the two that we give the really difficult kids to and-Now you know how First Grade Teacher A teaches: it's very open and noisy and undisciplined (now holding Su's picture).*

TEACHER 1: *Couldn't stand it—*

PRINCIPAL: *Well this is right. What kids will benefit by being—*

TEACHER 1: *Su should go right there (puts picture on First Grade Teacher B's card).*

PRINCIPAL: *All right you'd have Su over there, see. Now when you get these _____ you slip them in like this....*

The cards were put in the teacher's lounge by the principal for the teachers to consider the arrangement of students. If any of them did not want a particular student in their class or questioned the placement of a particular child, they were to signify this by turning the child's photograph on its side:

PRINCIPAL: *If during the time that this is up there somebody says 'I'm not so certain I want this child,' or 'this child with this teacher.' This is the signal (turns the picture on its side). Now that says, 'Hey, let's think about that. We may want to do it but we may want to move.'*

In this manner the tracking system at School A was initiated: Its foundations rested on the

36

instructions, typifications, and rationales given by the principal. There were three first-grade teachers at the school; only two were to continue the next year, and the third was to be replaced. Each of the three teachers is typified by the principal. One is typed as being 'strongly oriented academically'; the other teacher is typed as *"a warm Mother"*; and, the third is 'a new teacher'. The placement practices constitutive of this form of tracking (the Personality Track) will be examined in the third section of this chapter. I will confine my discussion to where the students were placed.

The two kindergarten teachers set about the task outlined by the principal in the following way. First, both teachers divided their classes into three groups of students: strong, average, and weak. The 'strong' students were those who, in the words of one of the teachers, *"...have the ability of being accurate and able to go rapid an' be able to respond to the concepts that are presented very quickly...".* The *"average"* students were those who demonstrated to the teacher that they knew the material presented in class but whose performance was flawed by slowness or messiness. The 'weak' students were those who interacted poorly with their peers and who did not verbalize in class. Then the students were placed in the following manner. All the 'strong' students were placed with the teacher who was typified as being 'strongly oriented academically'; the 'average' students were placed with the new teacher although some of them were placed with the 'strong' students while others were placed with the 'weak' students; and the 'weak' students were placed with the teacher who was typified as a 'warm Mother'.

School B

The kindergartens at School B were organized into two heterogeneous classes and within each class there were four homogeneous ability-groups. Two methods were used in forming the ability groups: interviewing the students and using routine classroom

37

activities to provide information about the students'
abilities. Selected students were interviewed during activity time. In the interview they were asked
to identify different shapes (squares, rectangle,
triangle, and circle), colors (red, blue, green,
yellow, and purple), and the letters of the alphabet.
They were also asked to count.

Classroom Activities. During activity time, the
teachers would walk around the room and interact with
the students as they played with games and other
available objects. The classification of these routine
activities and the manner in which the teachers interacted with the students provided them with information
about the students' abilities. For example, one of
the teachers was observed helping a student put the
blocks away after activity time. She asked the student
to put the larger of two blocks on one shelf and the
smaller on the other shelf. The student put the
wrong block on the top shelf. The teacher then asked
him to put a square block on the first shelf and a
round one on the second. The student couldn't tell
the difference between the two blocks. At the end of
the day I overhead the teacher relate this interchange to her colleague, but in her account she had
generalized the child's performance to difficulties
with shape perception and eye-hand coordination.

Another example of a routine activity used to
provide information about what the students know is
a color game played at the beginning of class. Each
student was given a little paper cut-out of Snoopy
attached to a little stick; some of these cut-outs
are red while others are blue, green, yellow, or
purple. A record is played by the teacher and on
the record the singer tells different colors to stand
up or sit down. The children are to identify themselves with the color of the cut-out they are holding
and respond accordingly. By watching and noting
which children failed to stand up or sit down when
their color was called, the teacher could evaluate
the student's recognition of colors. That the teacher

uses this classroom activity in this manner is suggested by the following incident. On my second day of observation the teacher asked me if I would like to *"play the game."* When I said I would she handed me a gree-colored Snoopy saying, *"I'll give you green, they have a hard time with that."* An interesting note is that no student mistakenly gave his Snoopy to the teacher (or to a student) when the various colors were collected at the end of the game. This raises questions of just what it is that the student has difficulty with: linking a name to a color or color matching.

During activity-time the students were watched to see which activities they chose and how long they stayed at any one activity before going on to another one. If a student consistently went to the playhouse (a chest full of 'grown-up' clothes and a wooden 'stove') the teachers regarded that student as being insecure and needing the role-playing activity which they connected with this activity. The teachers also noted which role the student took while playing in the play-house. The following account by one of the teachers suggests the underlying meaning that the students' participation in classroom activities has for the teacher.

> TEACHER: *Lu is a very, very quiet child. Shy but she does quite well in school. She's very quiet. She doesn't seem to play with the children very much and ahh but they seem to like her, it isn't that kind of thing. It's just that she doesn't seek out friends. I've tried to put her into situations where she'll have to become involved with other people: in the home. Mainly in the home because girls don't like the big blocks that well.*
>
> INT.: *How is she ahh what have your observations of her been when you have put her in those situations?*

39

TEACHER: *Well she's still pretty quiet but she'll do it, you know.*

INT: *She doesn't say she won't but she'll still kind of play quietly. She won't ever be one of the leading characters like the mother, you know. She'll never play the mother. She'll always play the child.*

If a student went from one activity to another in rapid succession without finishing one before beginning another, such a student was labeled *"immature."* The following incident illustrates this use of the classroom activities as a scheme of interpretation. One afternoon after the students had gone home I mentioned to the teachers that it was difficult to keep track of the students during activity time because they all went from one activity to another. One of the teachers made the further observation to her colleague that Li did this a lot and that it puzzled her because the student was large in size and should not have been behaving that way. She looked up Li's birthdate and announced to her colleague that Li was born on December 1st, meaning she was a 'young 5-year-old'. What this example points to is that a student who, because of her size, was expected to be 'mature' was redefined by exhibiting 'immature' behavior during activity-time and her birthdate was then invoked as pointing to the fact that she was immature.

For the casual observer, and maybe for the students who are engaged in them, these activities are just games to occupy one's time or to keep the students busy or out of trouble. To the teacher these activities represent something altogether different. The routine activities of the classroom are devices for assessing the levels of performance (and establishing levels of performance) of the different students. The activities tacitly embody for the teachers developmental requirements and signify to her different levels of the students' abilities.

The teacher's practical interest and task are the

location and identification of the students' abilities to form ability groups of homogeneous students. From her perspective as determined by these practical circumstances and practical interests, the child is not just playing but is behaving in ways that provide evidence of his abilities. The teacher's use of routine classroom activities in this manner is characteristic of her competence and characterizes her as a member of this particular setting as opposed to a casual observer.

Promotion. Another placement setting within the kindergartens at School B is the promotion of the students to either first or junior-first grade. At this school, no student is retained in kindergarten at the end of the year. He is promoted to either one of two first grades or to the junior-first grade. From junior-first a student is promoted either to a first grade or to second grade. The student's position within one of the four ability groups at the end of the year is the largest factor in this decision. The reader will recall that within the two classes there were four ability groups: (1) reading group, students reading in the first pre-primer; (2) high readiness group, students who know the beginning sounds and are ready to read by the end of the year but not actually starting to read because of lack of time; (3) average readiness group, students just starting to learn beginning sounds; (4) low readiness group, students who had not reached the basic readiness level and who were still working on recognizing different shapes, colors, letters of the alphabet, sounds and increasing their perceptual skills and practicing sequencing. Students who were in the first two ability groups were placed in one of the two first grades while the students in the low ability group were placed in the junior-first-grade.

AD HOCING IN THE SCHOOLS: PLACEMENT PRACTICES

I will now discuss the practicing used by the teachers within the placement settings for placing their students into specific classes, ability groups within those classes, and for promoting them into the next grade. Two kinds of placement practices were observed at the two schools participating in the study: Personality Tracking at School A and Ability-Group Tracking at School B. Both placement practices are characterized by the teachers' use of social knowledge in the form of social types and the teachers' use of tacit knowledge of human behavior and practical circumstances to assign meaning and find meaning in the students' behavior.

Social Types Used in the Schools

Before detailing the placement practices which constitute the tracking system at each school, I will review some of the social types used by the teachers at both schools to interpret and identify the student's behavior. By social type I mean an idealization used by members of a group to identify and interpret objects (including people), and events in their environment (Klapp, 1962; Strong, 1943). The importance of these social types comes from a conception of the tracking systems as products of the socially organized routine activities of the teachers. Some of those activities within the placement settings were described in the previous section (the elicitation practices and the use of routine classroom activities as devices for locating students' abilities) and additional activities will be described in this section. But before we begin such a discussion our first task is the description of the common-sense constructs (social types) used by the teachers to interpret their students' behavior. Four social types regularly used by the teachers at both schools were 'immature child', 'bright child', 'behavior problem', and 'independent worker'. I will give brief definitions of each of these types *from the perspective of the teacher,*[2]

---

[2]These definitions may well differ from those found in educational texts. My intent is to capture in these definitions, however, the teacher's use of these terms.

as an introduction to my analysis of the placement practices which form the basis of the tracking systems.

Immature Child. The 'immature child' is one who has a very short attention span as indicated by the fact that he cannot sit still during a lesson and is easily distracted by, and himself distracts, other students. The 'immature child' typically is called by the teachers a 'young 5-year-old'. Sex and size are also grounds for labeling a student 'immature'. More often than not an immature child turns out to be a small boy rather than a small girl. When a girl is termed *"immature"* it indicates that she is not acting in accordance with her chronological age which is used by the teachers as a tacit developmental model of the child. In the following example, taken from an interview with one of the kindergarten teachers at School B, we can see all of the above grounds for labeling a child *"immature."* The teacher in this section is describing one of two cases in answer to a question about what kind of behavior would require the teacher to send a student out of the room.

> TEACHER: *Then we have had one other little boy who is very very immature and he was a November birthday. Just a little, little boy and he was either practically sitting on my lap half of the time or running around the room and just making it—it they're so bad that you can't keep the rest of the class involved, if they're disturbing the rest of the class, that's when I feel it's necessary to get them out of the room, refer them for counseling.*

Bright Student. The *"bright student"* is defined by the speed with which he learns the material presented in class. He is a student who learns quickly and without the teacher having to dispense much time or effort as the following examples taken from

43

interviews with different teachers indicate:

TEACHER: *...but he's a bright child, he learns very quickly and umm at the first of the year he didn't know much about letters or anything but he learned them just like that (snaps her fingers) when they were presented.*

TEACHER: *He's performed very well amm he's confident, he grasps ahh concepts very readily and without any repetition.*

Another basis for labeling a student 'bright' is the student's high performance level despite what the teacher perceives to be poor social behavior in the class during the presentation of the material, as the following example suggests:

TEACHER: *Now this is Pa, is a very interesting child because he's one of the ones who's extremely bright but is a behavior problem in school. And umm one of the reasons he's probably a behavior problem is because he — well I guess I really shouldn't say he's a behavior problem but he's immature. Because he's young and we probably expect too much of him. He's an October birthday which would make him one of the youngest in the class....*

INT.: *What are some of the things that give you the impression that he was bright?*

TEACHER: *Ohh he has a fantastic memory: In the group I can read a story and he can be looking out the window or talking to his neighbor and I can ask him the question and he knows the anser like that you know. At first I would, he would be talking so after I read something or if we'd been discussing*

44

INT.:

TEACHER:

> *something I would say 'Pa, what have*
> *we been talking about?' And I was*
> *doing it because I figured he wouldn't*
> *know — and he did.*
>
> *Umm humm.*
>
> *And so it was in the total group that*
> *he's catching a lot of what they're*
> *hearing and if he's a child who can*
> *talk to his neighbor and still know*
> *the answer you know you've got a bright*
> *child on your hands....*

This account also reveals the grounds for labeling a
student 'immature'. In fact this is exactly what the
teacher does when she proposes:

TEACHER:

> *...Well I guess I really shouldn't say*
> *he's a behavior problem but he is im-*
> *mature because he's young and we*
> *probably expect too much of him. He's*
> *and October birthday which would make*
> *him one of the youngest in the class....*

Finally, the bright child is *"very verbal."* He
not only talks a lot, but his talk is heard by the
teacher as reflecting mastery of the materials presented in class, not just as idle chatter. For example during a reading lesson I was observing at
School A, one of the students interrupted one of her
classmates with the phrase *"that's fascinating,"* and
the teacher turned to me and said *"great vocabulary."*
In short, what would normally be sanctioned (inter-
rupting another student) in this case was taken as a
sign of the student's brightness: the action was not
seen as an interruption by the teacher but as a display of knowledge.

Behavior Problem. The *"behavior problem"* is
typified by a big boy who repeatedly engages in fights
with other children for what the teacher perceives as
[*"no reasons at all."*] The following example illustrates:

45

INT.: *What was the counselor's evaluation or haven't you received that yet?*

TEACHER: *Well he...Well I have and he was very worried about this child and called the mother right away. He came in and observed in the room about 15 minutes during our activity time and he said that in 15 minutes he found about 25 times that he got into a disagreement with a child. Just in that period of time. He'd walk past a child and go like that (teacher swings her arm with closed fist in hitting motion) for absolutely no reason at all or trip them or push them or try to get something going. You know. And we felt he should be removed from school if he continues to disrupt. So we've really been isolating him now and when he starts and send him over to the office. This kind of thing because he really does disrupt and get everybody else keyed up — as I said Thursday and Friday he wasn't here. It was just beautiful, it was great. It just takes this to get everybody going.*

The important points to note in this account are the repeated hitting of the child's peers and the teacher's inability to find a reason for this behavior. These two features of the child's behavior are what define him as a *"behavior problem."*

Independent Worker. The student who is an *"independent worker"* is defined by the teachers as one who can work with little or no supervision and who finishes the task begun before going on to another. The following example illustrates not only the grounds for labeling a student an *"independent worker"* but also suggests the practical reasons for the teachers' use of this social type.

46

INT.: *We are interested in knowing the kinds of abilities and achievements that you think a child going into the first grade from kindergarten should be able to have and do? Could you start by giving a few?*

TEACHER: *All right, well umm. Well I think they should be able to listen for a reasonable amount of time 15 to 20 minutes with a total group situation. Umm they're — how shall I put this — They're ready for, they could be ready for first grade and still be at different listening levels. Some will be able to listen for an hour and some won't. But they still would be ready for that kind of thing if they could listen for 15 to 20 minutes. I think they should be able to work independently for a reasonable length of time without having any direction from the teacher or having an adult right there with them. Umm they really should know how to work independently by the time they leave kindergarten because during activity time they're all choosing independent activities and some of them are out on the patio working with blocks without direct supervision and Mrs. (___) and I will take groups off to the side so they will be completely on their own. So in this way we're hoping they will be independent.*

The teachers' use of these social types to interpret and identify the behavior of the students constitutes a placement practice which is common to both schools. This placement practice forms the basis for two other practices which are specific to each school: the ability group track and the

personality track. The use of social types as a placement practice will be examined within the context of
these school-specific placement practices.

School B: The Ability Group Track
     These social types drawn from the teachers'
accounts form one of several practices which underlie
the ability-group tracking at School B. I will
examine the teachers' use of these social types to
identify a student within a particular ability group
level in the tracking system. In the following interview segment, standards for placement into the *"reading"* ability group and first grade are formulated by
one of the teachers at School B.

> INT.:   *What constitutes being ready to read
>   in terms of the readiness program.
>   What are the stadnards involved in
>   that?*
> TEACHER: *Being ready to read?*
> INT.:   *Uhh huhh, yes.*
> TEACHER: *All right umm well to begin with things
>   I've said: reasonable attention so
>   they can sit still in a reading group
>   and amm be able to work independently
>   enough on follow-up activity while the
>   teacher's working with another group —
>   these things are important.*

If the reader will refer back to the definition of
the 'immature child' he will see that a student so
defined does not meet these standards and consequently
is not placed in the upper ability groups unless he
shows the teacher on other grounds that he is both
very bright and immature. Such a student is unable
to sit still for an expected amount of time; his
attention span is short, and when outside the ability
group he cannot work by himself and thus distracts the
teacher from the ability group she is teaching. The
above passage also points to a particular feature of
both the teachers' use of social types to identify

and interpret the students' behavior: the social types and their use are grounded in the practical circumstances of teaching kindergarten with its particular form of classroom organization.

In the next interview segment a teacher is asked to justify her placement of a particular student in the junior-first grade class.

> INT.: *What were your reasons for putting him into junior-first as opposed to first.*
>
> TEACHER: *Well it takes him longer to learn things.*
>
> INT.: *Umm humm, I see.*
>
> TEACHER: *It takes him longer to learn letters and sounds and this kind of thing. But it could be just because he's the youngest you know. It's just another year for him to acquire — I don't believe in junior-first but since we have it there I have to put somebody in it.*
>
> INT.: *What do you mean by 'it takes him longer to learn letters? Do you have a schedule?*
>
> TEACHER: *No. It's just that we have to work more with him to learn. And not just with him but say with the whole lower group than we do with the others.*

Note the teacher's comment, [*"it takes him longer to learn letters and sounds and this kind of thing. But it could be just because he's the youngest, you know."*] Placement in junior-first as a result of the student's performance is linked to the student's *"immaturity,"* defined above as a social type. The teacher uses the social type 'immature' to 'explain' the student's performance without explicating the relation between them. The social type, then, becomes an interpretive aid for both placing a student within a particular ability group as well as the next grade.

In the following accounts in which the teacher

49

first describes the student and then justifies her
placement of the student in junior-first and then
first grade using the same social type.

TEACHER: *This is Ti and Ti's hard to describe
because he's a November birthday, one
of the youngest boys in the class
who's extremely verbal, just his
vocabulary must be fantastic. He's
the kind of child you can tell that
the mother has spent a lot of time
with him because he knows about everything and when he explains something
it's a long detailed explanation of
anything...And he knows all his sounds
and letters and he knew a good many of
them before he came and he's a Sesame
Street watcher and he knows everything
that's been present on that. So on
that side he's good but maturity-wise
he's very immature. He gets very silly
and he'll follow anyone who's getting
attention. He'll follow all the clowns
I have in the class: the ones that
are really showing off. Well he's
always there no matter who's doing
something he's doing it too. And if
someone during rest-time decides he's
going to lie down right here (pointing
to table we are seated around) instead
of over on the rug or at the table,
he'll be right here. But when he's
with a group that's mature he'll sit
and listen. So he's a follower and
wants to be he wants very badly to be
liked. He isn't really the best liked
child in the class because we have
mostly boys and Ti likes to play in
the doll house all the time (laughs)
and he likes to dress up in clothes
and most of the boys could care less*

50

*about that. And so he plays mostly
with the girls. I mean I try to encourage him to play a little more with
big blocks and things like this but
he's very disappointed if the home
isn't one of the activities of the day.
And ahh —*

INT.: *What other kinds of things do you know
about his family in terms of what the
father does?*

TEACHER: *His father owns a gas station and his
mother doesn't work. They seem to be
very well educated: they express themselves well and seem to be knowledge-
able about the correct way to bring up
children and this kind of thing and
things to do and things not to do.*

INT.: *Have you had several conferences with
them?*

TEACHER: *I've had two with her because he's a
child I wouldn't like to send to
junior-first but I have to.*

INT.: *Oh why is that?*

TEACHER: *Well, he's a follower for one thing
and most of those that are going to
junior-first are behavior problems,
that's one of the reasons they're
there — they haven't learned anything.
They're either immature or umm having
a hard time learning — things like
this....*

In the second account that follows the teacher is
again talking about Ti. This time within the context
of being asked where each student is in terms of the
work for the year and how prepared each is for going
on to the first grade.

TEACHER: *Ti's the one who's ready half and
half: one way he's ready and one way
he isn't. His eye-hand-coordination*

51

*is very poor and he can't do anything
with his hands and writing to him, to
teach him writing I think even in
September would be premature. He just,
it would be a real struggle for him,
he'd have a very hard time with it.
And yet reading I'm just sure he could
read. So one part hasn't caught up
with the other. So ahh he's the one
that is the follower and I would rather
like to see him in a room where he'd
have models to follow than in a room
where he'd have poor models to follow.*

INT.: *So he's going to be going where?*
TEACHER: *Well —*
INT.: *Or is he still a question mark?*
TEACHER: *He's going to be moving away.*
INT.: *Oh!*
TEACHER: *It would have been a question mark.
Ahh I would be inclined to put him into the first grade because I don't
like junior-first to begin with and
also he's the particular kind of child
that would, could go down in that kind
of situation because he, he's very
bright, very verbal. His body just
hasn't caught up with what he knows
and what he's learned.*

In the account that follows the teacher is talking
about the same student. In this account she was asked
to go down her list of students and tell the interviewer where she had placed them for the following
year and her reasons for the placement.

TEACHER: *Ti is, will not be in our school next
year. He's moving on the Mesa right
now. I'm not sure if the school he's
going to has a junior-first but he'd
be a question mark. He'd be one that
you'd almost have to wait until*

52

*September to really know how much
mature he ahh. He's very verbal umm
does well in anything verbal, well he
knows all of his letters and he knows
all of his beginning sounds and he
hears things well. His eye-hand-coordination is very poor and he is a
very poor listener and very silly and
immature.*

INT.: *Would you — Had he remained here,
where would you have put him?*

TEACHER: *I think I would have put him in a first
grade. Regular first would be amm the
high-low group. And alerted the
kindergarten err first grade teacher
that perhaps if he didn't work out
he'd be considered — Or it could work
the other way. But the problem with
putting Ti in a junior-first is he's
a follower —*

INT.: *Umm humm —*

TEACHER: *And he would tend to mimic the behavior
of the other children. And he could
grow a lot over those three months.
he's a young boy so he'd be a really
big question mark. But as it turns
out I really don't think the school
he's going to...I don't know if any of
the schools on the Mesa have a junior-
first. He may be in a regular first
anyway.*

These three accounts suggest that social types
are used in the placement of students and as justification for placement decisions. Furthermore, tacit
knowledge is used as an unexplicated link between the
social type and the student's behavior. In the first
account the teacher invokes the social type ["he's a
follower"] as justification for placing the student in
junior-first rather than first grade. Then in the
second account the same social type is used in

justifiying a first grade placement of the student.
The link between the social type and the student's
behavior is the conception of behavior as *"contagious"*:
certain people are more susceptible to the behavior
around them than others. It is just such a theory of
behavior which forms the tacit resource for the
teacher's statements:

> TEACHER: *So ahh he's the one that is the follower
> and I would rather like to see him in
> a room where he'd have good models to
> follow than in a room where he'd have
> poor models to follow.*

and

> TEACHER: *...but the problem with putting Ti in
> a junior-first is he's a follower —*
> INT.: *Umm humm —*
> TEACHER: *...and he would tend to mimic the be-
> havior of the other children.*

Another feature of the teachers' use of social
types as constitutive of ability group tracking is
that they are grounded in the practical circumstances
encountered by the teachers in teaching kindergarten.
This feature was mentioned in connection with the example on page 49 and is also revealed in the example
on page 50: The first instance is when the teacher
says, *"...I don't believe in junior-first but since
we have it there I have to put somebody in it."* The
teacher is pointing to the fact that the very existence
of junior-first is itself a practical contingency which
necessitates her placing students in it. It also
necessitates her finding students who can be placed
there. In her description of why this particular
student was placed in junior-first, the teacHer reveals further practical circumstances which underlie
her decision.

> INT.: *What are your reasons for putting him*

> *into junior-first as opposed to first?*
> TEACHER: *Well it takes him longer to learn things.*
> INT.: *Umm humm I see.*
> TEACHER: *It takes him longer to learn letters and sounds and this kind of thing....*
> INT.: *What do you mean 'it takes him longer to learn letters?' Do you have a schedule?*
> TEACHER: *No. It's just that we have to work more with him to learn. And not just with him but say with the whole lower group.*

When asked [*"Interviewer: What do you mean 'It takes him longer to learn letters?' Do you have a schedule?"*] the teacher does not say that the student has no idea of what the materials mean. Instead she invokes the practical circumstances of having to spend too much time with this student (and the lower group):

> TEACHER: *No it's just that we have to work more with him to learn. And it's not just with him but say the whole lower group.*

This example suggest that it is *in and through* these practical circumstances that the teacher identifies the student as having difficulty in learning and as a 'slow' student. The practical circumstances and practical interests of the teacher determines which social type she will use to interpret the student's behavior and place him at one level of the tracking system rather than another. Thus social types are not just theoretical abstractions; they are grounded in the practical circumstances and interests of the user.

This feature of social types and their use as constitutive of ability group tracking is revealed by re-examining the social types discussed at the beginning of this section. Underlying the teachers' use of the social type 'immature' is a very practical teaching concern — keeping the attention of 28 students while one of the students is misbehaving and diverting the attention of the others. This practical concern is revealed in the following excerpt taken from the example on page 43.

> TEACHER: *...if they're so bad that you can't keep the rest of the class involved, if they're disturbing the rest of the class, that's when I feel it's necessary to get them out of the room, refer them for counseling.*

This practical consideration also underlies the teachers' use of the social type *"bright child."* The time the teacher can spend in individual work with her students is limited; therefore, students who require less time free the teacher to work more with those students who need more individual help. This is reflected in the following example of a teacher talking about a *"bright child."*

> TEACHER: *He's performed very well amm he's confident he grasps ahh concepts very readily and without any repetition.*

The teacher's phrase [*"and without any repetition"*] suggests that such a student frees the teacher from working with this student.

The teachers' practical interest in having some free time during the day contributes to the use of the social type *"independent worker."* Recall the teacher's statement on page 47:

> TEACHER: *Umm they really should know how to work independently by the time they leave kindergarten because during activity time they're all choosing independent activities and some of them are out on the patio working with blocks without direct supervision and Mrs. (___) and I will take groups*

*off to the side so they will be com-
pletely on their own. So in this way
we're hoping they will be independent.*

If students cannot work independently the classroom
organization with its ability groups cannot function
because the organization requires both teachers to
be working with ability groups at the same time.
Students who fail to work independently and require
the teacher to monitor these 'free' activities draw
the teacher away from her work in the ability group.
In fact the 'free' activities are planned with just
this practical contingency in mind as strongly suggested by this account:

TEACHER: *We plan — First thing we usually talk
about is what our art activities are
we going to have because this is important to us because the art activities that the children can do independently are things that they can
do to release us to work individually
with children on other things. And
so it's important to us that we select
activities that they can do independently and that won't take us to be constantly wiping up after or that won't
involve any of our time for cutting for
them. It has to be something that they
can do on their own that they would
involve say a ten or even fifteen minute
period of time....*

The example given on page 48 is important because
it shows how the practical circumstance of the teacher
are transformed into criteria for judging the students'
performance.

INT.: *What constitutes being ready to read
in terms of the readiness program?
What are the standards involved in that?*

57

TEACHER: *Being ready to read?*
INT.: *Uhh huhh, yes.*
TEACHER: *All right umm well to begin with, things I've said: reasonable attention span so they can sit still in a reading group and umm be able to work independently enough on follow-up activity while the teacher's working with another group. These things are important.*

In the above account the teacher has linked the social types and the grounds for their use to the pragmatic task of maintaining the ability groups. This means that the social types and their definitions are not criteria which transcend the social setting in which they are used. Instead, the teacher's accounts demonstrate that the social types are embedded within the setting. They take on their specific sense from the setting and at the same time organize the setting through their use by the teacher to recognize and interpret the students' behavior in particular ways. The social types, then are not just a mere overlay on the setting by the teacher, rather they are an inseparable part of the setting which they organize through their situated usage. It is in this way that we say that the teachers' use of social types is constitutive of ability group tracking.

Preservation of the ability groups is also constitutive of ability group tracking. This preservation includes not only the group itself along with the differential exposure to curriculum but also refers to the label which the student carries with him as he moves from kindergarten to the first grade. There are several socially organized activities through which the ability groups are preserved. First, a little card goes with each student to the next teacher and is placed in his accumulative folder. On that card is a brief description of the student along with some anecdotal information and his final ability group position. In addition, there are recommendations from the teacher: *"consider him for first,"* if he is a marginal junior-first placement; and *"consider him for junior-first,"* if he is a marginal first-grade placement.

The major organizational activity which led to the preservation of the ability groups was the placement of the students into first grade. Once the decision had been made as to which students were going to first as opposed to junior-first, there remained the decision of which children would go into which of the two regular first grades. The kindergarten teachers explained that they wanted to place the students at random which would have split the ability groups. Their plan was not carried out at the request of the first grade teachers. One of the first grade teachers had a lot of *"behavior problems"* that year and to avoid a recurrence the following year requested that she be given all the students in the average ability group while the other first grade teacher take the students in the high and low ability groups. A consequence of this placement is that the ability groups will remain intact. An account of how the students were placed provides further features of how the ability groups were preserved at School B:

INT.: *One final question and that is how many first grade teachers do you have here not counting Mrs. (___) (the junior-first grade teacher)?*

TEACHER: *Two the other first umm humm.*

INT.: *How are the kids placed in the two?*

TEACHER: *The two?*

INT.: *The two classes yes.*

TEACHER: *Well they were placed in the two classes at the request of the two teachers, at their request they want — One of the teachers wanted all of the average children because she felt, for some reason I don't know why, that they would be better behaved. She had a lot of behavior problems and Mrs. (___) doesn't*

mind having behavior problems so she
just left it up to the other teacher.
So she wanted all the average children.
So she's getting all the low, medium
and high average children; and then
Mrs. (___) is getting all the lows and
highs. Now if we had it our way, we
would have just mixed them up and said
here are yours and here are yours, you
know they'd be high, average and low.
So that's what they're doing.

INT.: *Could you go over perhaps next time*
who's going into which class in terms
of you know going down the list again?

TEACHER: *Uhh huhh.*

INT.: *I think that will help. So in other*
words —

TEACHER: *That's how we did it. It's not the way*
we wanted to do it but as it turned out
the averages will have more of the
behavior — behavior problemwise it's
going to be a bad class because they
have a bad combination of children
that are, they really get into a lot
of trouble together you know. There's
a lot of very active boys in that
average group. We warned her but
that's the way they wanted it, they
wanted to have the groups they were
going to teach; and she wanted to
teach the average and (name of teacher)
didn't mind teaching the high's and the
low's.

INT.: *Let's see does that mean that your read-*
ing groups are going to be pretty much
intact?

TEACHER: *Yeah I guess so cuz they, they didn't*
want to shift too much so they think
they pretty much have them where they'll
be. Then of course Mrs. (___) is all
the immature slow children.

An examination of the preceding account reveals the following features of the perpetuation and justification of ability groups. First, it reveals that the labels that the students have at the end of the year will follow them into first grade. Second, the teacher's account reveals that even if kindergarten teachers had been allowed to proceed as they wanted the ability groups would have been perpetuated because the first grade teachers would be teaching the same ability groups as constituted in kindergarten with the first grade rooms merely being 'home rooms'. This is suggested by the following remarks:

> TEACHER: *I guess they didn't want to do much switching reading-wise, they wanted to have the groups they were going to teach; and she wanted to teach the average and (name of teacher) didn't mind teaching the high's and the low's.*

This section of the teacher's account implies that even if the ability groups were split and assigned to mixed home rooms, they would be reformed for the purpose of teaching reading. Third, the fact that the basis for maintaining the groups lay in one of the teacher's desire to avoid having another class of *"behavior problems"* suggests the notion that one of the pragmatic concerns orienting the teachers' decisions is *"avoiding trouble."* Fourth, the teacher's comment that [*"but as it turned out the averages will have more of the behavior — Behavior problem-wise it's going to be a bad class because they have a bad combination of children that are, that really get into a lot of trouble together, you know."*] suggests the use of a tacit theory of behavioral contagion as a resource for the placement decision or in this case a resource for predicting dire consequences from the decision. That is to say, embedded in her remarks is a theory of social behavior similar to the following definition of behavioral contagion offered by Shibutani (1969: 95):

In medicine a contagious disease is one
that is communicable by contact, and in sociology
the term behavioral contagion may be used to
designate the relatively rapid dissemination of
a mood or a form of conduct, generally through
direct interpersonal contact.

School A: The Personality Track

The personality Track is characterized by sorting
students into classes on the basis of matching typifications of the student and his future teacher.
Certain first grade teachers were known to receive
kindergarten students with certain characteristics.
But these characteristics are specified mainly in
the selection of one or another first grade teacher;
thus the teacher selected indicates the typification of the student. The foundations for this kind
of tracking were examined on pages 34-37 of this
study. The following examples provide some of the
essential features of this kind of tracking. All of
the teachers had been asked the following questions
by the interviewer:

> INT.: *Maybe the best way for you to give us an*
> *idea of what you must handle each day*
> *is to go over the children you have*
> *this year in your class. Can you give*
> *me a short description first and then*
> *give me some examples of how they be-*
> *have and handle the work in class.*
> *Why don't you just start with the first*
> *child that comes into your head.*

The first example comes from the teacher of the *"mature"*
class. In the example below she is talking about Ro
who is one of the students termed *"weak"* (see page 37)
by the kindergarten teacher.

Ro was one of the first students to come to the
mind of the teacher. After providing the interviewer
with some background on Ro's entry into her class,
the teacher comments that the student is not in the

62

average group (in contrast to the wishes of the
mother who wanted the student put in the top group):

INT.: *What is your impression of her?*

TEACHER: *Of her now?*

INT.: *I think she's a very slow worker and
I think that ahh she, she needs individual help in order to get the
concept of what I'm giving. And
that's a lot of time I say, 'Ro do
you understand?' I think that she's
just slow and needs a lot of help.*

    *She's a large child. Now here's a
case where even though she would not
be ready for first grade — she's
ready for a low first grade — but
even if she were not ready in other
ways, I still would pass her on to a
first grade because that girl another
year in kindergarten. Look how big
she'd be before she went into the
first grade! See so we would pass
her on.*

INT.: *What kind of ahh Have you had any
other contact with her mother and
father?*

TEACHER: *Ahh no. The mother just brought her
in just this one time an' the mother
brought her in just when we were
starting to have parent conferences
and I never had a conference with her
mother. Amm I have been meaning to
call and talk with her mother about
Ro and then I think well it really
does no purpose because Ro will go on
to first grade. And she will be
placed in a...where she will be comfortable. I believed I placed her with,
I have to look on the chart up there,
but as I recall I placed her with
Mrs. (First Grade Teacher B) where she*

*will be more motherly, mothered and
slower...*

There are several important features about the
operation of the Personality Track which are evident
in this discussion. The teacher placed the child
according to the principal's instructions (see pages
34-37). She links together two social types ('slow'
student with 'motherly' teacher) and that linking
provides the basis for the placement of the student
in a particular class. The underlying assumption is
that this kind of teacher is the best match for this
kind of student. This assumption is clearly invoked
in the teacher's justification for the placement:

> TEACHER: *...Ro will go to first grade. And
> she will be place in a...where she
> will be comfortable. I believe I
> placed her with, I have to look on
> the chart up there, but as I recall I
> placed her with Mrs. (First Grade
> Teacher B) where she will be more
> motherly, mothered and slower....*

A second feature of the Personality Track is
the use of circumstances which undercut academic
and social readiness for first grade. One of these
circumstances is mentioned in Ro's case: if a student
is disproportionately larger than her peers she is
advanced. One of the identifying characteristics of
the teacher's typification 'behavior problem' is the
student's physical size in comparison to his or her
peers. This was emphasized in a second interview in
which I questioned the teacher about this section of
transcript. She explained that were Ro to be kept
in kindergarten her larger size would lead to teasing
by the other students and might cause her to with-
draw from (become uncommunicative) or to become
aggressive toward her peers. In this reasoning we
can again observe the personality track placement
practice with its characteristic articulation of the

student's behavior and a social type. The social
type and the typical behaviors associated with it
then serve as the pivot on which the student's
placement turns.

Another student from the other kindergarten
was advanced to first grade because she was eight
years old. In an interview the teacher acknowledged
that the student was no better than the three students
who were being retained in kindergarten but that the
student was being promoted simply because of her age:

> TEACHER: *Now To ___. To in a way if you look
> at Jo and To you might say well if
> you're going to retain Jo why not To,
> you know. But To's eight see.*

The second kindergarten teacher at School A
also placed her students in accordance with the
principal's instructions. This became evident over
the course of several interviews which reveal further
features of the personality track. In one of these
interviews the teacher had been talking about Pe, one
of the more 'active' students when I asked the following question:

> INT.: *I noticed that you put him in (First
> Grade Teacher A's) room.*
> TEACHER: *Did I change his room? Oh now again
> in any of those children I can try to
> give my reasoning but I also tried to
> divide them 10, 10 and 10. I know
> there are a couple of children in
> (First Grade Teacher B's) room that I
> thought could very well go in the
> middle room. I call the middle room
> the unknown teacher (First Grade
> Teacher C) —*
> INT.: *Yes that's right.*
> TEACHER: *Amm but possibly not in (First Grade
> Teacher A's). If I've gotten the
> picture — I haven't spent a lot of*

65

time in (First Grade Teacher A's) room
just one or two times I've been there
to visit, and we took our class to
puppet shows and so forth.

INT.: *Umm humm.*

TEACHER: *But it's a different kind of room from*
(First Grade Teacher B's) room. And
we're trying to shield — I don't know
if this is good — shield the new
teacher (First Grade Teacher C) a
little bit so that she'll have a good
year and get off to a good start.

INT.: *How would you characterize the two*
rooms?

TEACHER: *Okay. Well let me just tell what was*
the one we were just talking about Pe
and....

INT.: *Pe and (First Grade Teacher A's)*
room —

TEACHER: *And (First Grade Teacher A's) room*
right. Well I felt amm I didn't mean
to put him in a loud noisy atmosphere
I don't want to encourage this in him
and yet I felt that he could take it,
you know, cuz I think he's used to
this kind of surrounding. Also amm
I think he's doing well in the phonics
approach to reading readiness. I
think he's hearing sounds an' this
kind of thing. And you know one of
the things we're supposed to look for
is children who learn this way maybe
better than other ways or at least
learn this way because (First Grade
Teacher A's) approach is much the
auditory phonics kind of approach...
and so I've got He in that room and who
else did I put St (___). Now some of
these kids...all these boys together
are very active and St my goodness he
can't shut up you know. He's just he's

66

ahh just talkative but sometimes this makes for a difficult situation if you have too many kids this way. Fr is active but they're not each one alone is ahh not what I'd call a behavior problem. So anyway there are several of those kids that are in that room but I thought maybe these kids could take a pretty active and noisy situation...And they didn't seem to me...well let's see some of those kids could go into the middle room if you wanted to but with (First Grade Teacher A's) approach I've picked out those are pretty good kids. Those are probably the cream of the crop as far as I can see grasping the numbers and reading concepts that we're teaching in kindergarten...I think if you look at those kids you'd think they're all... like Ma, have I got Ch there?

INT.:   *I think so.*

TEACHER: *Ch I might put in the middle one, he's kind of even going....*

This rather lengthy section of transcript reveals some of the features of the personality track placement practice which have already been described as well as some which have not been discussed thus far. This teacher, like her colleague, placed all of her 'strong' students with the teacher who had been typified by the principal as [*"strongly oriented academically"*]. This is clearly demonstrated when the teacher says of the students she placed in that teacher's room:

TEACHER: *Those are probably the cream of the crop as far as I can see grasping the numbers and reading concepts that we're teaching in kindergarten....*

67

She too placed all of the 'weak' students in her class with the teacher who was typified by the principal as [*"A momma, a warm mother"*]. This is strongly suggested by the following statement:

> TEACHER: *But I also tried to divide them 10, 10 and 10. I know there are a couple of children in (First Grade Teacher B's) room that I thought could very well go in the middle room....*

This statement suggests that the students who were placed in (First Grade Teacher B's) room were the weak students along with some of the *"average"* students who could have just as well been placed with the new teacher. The rest of the average students were placed with the new teacher. This is the same placement pattern as her colleague.

The rather long section of transcript that I have been examining also provides the reader with the characteristic features of the personality track placement practice. First, there is the feature of protecting the new teacher from the students who are [*"difficult"*] to handle as per the principal's instructions. This feature is strongly suggested by the following two passages one early in the account and the other from a later point:

> TEACHER: *And we're trying to shield — I don't know if this is good — shield the new teacher a little bit so that she'll have a good year....*
>
> TEACHER: *So that's why I put Pe there. I thought he might be a little hard for the middle teacher to handle....*

Second, there is the typifying of the two first grade teachers and then matching of the social type of the student with that of the teacher. The typification of the first grade teachers is embedded in the following statement:

> TEACHER: *I haven't spent a lot of time in (First Grade Teacher A's) room, just one or two times. I've been there to visit and we took our class to puppet shows and so forth...But it's a different room from (First Grade Teacher B's).*

The teacher does not come right out with a typification of the two teachers but she nevertheless suggests that the two teachers are different. There is also the matching of the student with the social type of the teacher as illustrated with the placement of Pe with the teacher who is [*"strongly oriented academically"*]:

> TEACHER: *Well I felt amm I didn't mean to put him in a loud, noisy atmosphere. I don't want to encourage this in him and yet I felt that he could take it you know cuz I think he's used to this kind of surrounding...So that's why I put Pe there: I thought he might be a little hard to handle for the middle teacher to handle....*

The placement of the student is accomplished through the teacher's use of typification of her students as matched with that of the first grade teacher. This matching involves the use of a behavioral contagion theory of social behavior as a tacit resource for matching the two typifications. This is suggested first, by the section of transcript just cited earlier [*"I didn't mean to put him in a loud noisy atmosphere. I don't want to encourage this in him"*]. It is also suggested by another section:

> TEACHER: *Now some of these kids, all these boys together are very active and St, my goodness he can't shut up you know. He's just, he's ahh just talkative but sometimes this makes for a difficult situation if you have too many kids*

69

*this way. Ti's active but they're
not each one alone is ahh not what
I'd call a behavior problem. So anyway there are several of those kids
that are in that room but I thought maybe these kids could take a pretty active
and noisy situation.*

What both of these sections point to is that the
teacher operates with a contagion theory of human
behavior and this tacit theory forms the background
or tacit resource for her use of the social types.
In the first example the teacher is clearly using
such a tacit theory of behavior for the passage implies that mere placement in such an environment will
lead or could lead to the student becoming noisy too;
especially if he is already that way. The second
example, the teacher's remark [*"He's just talkative
but sometimes this makes for a difficult situation if
you have many kids this way"*] clearly implies that
taken separately the students are *"all right"* but its
when they are together that *"things start to happen."*
In both of these examples the teacher is using a
theory of behavioral contagion which is similar to
the one proposed by Shibutani (1966: 95). This theory
of behavioral contagion is used by the teacher to
accomplish the articulation between the student and
the kind of teacher he is to be placed with. As such
the theory of behavioral contagion becomes an interpretive device for linking people and social types.
The theory becomes a members' method for making sense
of the environment. These examples also show that
the use of such tacit theories is context-bound in
that it is done within the pragmatic circumstances
and interests of the teacher, as suggested by the
remark [*"sometimes this makes for a difficult situation
if you have too many kids this way"*] .

70

CONCLUSION

The chapters which follow this one deal with students who are already in a classroom. In this chapter the topic has been: how do students get into and out of classes and ability groups. Using the ethnomethodological perspective, with its emphasis on how members define objects and events in their environments, I have attempted to locate and describe the placement practic es in the kindergartens of the two schools participating in the overall study. By way of concluding this chapter I would like to review the placement practices described herein in light of the perspective used in the study.

Ethnomethodologists stress the thoroughly accomplished character of social interaction including its sense as ongoing interaction. This accomplishment according to Garfinkel (1967) and Cicourel (1973) lies in the members' use of interpretive procedures. The description of how the teachers accomplished the screening interviews suggests that the use of elicitation practices by the teachers resulted in producing information to be counted as 'results'. Their 'seen but unnoticed' use by the teachers also resulted in the teachers' perception of the interviews as having an ongoing character. That is, through the seen but unnoticed use of elicitation practices, the teacher accomplished a sense of social structure. Furthermore, that discussion also revealed the indexical character of the screening results: they do not recover the situated practices of their accomplishment.

The use of elicitation practices also revealed what Garfinkel (1967) and Cicourel (1973) propose as one of the major properties of common-sense reasoning: reflexivity. When the teacher uses elicitation practices she is evaluating the information she receives from the student while simultaneously producing that information by using the practices. The elicitation practices provide "continuous (reflexive) feedback" enabling the teacher to sustain a sense of

71

"what's happening" or a sense of social structure (Cicourel, 1973).

Ethnomethodology also studies members' use of commonsense constructs. The member of society is conceived of as possessing a stock of knowledge consisting of typifications, recipes, and rules of thumb for negotiating everyday activities. Part of the teacher's stock of knowledge is a set of social types. A practice used by the teachers at both schools was to use these social types as interpretive schemes for articulating the student as being at one level of the tracking system rather than another. The Personality Track at School A consisted of the teachers' matching the social type of the student to those of the first grade teachers. At School B the teachers used social types to place the student into ability groups and the next grade. The tracking systems at both schools are constituted through the teachers' use of social types as schemes of interpretation.

The use of social types as schemes of interpretation involved practical circumstances. Embedded within the use of social types and their definitions (drawn from their situated usage) were a set of practical circumstances connected with teaching kindergarten. This feature of social types and their use suggests that the social types used by the teachers were 'invented' by them to recognize features of the students' behavior which if not recognized would result in the disintegration of the classroom situation (Wieder, 1969). This feature also supports Schutz' (1964) proposal that it is the practical interests and circumstances of the member that determines which part of his stock of knowledge will be used at a given moment. Finally, using social types as schemes of interpretation involved the use of tacit theories of social behavior as an interpretive resource to accomplish the articulation between a student and a social type.

In defining ethnomethodology, Garfinkel (1967) proposes that everyday activities are methods which members use to assign meaning to objects and events in their environments. The discussion of the teachers' use of routine activities of the classroom as devices for locating the students' abilities suggesting how this is accomplished. The indexical properties of the routine activities of the classroom enables the teachers to turn them into methods for locating and producing students of different abilities. Routine activities are transformed from play-activities to informal tests by the teacher supplying tacit meaning to those activities (seeing them as more than just playing but as embodying a set of developmental re-quirements) and through the way she interacts with the student.

Finally a word needs to be mentioned concerning the ontological status of the practices described in this chapter. The above list of practices is not a finite list — there are other practices which space does not permit mentioning and which await discovery. Further research is needed to determine which of these practices are situated and which are invariant to the situation. The practices described in this chapter are everyday activities which form 'seen but un-noticed' sense-making methods for locating and de-scribing students as possessing factual properties in order to place them into special classes, ability groups and into the next grade. Finally it would be a mistake for the reader to view these practices as 'faulty' or the result of poor teaching. These practices however faulty they may seem are part and parcel of the accomplishment of social interaction. Furthermore they are not to be conceived of as being capable of remedy through more formalized testing procedures. In the chapters which follow the reader will see that similar (but situated) practices are essential to the process of more 'standardized' tests as well.

APPENDIX

INITIAL INTERVIEW

NAME: _____
AGE: _____

How old are you? _____ Shows fingers: _____
Counts them: _____

When is your birthday? Month _____ Day _____

Did you have a party? _____ (who came) _____

    What did you like to do best? _____
    What was your favorite present? _____

How many brothers and sisters?
    Name   Age   Name   Age

_____ ____ _____ ____

_____ ____ _____ ____

_____ ____ _____ ____

What does your daddy do? _____
    (where does he work?)

* * * * * * * *

Incomplete man   Social expression
                            (How can you tell?)

                            How does he look?

                            How does he feel inside?

                            Happy or sad?

                            How can you tell?

74

APPENDIX
Incomplete Man Test

Incomplete man.

Chapter 3
ACCOMPLISHING CLASSROOM LESSONS

Hugh Mehan
University of California, San Diego

The evaluation of the child's performance in
school is being investigated in this book by videotaped analysis of interaction between: (1) children
and testers in the classroom; (2) children and testers
in tests; and (3) children, family members, and testers
in the home. Testing situations are reported on elsewhere (MacKay and Roth; this volume; Mehan, 1971).
This chapter reports on the classroom situation.

Teachers and other school officials continually
evaluate the child's school performance. The
educational method used to evaluate students'
abilities parallels the sociological conception of
social action. Sociologists typically describe social
action in terms of social actors following a set of
norms or rules in a social situation. (Parsons, 1937,
presents the most elaborate exposition of this model;
Wilson, 1970, documents its use throughout sociology.)
The components of this normative model include one
actor in a setting who produces talk or action. The
behavior is presumably guided or influenced in some
way by societal rules. A second actor, an observer
(or the first actor at a later point in time), judges
the a-propriateness of the first actor's behavior in
terms of the system's rules.

Applying this model to the educational setting,
the child is the producer of the action, which takes
the form of classroom talk or action. School officals,
in the person of teacher, tester, psychologist, etc.,
judge the appropriateness of the child's behavior in
terms of the educational system's rules. The rules of
the educational system, as they pertain to the child,
are primarily concerned with the 'correctness' or

'incorrectness' of the child's behavior. The following analysis is intended to shed light on the rule
interpretation process in the classroom.

Some of the characteristic demands on children
in the classroom will be explored in the following
sections by examining two "orientation lessons" which
took place in the first grade classroom of School A
described in Chapter 1. I will examine:
(1) the teacher's instructions to the children;
(2) the children's responses to these instructions;
and (3) the basis of the children's answers.

Methodological Notes

The materials presented in this chapter are
derived from transcripts of lessons made from the sound-
track of videotape recorded in School A. The following points are provided to clarify the procedures used
and the troubles encountered in videotaping, assembling transcripts, and analyzing materials.

Videotaping is not being recommended as a remedy
for sociological research problems. It is being used
to examine how measurement decisions and data interpretations in social science research and everyday
educational encounters are made. I locate my analysis
in transcribed materials so that the reader can have
access to the grounds of my analysis. With these
materials available, the reader can criticize my
interpretation and construct alternative interpreations.
The construction of alternative interpretations uncovers
the interpretive process itself, which is the ultimate
concern of this study.

Videotaping. The camera was set up in full view
of the participants in the classroom. The equipment
soon became a routine feature of the classroom scene.
The use of one camera limited study to small group
activities. Even when small group encounters were
recorded, it was often impossible to include all
participants within the field of focus. The omni-
directional microphone often made it difficult to
determine who the teacher was addressing, which child

77

was responding to the teacher, and what each participant was saying.

The lessons analyzed here were conducted when
the teacher arranged the class into small groups.
This arrangement reduced, but did not eliminate, the
problems of locating speakers, intended hearers, and
understanding utterances. These difficulties underline the point that varying interpretations of the
materials presented become available depending upon
the observer's familiarity with the materials, how (s)he
hears the tapes or sees the transcripts.

Transcript assembly. A transcript was made
after the lessons had been videotaped. A number of
practical decisions which have theoretical importance
have to be made during transcript assembly. If
grammatically correct, orthographically standardized
materials are included, the vocally or visually
provided information which is relied on to conduct
the analysis is omitted. If the duration of the
encounter of exchanges within it, grunts, hesitations,
hums and haws, pauses, false starts are included,
along with standard orthographical designations, a
different sense of the scene becomes available. Thus
the material included in a transcript influences the
reader's ability to reinterpret, criticize or expand
upon the analysis offered.

I include only words, and exclude gestures,
time references, and body movement designations in
the analysis which follows. Most exchanges between
teacher and children are included in the text. The
complete transcript is included as an appendix to the
chapter. I used a number of symbols in the text and
the appendix which are described below:

OL
| 1:1 | SW: | *Yes. Let's take...* | The transcript, page line, speaker, utter-rance |
| 1:6 | Di: | [*Hey, can you make*
[*it on -yours? -under?* | Two utterances spoken simultaneously |

5:16 Di:	*I know*		
		//SW: *Tell us*	An interruption
5:18 Ri:	_____		An unrecorded utter-
			ance
4:21 SW:	*The sun...*		A faded utterance
9:21 Pa:	*I put a, a, a*		An unclear utterance
	?madenta? under the		
	grass		

Although I am presenting the transcript as my
materials in this chapter, I am not suggesting that
the transcript captures the setting analyzed. As I
produced the analysis, I filled in information from
my memory of the surrounding events. It is difficult
if not impossible to separate the materials presented
or analyzed from the remembered experience, even
though I want to have the materials stand on their
own. In a sense, the transcript serves as documentary
evidence of the seen but not presented interactional
particulars of the situations analyzed.

The lessons studied. The orientations lessons
are concerned with spatial relations. The teacher
gathered a small group of children at a round table
in the corner of the room while the remainder are
occupied at their seats with other tasks. The teacher
presented the children with materials — drawing paper
and crayons in the first lesson, and flannel board
and objects of various shapes, sizes, and colors in
the second lesson. The teacher instructed the children
to orient certain objects in relation to other objects.
In the first lesson, the children are to draw lines
on their papers and then draw other objects on their
papers in relation to that line. In the second lesson,
the children are to place a piece of felt in relation
to a yarn line stretched across the flannel board.
There are behaviorally receptive and verbally
expressive comprehension tasks in each of the lessons.
Pressing the felt objects onto the board and drawing
objects on the worksheets is the behavioral portion of
the lesson, and represents receptive comprehension of

79

the instructions. There is also an expressive comprehension aspect of these lessons. After the children
have placed objects on the board or drawn them they
are asked to report on the activities they accomplished
during the behavioral portion of the lesson. There are
factual and grammatical aspects of the expressive
task. In accordance with the indefinite triangulation
procedure explained in Chapter 1, I asked the teacher
about the goals she had for the lesson and the expectations she had for the children's performance. She
reported that she expected the children to produce
answers which were both factually *correct* and grammatically *complete*. The teacher expected the children
to produce answers which *correctly* describe how they
placed objects in the behavioral portion of the lesson,
and the answer must appear as a complete sentence.

Characteristics of the Teacher's Instructions

In this section I examine the instructions which
the teacher gives to the children in the orientations
lessons. The teacher introduced the lessons by
demonstrating what she wanted the children to do
(OL 1:1; 7:12). In the first lesson, the teacher drew
a line on her paper, asked the children to do the same,
and then asked them to draw another object in relation
to that line. In the second lesson, she stretched a
piece of yarn across the flannel board, placed an
object above it, and then asked the children to place
a felt object on the board just above the line. After
this "behavioral" portion of the lesson, the teacher
asked the children to report on their work (OL 1:12;
7:12).

In both lessons, the dimensions and range of the
tasks were not described to the children. The children
in the first lesson were not told why they were drawing
worms, trees, and suns in relation to the line on their
papers. The children in the second lesson were not
told why a yarn was placed on the flannel board and
what was involved in putting felt beside the line.
Although later in both lessons the children are asked
to tell about the objects they had worked with, they

80

were not told what was going to be expected of them as they were drawing and placing the objects. When they were told to place objects in relation to the line, they were not told the distinguishing characteristics of the orientations prepositions. They were not told what it was to put something *above* or *below* the line, and how that action was different from putting something *"on there"* or *"doing what the teacher said."*

The teacher used vague, ambiguous, and incomplete instructions when she asked the children to report on their work. The teacher said: *Where is the orange worm, Do?* (OL 2:12); *Ri, where is the little seed? Where is the seed?* (OL 2:5); *Where is the worm, Je?* (OL 2:9); *Ok, all right, can you tell us, Pa, about what you did? What did you do?* (OL 7:12); *Listen, Ro, can you remember what I said?* (OL 7:23); *All right, Ro, tell us what you did* (OL 7:27).

When the teacher asked these *where, what,* and *when* questions, and others like them, she had a certain response in mind. The teacher told me in a post-lesson interview that she wanted the children to answer completely and correctly (see the description of a 'complete correct response' above). She wanted them to use certain prepositions (under, over, below and above) and not others (by, next to, on, in) while describing where the objects had been placed. However, the teacher does not tell the children about the intended answer form. The question *where did you put it?* or its equivalents *what did you do?* and *where is it?* (OL 9:2; 2:5-4:8) does not instruct the children: (1) to use the prepositions *under, above, below,* and *over* while describing the objects' placement; (2) to choose certain objects and not others; or (3) to construct a complete sentence.

The children's answers to the *where is it* question show there are many ways to formulate the location of the objects used in the lessons. Je said she placed her blue square *in the middle* (OL 7:18) of the flannel board. Pa said he *put a one on there* (OL 7:13), and that his pink diamond was *right by the sun* (OL 9:1). Je also said *The red flower is by the tree*

81

(OL 4:3) when asked where the red flower was located (OL 4:2). Do combined proterms with ostensive pointing while locating her orange worm *right there* (OL 1:13). Other answers to the question *where is the seed (worm, flower...)* could have included *on the paper, in the room, in the garden, at home.* Questions like *where is the...* do not tell the children how to choose the expected answer from among the many possible ways to formulate the location of the objects placed during the lesson.

The child's problem in this lesson is similar to what Schegloff (1971) describes as the member's problem in formulating location. Schegloff notes that even though places, objects, or activities can be adequately and correctly described by one of a set of terms, on a particular occasion there are some formulations which are more appropriate than others. The child in these lessons must determine what the teacher considers to be the appropriate formulation of the location of the items on the board or on the paper.

The question *what did you do?* asks the children to report on activities which had taken place previously, but which had not been marked as activities which were to be reported on later. To answer a question like this, the child must remember previous instructions across time, interruptions, and intervening tasks. The child has done many things while at the work table, in school that morning, that week, that year. Instructions like *tell us what you did* require the child to select and report on one action from among the many he has performed; however, there are no hints or cues in the instruction which help the child decide which of the many activities he has performed should be reported on.

The children must be able to make the same 'sorting decisions' when asked *...can you remember what I said?* (OL 7:23). The teacher has said a lot of things during this and other lessons. Now the teacher is asking the child to search the entire corpus of *things the teacher had said* to locate an appropriate item for this occasion. The teacher has not refered to the one appropriate of the many instructions she has given.

Furthermore, when the instruction was given to the group (OL 6:13-14), there was no indication that it would be important subsequently.

The instruction *Ro, put something yellow above the green line. All right, Pa, put something pink above the green line* (OL 8:10), given in the second orientation lesson has the same properties. The term *something* can refer to a wide range of objects. There are a lot of *"things"* in the room, the school, the world which potentially could be a *"something."* There are no explicit boundaries which establish the domain from which the children can choose a *"something"* to place on the board. Nevertheless, without fail, the children go to the shoebox on the table to choose a *"something."* The information which the children need to carry out that instruction is not found in the verbal instruction, but comes from previous work with the materials, the nonverbal actions of the teacher, and other children.

In the general model of classroom interrogation, the teacher asks a question and the child answers. If the child produces an acceptable answer then the teacher asks this child another question, or asks another child a question. If the child doesn't answer correctly then the teacher continues to question the child until a correct answer is obtained. In the lessons under review, when a child did not answer acceptably the teacher typically asked the child to answer again. However, the teacher's supplemental instructions or questions contain little (if any) more information about what is expected than the original request did.

After all the children in the second lesson had placed an object on the flannel board, she asked them to explain their work:

OL
7:12　SW:　*...can you tell us about what you did? What did you do?*
　13　Pa:　*I put a one on there*
　14　SW:　*Ok, where did you put it?*
　15　Pa:　*On there*

16 JE: *In the middle*
17 SW: *Where did you put it on there?*
18 JE: *In the middle*
        //Ro: *up above*//Pa: *in the middle*
        //Ro: *above.*

Pa's reply (7:13) is an *adequate* answer to the
teacher's question (7:12). However, the teacher had
an unstated expectation for the answer form which
made Pa's response *unacceptable.* The teacher continued to ask Pa about his performance. She continued
to get adequate but unacceptable formulations of the
object's location: *on there, in the middle, up above.*
        On other occasions when the children did not
answer to the teacher's satisfaction, the teacher
provided a model of the complete, correct response for
the children to imitate. She said the equivalent of
*can you say that in a sentence: The seed is under the
grass* many times. That kind of supplemental instruction *does* provide the child with more information about
expected answers, but the features which make that
sentence exemplary by comparison with the ones submitted but not accepted are not made clear to the child.
When a child produces an answer which meets the requirements of a complete correct response, the child
is not told: *"That is the kind of answer I want; from
now on answer questions like that."* The teacher merely
goes on to the next step in the lesson.
        On some occasions when the children did not pro-
duce a CCR, the teacher did not ask them to reproduce
a model sentence, but asked them to expand their
elliptical version into a complete sentence. (To do
this, the teacher asked, for example, *Can you say that
in a sentence?* (OL 2:11).) When a child is presented
with a model, he can imitate it without necessarily
knowing why that sentence is preferred over other
productions. Likewise, when a child is asked to expand his answer, he is not provided with information
that tells him what the desired answer form is.
        The child does not understand the expected
answer form because the teacher does not indicate *why*

84

answers are correct. Not every answer which is accepted is marked for the reasons it was accepted. The model of the correct answer is supposed to be a complete sentence. Yet, as I will show in the following section, a complete sentence is not obtained every time an answer is accepted. Sometimes incomplete sentences are accepted. For example, Do was asked where she had drawn her orange worm (OL 1:12). Her first response, *right there*, was not accepted (OL 1:13-14), presumably because it did not meet the specifications of a 'complete, correct response'.

Her second response, *under the grass* (OL 1:15), did not meet the requirements of a complete, correct response either, yet it was accepted. For now, I am not concerned with the differential treatment of similar answers by the teacher; I will take that point up in the following section. I wish to point out that Do, although told her answer is acceptable, is not told *why* her answer passes.

The same is true in the following sequence. The children in the first lesson are asked to make a red flower under the tree they have drawn on their worksheets (OL 3:4). Then they are asked to *tell...where the red flower is* (OL 3:4). Do is selected to tell about her flower first, and the following transaction took place:

OL
3:5	Do:	*Under the tree*
6	SW:	*Tell me in a sentence*
7	Do:	*It's under the tree*
8	SW:	*What's under the tree, the flower, Do? Tell me. The flower*
9	Do:	*The flower is under the tree.*
10	SW:	*Where is the red flower Ri?*

The teacher's initial instruction to tell about the placement of the flower in relation to the tree does not contain information about how the child is to choose from among all the available ways to formulate the location of the tree and flower. When the

85

child produces answers which do not pass, but then
finally submits one which does, she is not told what
differentiates between her incorrect and her correct
response.

I have been describing teachers' instructions
which do not tell the child how to choose the one
'correct' answer from among a number of possible
answers. Now I will describe instructions which produce answers from the children which *are* correct under
the guidelines of the instruction, but are not the
responses the teacher wanted. These answers are not
factually wrong; they are inappropriate in terms of
the teacher's unstated expectations. The answers are
not appropriate because of the ambiguity of the instruction to which they are a response.

In the first orientations lesson, after the
children had all drawn flowers on their worksheet, they
were then asked to describe their work. The teacher
had trouble getting Ci to explain her work in a complete sentence by asking her standard questions, so
she changed her question format a little. She provided
an *incorrect* formulation of the location of the flower
in relation to the grass: *"Can we say the red flower
is above the grass?"* (OL 3:24). Her intention was
to have the child correct this factually incorrect
statement by saying *"no."* However, the phrase *"can
we say"* is apparently at least two ways ambiguous,
for Ci does not deny or correct the erroneous statement, she imitates it: *"The red flower is above the
grass"* (OL 4:1). Whereas the teacher is asking
whether it is factually correct to say such a thing as
"flowers are above the grass," Ci follows the routine
established previously and gives a grammatically correct answer form. In these earlier question-answer
frames, such an answer would have been correct, for
it has the correct syntactic form. However, her
choice of prepositions makes this a factually incorrect, though grammatically correct answer.

The same sense of ambiguity in instructions is
found in this sequence taken from the first orientations
lesson:

86

OL
4:19 SW: *All right, Di, can you tell me something*
            that the sun is above? The sun is...
  20 Di: *Above the ground um ground*
  21 SW: *The sun...*
  22 Di: *is above the* ⎡ *tree*
      Ci: ⎣ *tree*
5:01 SW: *All right, can you say it in a sentence*
            now? All together?
  02 All: *The sun is above*
                //SW: *Let Di do it and*
                       say all of it.
                       The sun...

In line 4:21, the teacher is attempting to get Di to
give her answer in a complete sentence. She wants Di
to say *"The sun is above the tree."* To aid Di in the
production of that sentence, the teacher begins the
sentence: *"The sun..."* However, Di interprets the
teacher's question as a request for another object
the sun is above. She *completes* the sentence by
building on the phrase provided by the teacher. Both
'sentence completion' and 'sentence repetition' are
logically possible and feasible answers to the instruction *"the sun..."*. Although one of the possible
answers, sentence repetition, and not sentence completion is expected and preferred by the teacher, the
children are not provided the means by which they can
come to that conclusion.

    The question *"can you say it in a sentence now?*
All together?" contained in line (5:01) is another
example of a request which has one intended meaning
for the teacher and another for the children. When
the teacher asks this question, she wants *Di* to *com-*
plete the sentence she had given in (4:22). The
children, however, interpret this instruction as a
request for an answer to be given in *unison*.

    This analysis shows teachers' instructions dur-
ing classroom lessons do not provide children with
all the information they need to follow the instructions.
The child must look elsewhere for assistance in interpreting verbal instructions, commands, and questions.

He must attend to the materials he is working with,
his classroom experiences, other children's activities,
the teacher's gestures, body orientations and voice
intonations. The child must call on instructions given
to him on previous occasions; he must decide which,
among the many instructions given to him previously,
applies in a particular situation.

Garfinkel (1967; Garfinkel and Sacks, 1970) and
Cicourel (1973) (following Bar-Hillel's 1954 usage)
call utterances with these characteristics "indexical
expressions." Indexical expressions are tied to the
context in which they are used. The meaning different
interpreters (e.g., participants in the lesson, such
as teachers and children, observers of the lesson,
such as principals and researchers) derive varies
with their perspectively provided knowledge of contextual features. Because teachers' classroom talk
(like parents' talk in the home) is indexical, the
child must learn to rely on contextual features to
negotiate teaching-learning situations. (I will
discuss some of the contextually based interpretive
practices which children use to understand teachers'
indexical expressions below in the section entitled
"the source of the children's answers.") Reliance on
contextual features to understand utterances is an
integral feature of classroom learning. However, the
child's opportunities to utilize contextually provided information is purposefully limited in the formal
testing situation. The implications this suppression
has for the evaluation of the child's school performance
is discussed briefly below and more extensively elsewhere (MacKay and Roth, this volume).

The Teacher's Treatment of Children's Answers

I have described the way in which the teacher
requests children to perform actions and respond to
questions. I will now examine the children's responses
to such requests and the teacher's reactions to these
responses.

In the expressive portion of these two orientation
lessons, the teacher consistently uses a question like

"where is the triangle?" to elicit the children's responses. The teacher expects the children to produce answers which *correctly* describe how they placed objects in relation to other objects in the behavioral portion of the lesson. The answer is to take the form of a *complete* sentence, diagrammed in phrase structure in Figure 3.1.

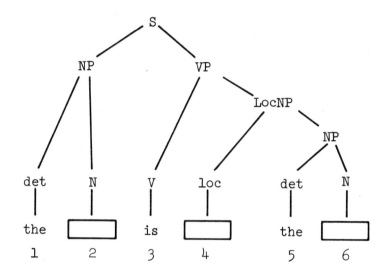

FIGURE 3.1. "The Complete Correct Response" (CCR)

That is, the child is expected to produce a response like *"the triangle is under the line."* The child is not supposed to submit: (a) Subject NPs (represented by slots 1 and 2), e.g., *"the chair;"* (b) Proterms (e.g., *"it," "my"*) in the place of the Subject NP, e.g., *"It's under the table," "On there," "here;"* (c) LocNPs (represented by slots 4,5 and 6), e.g., *"under the chair;"* or (d) final NPs (slots 5 and 6) e.g., *"the chair."* If the child does submit one of these (or other) unacceptable answer forms, the teacher is supposed to continue questioning the child until the

CCR is obtained.

I will now examine the teacher's application of this 'correctness and completeness' rule to children's answers. I will confine my analysis in this section to the children's responses to instances of the question type: *"Where is the triangle?"* All such exchanges between the teacher and the children are discussed below. The numbers in parentheses without colons in the margin next to an excerpt from the transcript designate the sequence being discussed, e.g., (3). Numbers in parentheses with colons, e.g., (OL 1:1) refer to the *"Orientations lesson"* transcript page and line numbers. Once a segment is discussed, it will be referred to later in the text by its *"sequence number."* All conversation between teacher and children which intervenes between segments analyzed is omitted. It may be found in the *"Orientations Lessons Transcript"* (Appendix 1) from which the segments are taken.

The children's answers. After the children in the first lesson have all drawn objects on their pages *"under the line,"* the teacher asks Do to report on what she has done:

OL
```
    1:12  SW:  ... All right, where is the orange
                  worm, Do
      13  Do:  Right there.
(1)   14  SW:  Ok, tell me where he is
      15  Do:  Under the grass
      16  SW:  Ok...
```

Do is the first child asked to respond to this question type. She answers by pointing and provides *"proterms,"* i.e., *"right there."* This response is not accepted, and on her second turn, Do provides a LocNP. Because the teacher goes on to the next phase of the lesson, instructing the children to draw other objects on their paper, I take it (and assume the children also take it) that this response passes as correct.

After the children have all drawn seeds under

90

the grass on their papers, the teacher asks the children to describe their location. Ri is asked first:

OL

	2:5	SW:	*Ri, where is the little seed? Where is the seed?*
(2)	6	Ri:	*Under the grass*
	7	SW:	*Can you say that in a sentence? The seed is under the grass?*
	8	Ri:	*The seed is under the grass seed*

Ri, like Do ahead of him, provided a LocNP, but unlike Do's, his response did not pass. He was asked to provide his answer in a complete sentence, which he did on his next turn. Both children took two turns to provide an acceptable answer, but a LocNP was judged acceptable for one child, while a complete sentence was demanded and obtained from the second child. Note that the child added a word, *"seed"* to the sentence he was asked to imitate, *"the seed is under the grass."* This violation of the correct answer form (which actually resulted in a meaningful sentence) was not challenged, though the submission of a LocNP was.

As soon as Ri has answered this question, the teacher calls on Je to do the same:

OL

	2:9	SW:	*Where is the worm, Je*
	10	Je:	*Under the grass*
(3)	11	SW:	*Can you tell me in a sentence?*
	12	Je:	*The the worm is under the grass*
	13	SW:	*All right now...*

Je, like Ri and Do, takes two turns to reach an answer the teacher considers acceptable. Je, like Ri, was expected to produce a complete sentence. Like Ri, Je modified the complete sentence, but not enough to be challenged.

The children are then asked to make red flowers under their trees and to report on their placement. Do is asked to tell about the flower she drew first:

OL

	3:4	SW:	*Ok, let's look at the red flower. Can you tell me where the red flower is Do?*
		All:	*right here, right here*
	5	Do:	*Under the tree*
	6	SW:	*Tell me in a sentence*
(4)	7	SW:	*What's under the tree? Do Tell me, the flower... The flower*
	9	Do:	*The flower is under the tree*

The teacher, ignoring the chorus of *"right here's,"* designates Do to locate the flower. Do produces a LocNP which is not accepted. Do extends the complexity of the sentence, but presumably, because she uses a pronoun (it, in line 3:7) instead of a NP, that response is not accepted either. The teacher asks for the name of the object which is under the tree, ex-pecting, presumably: *"The flower is under the tree."* Do provides the Noun Phrase *"the flower"* instead, which, although an answer to the question, is not in the form of a complete sentence. Therefore, the teacher prompts Do with the phrase she has just given her, and Do then gives a complete correct response. Do has now responded twice in this lesson. The first time (1) the LocNP she provided was accepted; the second time she was extended until she produced a complete sentence.

Finished with Do, SW turns to Ri.

OL

	3:10	SW:	*Where is the red flower, Ri?*
	11	Ri:	*Under tree*
(5)	12	SW:	*Can you tell me in a sentence?*
	13	Ri:	*The flower is under the tree.*

This response set is essentially the same as the one Ri gave when asked the first time. On both occasions, he took two turns to produce a complete correct re-sponse.

Ci is next:

92

OL

> 3:14 SW: *Ci, where is the red flower?*
> (6) 15 Ci: *The red flower is under* ⌈ *the tree*
> *Hey, that's*
> ⌊ *not red*

On her first turn, Ci produces the desired answer form.
The teacher's questions consist of a factual and
a grammatical dimension. Although the teacher presumably demands adherence to both factual and grammatical standards of correctness, sometimes the teacher
only deals with one kind of violation, and lets the
other kind of error pass without correction. In this
case, the flower Ci drew was not in *fact* red; she had
used a crayon of a different color to draw her flower.
So, although her sentence was grammatically correct
and complete, it did not factually report on the actual
state of affairs which existed on her work sheet. The
answer met the grammatical requirements of a complete,
correct response, but violated the factual requirements.
Yet, the teacher, concerned with grammatical construction, did not correct the inaccurate account.

The teacher's practice of correcting matters of
grammar while sometimes ignoring matters of fact is
interesting in light of the psycholinguistic observation (McNeill, 1971) that parents are often more
concerned to correct factual mistakes in their children's
descriptions than they are concerned to correct any
syntactic irregularities in sentences. Schutz (1970)
provides assistance for the interpretation of such
seemingly contradictory empirical observations with
his concept of "perceptual relevance." Attention
directed to one feature of a scene often prohibits
attention to other features simultaneously. While one
problem is in the foreground of perception, others slip
into the background of features. As systems of relevance
are modified, the problem which was of little concern
can be brought from the background and placed at the
center of focus. When the children around the teacher
make demands on her attention, when she has to keep
a watchful eye on children in other parts of the room.

Because she is unable to record each child's answer as he gives it, the teacher's attention is drawn away from the multiple dimensions of her question. They slip into the background of her perception. But, in the very next moment, the teacher may be freed of these pressures and her attention can be focused more intently on the question she is asking. When her attention is not divided, she is able to focus on individual children's needs and mistakes. Descriptions (and criticisms of the teacher's evaluations of children must take these situationally based, moment-to-moment shifts in the teacher's attention into account.

Continuing around the table with the same question, the teacher asks Di about the flower she drew:

OL

	3:16	SW:	*Di, where is the red flower?*
	17	Di:	*The red flower*
(7)	18	SW:	*The red flower*
	19	Di:	*Is under the tree*

Di takes two turns to complete the desired sentence form. On her first turn, the LocNP is given. In (2), (3), (4), (5) the children gave less than complete sentences, and were asked to bring them up to the desired level of correctness. That request was not made of Di here.

Je is the next to be asked to formulate the flower's location under something:

OL

4:2	SW:	*Je, can you tell me where the red flower is?*
3	Je:	*The red flower is by the tree.*
4	SW:	*Yes, the flower is by the tree. What can we say about it when we talk about the flower and the tree? Where is the red flower in relationship to the grass? What can we say about it when we talk about the flower and the grass? Do you know what, can you listen to each other now?*

94

5	Ri:	*Can we make mud under here?*
6	SW:	*Maybe we can make mud under here. Right now it's Je's turn to talk. Ci can you put your crayons on the table? Where is the red flower, is it under the grass?*
	Di:	*My name is Mrs. Crayon*
7	Je:	*No*
8	SW:	*Where is it?*
9	Je:	*On the grass*
10	SW:	*All right, it's on the grass. Is it above the grass?*
	Di:	*My name is Green Grass. Can you talk to me? My name is Green Crayon. I am sticking a crayon in my earphone.*
11	Je:	*No*
12	SW:	*Ok...*

(8) appears to the left of the transcript.

Je's response (OL 4:3), though in the form of a complete sentence is not accepted because of the presence of the preposition *"by."* The teacher's attempts to have Je substitute an *"under phrase"* for the *"by phrase"* are confused by interruptions from other children. After a series of questions to which Je provides *"no's"* she produces a locNP which is accepted as an answer. This sequence contrasts with (3), where Je produced a complete, correct response after two turns. Here a LocNP was accepted.

The teacher next instructs the children to draw suns above the trees on their worksheets (4:12). Ci is first to tell where she drew the sun on her paper:

OL

4:16	SW:	*All right, can you tell* ⎡ *where the sun is?*
(9)	Ci:	⎣ *above the grass*
17	SW:	*All right, Ci, tell us where the sun is.*
18	Ci:	*It's above the tree.*

This sequence initially follows the pattern seen in (4) where Do first provided a LocNP, then when she was asked *what* was under the tree, provided the pronoun *"it."* This sequence differs from (4) in that the

95

pronoun *"it"* is accepted, whereas, in sequence (4) it
was rejected and a complete sentence was demanded.
In one sequence (4) a proterm is an acceptable referent
for an object; on another sequence (9) it isn't.

The teacher now changes the task slightly. She
wants Di to tell her the name of another object which
the sun she has drawn on her page is above.

OL

4:19	SW:	*All right, Di, can you tell me some-thing else that the sun is above? The sun is...*
20	Di:	*Above the ground um ground*
21	SW:	*The sun...*
22	Di:	*Is above the　　　tree*
	Ci:	*　　　　　　　　tree*
(10) 5:1	SW:	*All right, can you say it in a sentence now? Altoghether?*
2	All:	*The sun is above*

　　　　　　　//SW: *Let Di do it and say all of it.*

　　　　　　　　The sun is　　above the tree
　　　Di:　　　　　　　　　　*aobve the tree*

| 3 | SW: | *Can you say it* |
| 4 | Di: | *The sun is above the tree.* |

Di succeeded at first in providing the name of another
object the sun was above (OL 4:20). But because she
used a LocNP and not a complete sentence, the teacher
continues to question her. She starts the sentence
which she wants Di to add the phrase *"is above the
ground."* With help from Ci, Di *completes* the sentence
begun by the teacher, rather than *repeating* it from
the beginning, as the teacher wanted. Therefore, the
teacher asks Di to provide a complete sentence, which
she obtains (OL 5:4). This is the second time Di has
been asked to respond to the question *"where is ＿＿＿."*
The first time (7), the LocNP which she provided was
accepted; this time it was not.

Note that Ci's addition changed Di's response
from *ground* to *tree*. Ci had already provided *tree*

96

as an answer to the question: tell me something *else*
the *sun* is above. By changing her response from
ground to *tree*, Di was in effect, violating the factual
aspect of the question-answer frame, while satisfying
the grammatical aspect. (See sequence (6) for a
similar occurrence.)

The teacher continues to ask the children for
other things the sun is above (OL 5:5). After Ri
says he doesn't know, (OL 5:6) Do is asked to answer:

OL

     5:07 SW: *All right, Do, can you try it?*
       08 Do: *Try what?*
       09 SW: *Is the sun above something else*
(11)   *besides the tree?*
       10 Do: *Yeah, the line*
       11 SW: *Say it in a sentence*
       12 Do: *The sun is above the line.*

Do's production of the final NP is once again not
accepted; she has been asked to produce a LocNP each
time (1), (4), and (11) she has answered. She produced
a LocNP each time; it was accepted as an adequate
response once. She was asked to complete the sentence
the two other times.

The teacher then changed the task. Instead of
asking the children to represent objects on their
worksheets, the teacher asked them to find similar
things in the classroom. Je responds first, followed
by Ri:

OL

     5:13 SW: *Now, listen to me. I'm looking around*
            this room, and I'm going to try to find
(12)   *some things that are above me, that are*
            up above me. And I can say...
       14 Je: *The ceilin'. The ciling is up above me.*
       15 SW: *Ok, the ciling is up above me. Can you*
            tell me something that is above
                ⌈ *you. Ri look around*
         Di: ⌊ *you*

```
      16   Di:   I know
                 SW:   Tell us
                              //Ri:   I know what's above
                                      me:   a light
(13)  17   SW:   Say it in a sentence        //the light...
                              //Di:   A garbage can
      18   Ri:   _____
      19   SW:   Ok, Ri, just tell me something that is
                 above you and then you can go to the
                 bathroom.
      20   Ri:   The light is above me.
```

Je for only the second time in the lesson produces a
complete correct response on her first try. Ri then
produces the initial noun, "light," which the teacher
asks to be put into a complete sentence. This is the
third response by both Je and Ri. Ri has been asked
for a complete sentence each time he answered (2), (5),
(13). Of je's three responses (3), (8), and (12), a
LocNP was accepted once (8); the other two times, she
was asked to provide a complete sentence.

Continuing the sequence, Ci is asked to report
on things that are above her:

```
OL
      5:21   SW:   ...Can you tell me something, Ci?
      6:01   Ci:   _____
        02   SW:   Those are kind of hard to say.  Those
(14)              are acoustical tile.  Why don't you just
                  say the tile.
        03   Ci:   The tile is above us.
```

The videocorder was not able to pick up Ci's response
(6:01), so my record does not show whether she produced
a complete correct response. Insofar as the teacher
provided the name of the ceiling tile, I take it that
Ci asked a question rather than produced a response.
Nevertheless, she was able to produce a complete
sentence in her next turn, marking the second time she
did so (6). During her other response sequence (9),
Ci's incomplete utterance passed.

Do is asked next:

OL

    6:4 SW: *Ok, Do, can you find something that is*
(15)   *above you? Look around you and find*
               something that is above you.
      5 Do: *The light is above me.*

This is Do's fifth response. For the second time in a row she has produced the expected answer form.

The following request made of Di is the last in the lesson:

OL

    6:6 SW: *All right, Di, can you find something*
              that's above you?
      7 Di: *A table*
      8 SW: *Can you tell me something that's above*
              you, Di?
(16) 9 Di: *Table*
     10 SW: *Is that above you? What table is above*
              you?
     11 Di: *It's above*
     12 SW: *I can say something...*

The teacher is not happy with Di's choice of *"the table"* as an object which is higher than she is. She tries to explain to Di what is wrong with her answer. However, she does not require Di to produce a complete response. Her last phrase *"It's above"* (OL 6:11) stands as an acceptable utterance.

The following exchanges occur in the second orientations lesson given immediately following the lesson just discussed. The task and materials have changed, but the question frame and CCR rule remains in effect. After all the children in this second group have placed objects on the flannel board in response to the instruction *"put something above the green line"* Pa is the first asked to explain what he had done:

OL
```
        7:12   SW:   ...can you tell us, Pa, about what you
                     did?  What did you do?
          13   Pa:   I put a one on there.
          14   SW:   Ok, where did you put it?
          15   Pa:   On there
          16   Je:   In the middle
          17   SW:   Where did you put in on here?
(18)      18   Je:   In the middle
                        //Ro:  up above              //above
                           //Pa:  in the middle
          19   SW:   Did I say put a one in the middle, or
                     put something in the middle:  What did
                     I tell you to do?
         20:   Pa:   Put anything
         21:   SW:   Where did I tell you to put it?
          22   Pa:   On the bottom
          23   SW:   Listen...
```

The first of Pa's five responses in this sequence meets
all the requirements for a grammatically correct response but one: he uses the preposition *"on"* rather
than *"above."* When further questions which incorporate
parts of the correct answer do not elicit a proper speci-
men, the teacher allows the erroneous utterance to pass,
and turns to Ro:

OL
```
        7:23   SW:   Listen, Ro, can you remember what I
                     said?
          24   Ro:   Put it above
          25   SW:   Above what?
(18)      26   Ro:   The green line
          27   SW:   All right Ro, tell us what you did.
          28   Ro:   Put a square a:a:a  Put a square above
                     the green line
```

Ro, across her first two turns, produced the components
of the complete correct response. The teacher then
asked her to answer in a complete sentence. This request
stands in contrast to (7), where Di had also produced

the components of the correct answer across two turns, but was not asked to produce a complete, correct response.

Having obtained the desired response from Ro, she turns to Je:

OL

	8:3	SW:	*Ok, Je, can you tell me what you did ?*
	4	Je:	*I put a blue triangle above*
(19)	5	SW:	*Above what?*
	6	Je:	*The green line*
	7	SW:	*Ok...*

In her first reply, Je gives all information but the final noun (line, grass...). The teacher prompts her a bit and Je provides the ending of the sentence. As with (7) and unlike (18) the child was not asked to put the components together in a complete sentence.

A new round of object placement is begun, and Je is the first child to be asked where she placed objects on the flannel board:

OL

8:17	SW:	*All right, Je, tell me what you did.*
18	Je:	*I put a blue u:n:n: //square*
		//SW: *square*
		//Ro: *square*
19	Ro:	*I'm not going to tell you guys*
20	Je:	*Above the green line*

This is the second time in a row that the teacher has not asked Je to combine the parts of the complete answer. If Je's two parts are combined, the name of the object which had been placed above the line is missing. It can be found in Ro's addition to Je's first response and the teacher's reinforcement of it. In fact, then, Je has not produced a complete response, even across two turns, as she did immediately before (19). The teacher allows the *incomplete* response produced across two turns to stand, and goes on to Pa:

101

OL

   8:21 SW: *Pa, what did you do?*

     22 Pa: *I put a pink //I mean no, what was it?*
                      //Je: *yellow*

     23 SW: *A pink*
                 //Ro: *diamond*
                          //Pa: *a pink diamond*

     24 SW: *Where:*

  9:01 Pa: *Right by the sun*

      2 SW: *All right, it's right by the sun, but where is it?*

(21)   3 Ro: *Up above the line*
                       //Je: *the green line*

      4 Pa: *The line*

      5 SW: *Where did I tell you to put it?*

      6 Pa: *Above the*

      7 SW: *above what?*

      8 Pa: *Above the green line*

Pa's initial attempt to answer this question, like Je's earlier (8), contained a *"by phrase"* and so was rejected. The teacher succeeded in directing Pa to use the preposition *"above,"* but the sequence stopped short of a complete response. Insofar as this sequence ends with a LocNP accepted as an adequate formulation, it is similar to (1), (7), (8), (20). Insofar as an answer produced across turns is accepted as adequate it is like (7), (19), and (20); see (27) below as well.

     Ro is the last child to be asked about her placement of an object above the line:

OL

   9:09 SW: *All right, Ro, what did you do?*

(22) 10 Ro: *Put a yellow rec, I put a yellow rectangle above the green line.*

Ro gives a complete, correct response on her first try. On her previous answer in this lesson (18), she was asked to complete a sentence which had contained only a LocNP.

When Ro completed her answer, the teacher removed the objects from the flannel board and asked the children to place objects *under* the line, rather than *above* it. As each child places his object on the flannel board, he is asked to report on its placement.

Ro leads off; followed by Pa:

OL

	9:18	SW:	*...Ro, what did you do?*
(23)	19	Ro:	*Put magenta under the grass*
	20	SW:	*Ok. Ma:a:genta. (Ro: magenta). All right, Pa. Would you find something magenta and put it under the grass? Ok. What did you do Pa?*
	21	Pa:	*I put a a, a, ?magent? under the grass*
(24)	22	SW:	*Magenta what? Is it a circle? (Pa: No). Did you put a magenta circle under the grass?*
	23	Pa:	*I put a magenta square under the grass.*
	24	SW:	*All right...*

Ro treats the word *"magenta"* as a noun and this use passes, perhaps because the teacher is intent on correcting her mispronunciation of the word. When Pa uses the word in the same way, the teacher corrects him, and makes him use it as a modifier. Thus the teacher treats the same error differently though they occur immediately after one another.

When the children finished placing *magenta* objects, the teacher asked Je to choose a *blue* object to place on the flannel board below the grass 10:3:

OL

	10:3	SW:	*Je, what did you do?*
	4	Je:	*I put a blue*
	5	SW:	*A blue what? Blue*
(25)	6	Je:	*A blue*
	7	SW:	*A blue what?*
	8	Je:	*A blue rectangle*
	9	SW:	*Fine.*

Je struggles to name the object she placed, just as
she did in sequence (20). When she produces the name
of the object, the teacher does not interrogate her
further. Je has been questioned three times during
the course of this lesson. On none of those occasions
was she asked to answer in a complete correct sentence.
Her component answers across turns (19), (20), and NP
(25) were considered acceptable.

Just as in the first orientations lesson, the
teacher finished this lesson by asking the children
to examine objects around the room. Ro provides the
first audible answer to the question about locating
objects which are under other objects:

OL

	10:13	SW:	...*Ok, Ro*
	14	Ro:	*The rug*
	15	SW:	*Ok, tell me about it, the rug is*
	16	Ro:	*On the floor*
	17	Pa:	*under*
	18	SW:	*Under what? What is the rug under?*
	19	Pa:	*Under the floor*
	20	SW:	*the rug is under the...*
	21	Ro:	*...floor*
(26)	22	Ri:	*I'm finished Mrs. Wa*
	23	SW:	*Is it under the floor?*
	11:01	Pa:	*Under the ground*
	02	Ri:	*I'm finished Mrs. Wa*
	03	SW:	*Is the rug under the ground?*
	04	Ri:	*Mrs. Wa, I'm finished.*
	05	Pa:	*On the ground.*
	06	SW:	*Not now Ri. The rug is under...it's on the floor. Is it under the floor? My hand is under the table. Is the rug under the floor? What is the rug under?*
	07	Je:	*On the floor*
	08	Ro:	*It's on the floor.*
	09	SW:	*It's on the floor, and we could also say it's above the floor, couldn't we? But the rug is under something too.*

> *In some places I can see the rug is*
> *under the...*

10	Ro:	*Cabinet*
11	SW:	*Right*
12	Ro:	*Under the cabinet*
13	SW:	*Ok, say it all by yourself now.*
14	Ro:	*The rug is under the cabinet and the TV.*

Pa responds next:

	11:19	SW:	*Pa, can you tell me something that is under something else?*
	20	Pa:	*The boxes*
(27)	21	SW:	*What are they under?*
	22	Pa:	*Under the flat blocks*
	23	Ro:	*They are under the wood.*
	24	SW:	*Ok, the big blocks are under the flat blocks*

Pa produces the components of a complete answer across two turns. As in sequence (7) with Di, (19) and (20) with Je, he is not asked to put the components together in one sentence.

The teacher continues to ask the children to explore the room. Pa responds once again:

OL

	11:25	Pa:	*The clay*
	12:01	SW:	*Ok, the clay what*
(28)	02	Pa:	*The clay is under the stuff*
	03	SW:	*What stuff?*
	04	Pa:	*The toys and stuff*
	05	SW:	*Ok...*

Pa's initial response in this sequence is like his initial response in the immediately preceding sequence: he provided only the initial NP. In both cases, the teacher wants Pa to provide a more complete answer. Whereas in sequence (27) when he was questioned further, he only produced a LocNP, in this sequence he

105

produced a complete sentence. But this sentence is flawed. The teacher wants a better descriptive term than *"stuff."* While Pa finds a substitute term for *"stuff,"* he loses the *"complete sentence"* answer form. The teacher accepts the detraction, and does not ask him to complete the sentence.

Ro's response to the request for information about objects *under* other objects completes the lesson:

OL

12:07	SW:	*Ok, Ro, can you tell me?*
08	Ro:	*The tables are on the ground.*
09	SW:	*On the ground. What is the table under? Is it under the floor?*
10	Ro:	*On the floor*
11	SW:	*Ok, the table is under something.*
12	Ro:	*The ceiling*
13	SW:	*Right, you may go to your seats.*

Although Ro's first response meets the requirements of completeness, the preposition *"on"* causes the teacher to request another answer (see 8, 17, 21, 26). The teacher accepts *"the ceiling"* as satisfying the request for an object which is *"under"* something else.

Negotiated performance assessment. Examination of the children's responses to the teacher's requests shows: (1) the desired answer form was not uniformly demanded or obtained, and (2) tokens of the same answer type are treated differently.

(1) The teacher demanded and obtained the desired answer form in sequences 2, 3, 4, 5, 6, 10, 11, 12, 13, 14, and 15 from lesson 1, 17, 22, 24 and 26 from lesson 2. She did not continue to question the children until the desired answer form was obtained in the remaining question-answer sequences in the two lessons. This means the teacher obtained the kind of answer she wanted only 51% of the time in both lessons (see Table 3.1).

Table 3.1. Complete Correct Responses (CCR)
Obtained in Orientations Lessons

	Responses			
Lessons	Total sequences	CCR obtained	CCR not obtained	% CCR obtained
First	16	11	5	68.7
Second	13	4	9	30.0
	29	15	14	51.0

(2) The teacher's judgments about acceptable responses vary. Sometimes answers which did not meet the specifications of the complete correct responses were rejected; other times, tokens of the same response type were accepted.

The teacher in both pre- and post-lesson interviews supplied me with the features of the correct responses she expected from each of the children during these lessons. According to a 'rational' model of decision-making, indeed, according to the teacher's own expectations for the lesson, each and every response which matched the features of correctness would be treated as correct; each and every deviation would be treated as erroneous. Thus, according to the teacher's own criteria of acceptability, the child is not supposed to submit (a) Subject NP's represented by slots 1 and 2 (e.g., *"the chair"*), (b) Proterms (e.g., *"it," "my"*) in the place of the Subject NP (e.g., *"It's under the table," "On there," "here"*), or (d) final NP's (slots 5 and 6) (e.g., *"the chair"*) (see Figure 3.1). If the child does submit one of these (or other) unacceptable answer forms, the teacher's rule indicates she would continue questioning the child until the CCR was obtained.

Examining the seventy-four question-answer exchanges between the teacher and children shows that

107

instances of each of these three deviant types were
accepted as answers. When asked the prototypical
question the children answered with Subject NP's 16
times (see sequences 4, 7, 11, 13, 16 (twice), 19,
20, 21 (twice), 25 (three times), 26, 27, 28). This
answer form was rejected 15 times and accepted once
(see 25). Proterms were submitted instead of Noun
Phrases nine times (see 1, 4 (twice), 9, 16, 17 (three
times), and 26); two of those (sequences 9 and 16)
were accepted as answers while the remainder were
rejected. The children answered with only a Locative
Noun Phrase 20 times (see 1, 2, 3, 4, 5, 7, 8, 9, 10
(twice), 20, 21 (three times), 26 (twice), 27, and
29). Six of these (1, 7, 8, 20, 21, 27) were allowed
to pass even though they did not meet the teacher's
previously stated expectations for correctness. Likewise, of the seven *"final NP's"* submitted as answers
(see sequences 18, 19, 21, 26 (twice), 28, and 29)
three (19, 28, 29) were accepted as answers.

The teacher's differential treatment of instances
of the various deviant answer types is summarized in
Table 3.2.

Table 3.2 The Teacher's Treatment of
"Deviant" Answer Types

Type of deviant answer	Teacher's treatment			% Deviant Accepted
	Total	Accepted	Rejected	
SubNP only	16	1	15	
Proterms	9	2	7	
LocNP only	20	6	14	
Final NP only	7	3	4	
Wrong Loc or no SubNP	5	2	3	
	57	14	43	23%
CCR	17	15	2	
	74	29	45	

108

Of particular interest is the teacher's treatment of seemingly correct responses. On two occasions (24 and 28), the child submitted an answer which appears to meet the criteria of a complete correct response, but the teacher rejected them.

> (24) 9:21 Pa: *I put magenta under the grass.*
> (28) 12:02 Pa: *The clay is under the stuff.*

In the first case (24), the rejection seemed to be based on the misuse of *"magenta"* as a noun. In the second case (28), the rejection seems to be a response to the *"inappropriate"* noun *"stuff."* It is instructive to examine sequence (24) by comparison to (23).

> (23) 9:19 Ro: *Put magenta under the grass.*
> (24) 9:21 Pa: *I put a, a, a, a madenta?*
> *under the grass*

Pa's response is almost a duplicate of Ro's; however, Ro's response was accepted, while Pa's was not. Likewise, examining the answer that the teacher accepts from Pa in sequence (28) is interesting for it shows she allowed the 'unacceptable' noun, *"stuff,"* to appear, and it appeared in an unacceptable grammatical form. The response which the teacher accepted was: *"the toys and stuff"* (12:14). That means the teacher rejected a CCR for a Final NP.

The child is supposed to produce the complete, correct response in one turn; he is supposed to say, for instance, *"the tree is under the sky"* all at once. On six separate occasions (see sequences 7, 18, 19, 20, 26, and 27) the children produced all of the correct parts of the answer, but they appeared across two or more turns. Di's conversations with the teacher in sequence (7) illustrates this point:

OL
> 3:16 SW: *Di, where is the red flower?*
> 17 Di: *The red flower*

(7) 18 SW: *The red flower*
     19 Di: *...is under the tree*

When the child's answer is spread across a number of
turns, the teacher's plan was to have the child combine the parts into a complete sentence, as she did
in sequence 26:

OL
    10:13 SW: *...Ok, Ro*
      14 Ro: *The rug*
    11:09 SW: *...But the rug is under something,*
             too. In some places I can see the rug
             is under the...
(26) 10 Ro: *Cabinet*
      11 SW: *Right*
      12 Ro: *Under the cabinet*
      13 SW: *Ok, say it all by yourself now.*
      14 Ro: *The rug is under the cabinet and the*
             TV.

However, on only two of the six occasions where answers
appeared across turns did the teacher demand the child
complete his answer (see 18, 26). On the remaining 4,
the child's incomplete answers were allowed to stand.
    The teacher's differential treatment of the same
answer type cannot be explained by the differences
between the lessons, the differences in the children's
performance, the deviant answer types, the teacher's
expectations for each child.
    As Table 3.3 shows, answers which do not attain
the level of a complete correct response are found in
both lessons. Of the eight children, only Ri was
asked to produce a CCR each time a question was asked
of him; only Je was never asked for a CCR. Table 3.2
shows each type of answer was both accepted and rejected
in both lessons.
    The teacher's differential treatment of children's
answers cannot be explained by saying she is careless,
had a bad day, does not have a lesson plan, or by
saying she had different expectations for each child's

Table 3.3.   The Teacher's Treatment of
Children's Answers

	Teacher's treatment		
Child	CCR demanded and obtained	CCR not demanded or obtained	Total
(first lesson)			
Do	3	1	4
Ri	3	0	3
Je	2	1	3
Ci	2	1	3
Di	1	2	3
	11	5	16
(second lesson)			
Pa	2	3	5
Ro	2	3	5
JE	0	3	3
	4	9	13

performance. A self-fulfilling prophecy argument
(e.g., Rosenthal and Jacobsen, 1968) would suggest
that the teacher has a preconceived notion of each
child's ability, and treats the child such that he
performs in accordance with that expectation.

The teacher's ranking of these children according to their ability at the time of these lessons was:

1.	Je	5.	Pa
2.	Ro	6.	Do
3.	Ri	7.	JE
4.	Ci	8.	Di

If a self-fulfilling prophecy was operating, one would
expect the teacher to demand complete correct responses
of the children at the top of that list more than the

111

children nearer the bottom of it. The teacher demanded
complete, correct responses of these children according to the following ranking:

1.	Ri	100%	5.	Ci	67%
2.	Ro	80%	6.	Pa	40%
3.	Do	75%	7.	Di	33%
4.	Je	67%	8.	JE	0%

The matched rankings for Ro and Ci provide support
for the self-fulfilling prophecy interpretation of
the teacher's differential treatment of the children's
answers. The remaining mismatches operate against
this interpretation.

The statement of the correctness rule does not
capture how this teacher used the rule in this lesson.
The completeness and correctness features of the rule
are not the only features that the teacher relied on
while judging the appropriateness of the children's
responses. These features of the rule are seen against
a back-drop of situational features. The situational
interpretation of action accounts for the differential
treatment of *"similar"* displays.

Before a lesson starts, the teacher may have an
overall lesson plan in mind. She may know the criteria
she will use to judge correct answers. But, the goals
for the lesson change as the lesson gets underway.
The decision to accept or reject a child's answer becomes influenced by events that emerge within the
situation, like the child who is answering the question,
when in the lesson the request occurs, the child's
immediately past performance. Although the history of
the child's performance in a lesson, on a particular
day, or previous days all contribute to the teacher's
moment to moment decisions about answers, these and
other factors do not enter neatly into a calculus of
previously weighed values. Classroom interaction does
not proceed like a play, game or orchestra performance.
In Goffman's (1959) dramaturgical model, actors
meet before an encounter (performance) to be assigned

their parts and to learn their lines. They come on stage to present the results of this accomplishment to a passive audience. Negotiation occurs in the rehearsal stage of interaction where actors decide on lines and parts, but once a shared definition of the situation to be presented is reached, parts are played out according to the script. The teacher does not prepare a script of lines to read (questions to ask) in backstage rehearsal (lesson planning) and then read them on stage (during the lesson). Questions to ask, the direction in which to take conceptual points, evaluations of children all emerge as the lesson is underway. The innovation and emergence found in classroom interaction is not captured by a dramaturgical model (cf. Garfinkel, 1963).

Game metaphors (Goffman, 1961; Scheff, 1967a, 1967b; Schelling, 1960) used to explain social interaction also rest on the existence of a prior conventional agreement. When social interaction is equated with a game, game players are assumed to know of the rules of the game prior to play and are motivated to conform to them. Social actions, equated with moves in a game, are drawn from a range of actions specified and agreed on in advance of play by the rules of the game. Although strategy may dictate the expeditious choice of a certain move in a special circumstance, that move will always be one specifiable under the rules of the game. The spontaneous classroom occurrences cannot be captured by analogy to games. The teacher does not have time to keep track of the course of each child's answers. The teacher's attention is demanded in too many places to make rationally calculated, statistically valid decisions during the flow of conversation with the children. The child's contextually situated understanding of instructions, and the teacher's interpretation of the child's performance is accomplished anew each time questions are asked and answers are given to them.

The differential treatment of the children's answers can be explained, then, by saying the determination of the child's performance is negotiated each moment of teacher-child interaction. Each question-answer sequence has its own organization and features which contribute to decision making. This conclusion should not be interpreted as saying the teacher is not operating rationally, is incompetent, etc. Rather, situational negotiation is a comment on the nature of rule interpretation. It is an unavoidable feature of the process of fitting an instance of behavior together with a normative rule in a social situation.

The Source of Children's Answers

Teachers ask children questions and request information from them to see whether they understand materials presented in lessons. Teacher's take children's answers, completed worksheets, and homework problems, as evidence for the children's understanding. When questions are answered correctly, the teacher concludes the child *"understands"* or *"knows."* If he doesn't answer correctly, then the teacher may conclude the child cannot understand, needs more training or help.

In this section some teacher-child question-answer sequences are being examined to see if the child's performance derives from the teacher's request for information and the child's knowledge of the task at hand. That is, the context of interrogation is being examined to see what the child attends to in order to answer questions. In the instances which follow, children employ practices which I call 'imitating', 'cohort production', and 'searching'. While using these practices, the children are found to rely on the sequence of questions, hints from others, the teacher's tone of voice to answer questions. Since the child's answers are influenced by cues in the situation around him, it is difficult to conclude that his answers come only from underlying conceptual knowledge.

Imitation. In the first orientations lesson the teacher is asked the children to report in a full sentence about where they drew certain objects on their pages:

OL
2:5   SW: *...Ri, where is the little seed?   Where is the seed?*
6   Ri: *Under the grass*
7   SW: *Can you say that in a sentence: the seed is under the grass?*
8   Ri: *The seed is under the grass seed*
9   SW: *Where is the worm, Je?*
10   Je: *Under the grass*
11   SW: *Can you tell me in a sentence?*
12   Je: *The the worm is under the grass*

After Ri has successfully accomplished what the teacher wants, Je is asked to respond to the same question. When Je produced her answer, she had available the work she had done while drawing the worm under the line. She also had access to her past experience with tasks of this sort, and the first child's responses which the teacher has just tacitly acknowledged to be a correct response. Although one can conclude Je understands the concept *"under,"* it is also possible that Je was able to produce her correct answer because she imitated Ri's correct response.

The second orientation lesson begins with the teacher's request to place felt objects on a flannel board. She first demonstrates the task which she wants the children to accomplish by placing a pink diamond above the green line. Then she places an orange felt piece in the upper left hand corner of the flannel board and explains that the felt piece is the *"sun"* and that it is *"above the green line"* (OL 6:13). Ro, JE, and Pa are each asked to choose an object and place it on the flannel board above the green line. When they are finished, the board looks as it is shown in Figure 3.2 (as viewed from the perspective provided by the camera).

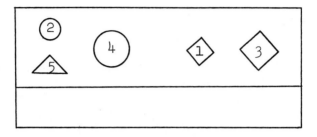

1. A pink diamond placed by SW (6:13)
2. *"the sun"* placed by SW (6:13)
3. A *"square"* placed by Ro (6:14)

4. A   *"stoplight"*   placed by Pa (7:4)
      "one"

5. A *"triangle"* placed by JE (7:9-10)

All of the children's placements are appropriate
responses to the instruction *"place something above
the line."* Therefore, one can conclude each of the
children understand that concept. It is also possible
to conclude that the children were able to place the
objects appropriately because the teacher placed the
first two objects properly.

Cohort production of answers. Both teachers and
children contribute to a child's production of responses by supplying information which becomes incorporated into answers. The most dramatic illustration
of the 'cohort production of answers' occurs in this
sequence from the second orientations lesson:

OL
10:09 SW: *Fine. Now, can you look around the room
           and see what you can see and tell me
           about something that is under something
           else?*
  10   Pa: *Under?*
  11   SW: *Raise your hand when you see something
           that is under and tell me. Ok, good, you
           are thinking. Stay here, JE. Stay here.*

116

12	Pa:	*I know what's under*
13	SW:	*Sit down at the chair. Sit down. Ok, Ro*
14	Ro:	*The rug*
15	SW:	*Ok, tell me about it. The rug is...*
16	Ro:	*On the floor*
17	Pa:	*Under*
18	SW:	*Under what? What is the rug under?*
19	Pa:	*Under the floor*
20	SW:	*The rug is under the...*
21	Ro:	*Floor*
22	Ri:	*I'm finished Mrs. Wa*
23	SW:	*Is it under the floor?*

11:01	Pa:	*Under the ground*
02	Ri:	*I'm finished Mrs. Wa*
03	SW:	*Is the rug under the ground?*
04	Ri:	*I'm finished Mrs. Wa*
05	Pa:	*On the ground*
06	SW:	*Not now Ri. The rug is under it's on the floor. Is it under the floor? My hand is under the table. Is the rug under the floor? What is the rug under?*
07	JE:	*On the floor*
08	Ro:	*It's on the floor*
09	SW:	*It's on the floor, and we could also say it's above the floor, couldn't we? But the rug is under something, too. In some places I can see it's under the*
10	Ro:	*Cabinet*
11	SW:	*Right, Tell us now, Ro, the rug is...*
12	Ro:	*Under the cabinet*
13	SW:	*Ok, say it all by yourself now.*
14	Ro:	*The rug is under the cabinet and the TV.*

The teacher has requested the children to examine the room for instances of objects which are under other objects. Because she wants the report to take the form of the complete, correct response outlined above, Ro's first response, *"the rug"* though an answer to the question, is not accepted. The teacher begins

the sentence form she wants to elicit. Although Ro
is being encouraged to start that sentence from the
beginning, she completes that sentence instead:

OL
   10:15 SW: *Ok, tell me about it. The rug is...*
     16 Ro: *On the floor*

This answer, like her first answer is a *factually*
correct answer to the request, *"tell me something that
is under something else."* The rug is indeed on the
floor. Once again, because the sentence form does not
fit the intended paradigm for a complete, correct
response, it is not accepted.

    Now Pa introduces the desired preposition,
"under" (10:17). Pa has not supplied the names of
objects to go along with his choice of the correct
preposition. There is no information available which
tells what "underlying sentence" Pa is constructing.
Ro has supplied the names of some objects; the teacher
combines parts of the two children's answers to form
most of the sentence form she is looking for:

OL
 10:17 Pa: *Under*
   18 SW: *Under what? What is the rug under?*

The teacher is looking for a noun which could appropriately be place into the *"LocNP"* slot, which I have
indicated as #6 in Figure 3.1.

    Pa answers this question. He retains the prepo-
sition *"under"* from his first answer. The NP *"the
floor"* possibly comes from Ro's earlier answer. The
phrase *"under the floor"* though grammatically acceptable, is not factually appropriate when it is considered to be a part of the sentence begun with *"the
rug is under...".* Therefore, the teacher repeats the
sentence form she wants; the same results accrue:

OL
 10:18 SW: *...what is the rug under?*

19   Pa: *Under the floor*
20   SW: *The rug is under the*
21   Ro: *floor*

The answer, if assembled from the parts alternately
provided by children and teacher, reads: *"The rug
is under the floor."*
　　　　The teacher uses that faulted production to
question it.   She asks the children to find a noun
for floor in slot #6.   Pa does substitute a noun, but
the new candidate is no better than its predecessor:

OL
10:23   SW: *Is it under the floor?*
11:01   Pa: *Under the ground*

To question that production, the teacher says the
faulted sentence to call for an appropriate noun in
the final-noun slot.   Pa substitutes *"on"* for *"under,"*
in his answer, but it is a wrong word in the wrong
slot.   This addition makes the sentence factually
correct once again.   The rug *is* on the ground, but
once again, the preposition *"under"* is not employed
in the answer:

OL
11:3   SW: *Is the rug under the ground?*
　5   Pa: *On the ground*

Reestablishing interest in *"under"* (11:6) does not
produce the desired results from either Ro or JE:
they both continue to say the rug is on the floor:

OL
11:6   SW: *...is the rug under the floor?   What is
　　　　the rug under?*
　7   JE: *On the floor*
　8   Ro: *It's on the floor*

When the teacher finally provides the first five slots
of the sentence, which asks for an insertion into the

final slot. Ro provides an acceptable entry:

OL
11:9   SW: *...the rug is under something, too? In some cases I can see it's under the*
  10   Ro: *Cabinet*

She is coaxed into providing the answer in a complete, correct response (11:11-14).

    This instance bears a strong family resemblance to one student-teacher question-answer practice which Holt (1964:24-25) identifies in his penetrating and insightful description of the educational process. Holt describes the child who elicits the teacher's help in order to perform different tasks. This child, when asked questions which are too difficult for him, remains silent but attentive. The teacher modifies the problem to make it easier. Still, the child doesn't answer correctly. Finally, the teacher asks an even easier question to which the child can respond.

    This entire *"under the ground"* sequence (10:9-10: 14) provides directly observable confirmation of Holt's general descriptions of the negotiated character of the classroom question-answer encounter. The issue at hand in this sequence, the other sequences examined, and in teaching-learning situations in general, is the basis upon which the child provides acceptable answers to questions. Ro provided an acceptable response at (11:14), but neither she nor the other children did so earlier in the sequence. If retrieving information from the child involves triggering the child's store of underlying knowledge by the teacher's verbal instructions to provide an answer, then, it is unclear why Ro, or any of the other children should not have been able to produce an acceptable answer at some other point in the sequence.

    Searching. During the course of a lesson or test, the expected sequence or series of exchanges between an adult interrogator and the child respondent is supposed to be:

120

Turn	Speaker	Response
1	adult	question
2	child	answer
3	adult	question
4	child	answer
etc.		

However, during the course of the adult's interrogation of a child, the child can initiate action which introduces variation into this sequence. The child can present an action to the adult in such a way that adult comment on it is demanded. The adult's response to the child's question provides supplemental information to the child which helps him to respond to the original question, so that instead of the interrogator initiated q-a, q-a sequence, a respondent controlled "embedded question" sequence (Schegloff, 1971) results:

Turn	Speaker	Response
1	adult	question ⌐
2	child	question ⌐
3	adult	answer ⌐
4	child	answer ⌐

That is, the child is able to utilize the teacher's response (which appears in turn 3) to his demand (made in turn 2) to provide an answer to the original adult question (during turn 4). An example of the child's "searching" practice occurs early in the first lesson:

121

OL

1:1　SW:　*Yes.　Let's take our green crayon and make a line at the bottom of your paper.　Just take your green crayon and make a green line at the bottom.*

2　Ci:　*Like that?*

3　SW:　*Yeah.*

4　Di:　*Now what are we going to do?*

5　SW:　*Now take your orange crayon and make an orange worm under the green line.　Pretend that's grass.　Just a little wiggle.　Here let me show you on this one.　An orange worm.*

6　Di:　*Hey, can you make it on* ⌈ *yours?*
　　Je:　　　　　　　　　　　　　　　　⌊ *yours?*

7　SW:　*No, I'm watching you make yours*

8　Je:　*Over here?*

9　Ci:　*Under?*

10　SW:　*Listen, I'm going to say it just once.　Make an orange worm under the green line.*

11　Di:　*Like that?*

12　SW:　*Beautiful.*

While the teacher is introducing the behaviorally receptive aspect of the lesson, she draws a line on her paper and instructs the children to do the same (OL 1:1).　Ci, sitting to the teacher's left, and fully able to see the display produced by the teacher, draws a line across the vertical edge of her paper and asks, *"Like that?"* (OL 1:2).　The teacher responds affirmatively (OL 1:3).　Ci has produced a correct response to the teacher's request to draw a line at the bottom of her paper, but she was aided in that production by the teacher's comments.　The teacher's comments, obtained by the children's request for confirmation of their work, are incorporated into the children's responses in the very next sequence.　There the teacher is asking the children to make orange worms under the lines they have drawn.　First, Je (OL 1:8), then Ci (OL 1:9), and then Di (OL 1:11) place their crayons on their papers and inquire about the

122

appropriateness of the placement. The teacher says
"beautiful" (OL 1:12), and the children then actualize
the "trial responses" they had begun when they indicated the place they were considering drawing their
answers. These children, then, have produced correct
answers to the request to draw objects under lines, but
what contributed to their productions? Their answers
may have been based on prior knowledge of that concept,
or these answers may have been produced by incorporating
the teacher's reinforcing comments. Examining only the
child's completed work does not provide an answer to
that question.

The child's "searching practice" should be compared to Rose's "glossing practice" (Garfinkel and
Sacks, 1970:366). Rose's gloss occurs when a question
or comment is made and the answer returned to it gives
the original comment or question sensible meaning. An
example:

> On a visit to a city he has never seen
> before, Rose is met at the airport by his host.
> They are driving home when Rose (looks) out the
> window — which is to say that Rose, after doing
> (looking ahead) then does (watching something go
> by) by turning his head to accord with the
> passage of the auto. Rose's problem is to get
> his partner to provide him with what he has
> been looking at. Doing the notable particulars
> (looking ahead) and (watching something go by)
> and their serial arrangement are the crux of
> the matter, and make up Rose's artfulness.
> Continuing to do (looking out the window) Rose
> remarks, *"It certainly has changed,"* finds in
> the reply, and with the use of the reply, what
> he, Rose, was talking about in the first place.
> Picking that up he formulates further the con-
> certed, sensible matter that the two parties are
> making happen as the recognizable, actual, plainly
> heard specifics in a course of conversation:
> *"You don't say. What did it cost?"*

The child's use of practices like "imitating', "searching," and "cohort production," indicate that the child is paying attention to much more than the teacher's presentation of stimulus items in order to answer questions. The context-bound nature of answers makes it difficult for educators to subscribe to theories that say the child's answers come exclusively from an underlying knowledge of the materials presented. As Holt (1964:19) says, *"...we can see that a 'successful' student can give the answer and the chatter (the explanation of what they do) without understanding at all what he was doing or saying."* If the teacher looks just at the child's answers to her questions, she cannot decide about the child's mastery of the materials. When only completed documents — test scores, worksheets, answers-to-questions — are examined, the reasoning abilities and sources of information children use to answer questions and to follow instruction is not available. The teacher and tester must examine the practices and procedures which children use to produce answers as well as the answers themselves in order to make judgements about the child's competence.

Summary

The teacher's statement of the requirements for a "complete, correct response" is the "rule" in the analytic scheme being employed in this chapter. Normative social theory suggests such rules are applied in the following way: The teacher has a conception of the correct response in mind when she asks each child a question. The child responds. The teacher matches the particular response with her conception of correctness. The negotiated performance assessment observed in these lessons does not match the normative model of action. In both pre- and post-lesson interviews, the teacher was able to provide me with a description of the correctness rule. However, my analysis of this lesson shows that the statement of a rule does not account for its use in social situations.

Rule use in a social situation is an interpretive process. The "correctness" rule had to be interpreted against a constantly changing background of features of the setting which might include the child's behavior, the teacher's expectations, the question structure. Because the rule cannot anticipate these background features, the formal statement of the rule is incomplete. Rule incompleteness suggests that teachers must go beyond the formal definition of the rule in order to interpret the children's behavior in terms of the rule. The teacher must supply the unstated background features when the rule is juxtaposed with the situation and a child's response. Hence, any discussion of normative action must not include the situationally provided features related to the interpretation of the rule as well as the normative rule.

The indexical features of teacher's instructions have implications for the child as well. In the orientations lessons designed to teach children how to use prepositional phrases, the teacher asked the children to place objects in relation to a focal point, and then asked them to tell her where the objects were. The teacher asked questions like *"Where is the triangle, Joey"* in order to achieve these objectives. The children's answers to the teacher's questions show there are many adequate ways to formulate the location of the objects used in the lesson. *"Right here,"* *"The red flower is by the tree,"* *"On there,"* *"In the middle,"* *"Off the grass,"* *"Up above,"* *"Right by the sun,"* *"Under the grass,"* are all candidate answers along with the preferred form. Other answers to the teacher's questions could have included *"on the paper,"* *"in the room,"* *"in the garden,"* *"at home."* The indexical features of the teacher's instructions present the child with a problem which the instructions do not tell him how to solve: he must find one answer or formulation from among the many available which matches the teacher's unstated expectations.

Although there are many adequate ways for the child to convey information which answers the teacher's questions (i.e., there are many formulations of the location of the instructional objects), the teacher has selected one of the adequate formulations as the appropriate one. The teacher wanted the children to use certain prepositions (under, below, over, above) and not others (by, next to, on, in) and to use a complete sentence (e.g., *"The sun is above the tree"*), and not a phrase (e.g., *"by the tree"*), a gesture, 'proterms' (e.g., *"on there"*) while describing where the instructional objects had been placed.

However, the teacher's questions did not tell the child *how* to arrive at the expected answer form. Wood (1969) says Garfinkel calls this feature of verbal utterances "the structure of essential difference." No matter how voluminous or explicit the definition or description, Garfinkel claims they will always be incomplete in the sense that the activities which must be accompanied to follow the instruction will always be left out. Garfinkel says that it is an invariant property of rules and instructions that they do not include a description of the work which constitutes following the rules. Because teacher's expressions are essentially incomplete, all the information the child needs to follow the teacher's instruction is not found in the instruction itself. The child must locate this needed information in such contextually provided features such as the teacher's non-verbal behavior, teaching materials, the previous course of this lesson, his past experience. The child must utilize interpretive practices like imitating, cohort production, and searching to interpret teacher's instructions.

Because the teacher's instructions are indexical expressions, their meaning changes for the child as the lesson unfolds. This emergent sense of meaning defies a static description which presumes that the meaning of instructions is clear at the outset of an exchange and remains constant throughout; it requires a description which openly includes retrospective and prospective assignment, indefiniteness and indeterminancy as features of meaning (see Cicourel, 1973; Garfinkel, 1967; Schutz, 1970).

The child's use of context-bound interpetive practices has consequences for measurement in educational settings. The primary instrument used to evaluate child's school performance is the standardized educational test. The educational test, like the questionnaire and laboratory protocol, is presumed to have objective stimuli and clear instructions. Therefore, the respondent does not need to rely on contextual information to respond. However, the organization of testing (and research) settings does not allow the respondent and observer's interpretive work to be examined. If test items, like classroom instructions, have indexical features, then respondents and observers can be expected to use context bound interpretive practices in testing settings as well. MacKay (this volume) present some of the indexical and negotiated features of educational testing situations. These findings point to the practical necessity of examining tester's and children's interpretive work as well as the products of interpretation within educational decision-making situations.

One other feature of these lessons remains to be addressed. Although my analysis shows that the teacher did not uniformly demand or obtain the desired answer form from the children, she thought she had consistently applied the correctness rule. When I interviewed the teacher after I had completed my analysis of these lessons, I asked her if she thought she had obtained the desired answer form from all the children. She replied that she thought she had. When I told her that my analysis showed differential treatment of answers, she was genuinely surprised.

The teacher's ability to retain the view of consistent treatment despite the presence of evidence to the contrary which became visible upon analysis is a further comment on the relationship between the statement of a rule in the abstract, and its use in actual social situations. Accounts, whether given before or after activities, are divorced from the situation in which the activities they report are produced. This idealization strips away the situational variations, the confusions, the contradictions, and arrives at a *"clean"* version. This is no devious plan. This is no forgetful teacher. Idealization is a feature of the accounting process. Garfinkel (1959:55) provides an explanation of this phenomenon in his description of the documentary method:

> The documentary method consists essentially in the retrospective prospective reading of a present occurrence so as to maintain the constancy of the object as a sensible thing through temporal and circumstantial alterations in its actual appearances... The documentary method occurs as a feature of situations of incomplete information in which effective actions nevertheless must be taken, matters of fact decided, and interpretations made. The method would seem to be an intimate part of a social process wherein a body of knowledge must be assembled and made available for legitimate use despite the fact that the situations it purports to describe (1) are, in the calculatable sense of the term, unknown; (2) are in their actual and intended logical structures essentially vague; (3) are modified, elaborated, extended, if not indeed created by the fact and manner of being addressed.[1]

That is, the teacher's differential treatment of children's answers, coupled with her simultaneous perception of uniform treatment, is a natural feature of the constantly changing course of the teaching-learning situation. Although the teacher has certain answers and goals in mind before the lesson starts, the demands on attention, memory, and information processing are so great, and action happens so quickly, that a statistical ly reliable accounting of the children's activities is rendered impossible; an idealized account is the only account possible.

In brief, this analysis of teacher-child classroom interaction has shown that the interpretation of

---

[1] I am grateful to Marshall Shumsky for showing this quote to me.

rules is a negotiated process; teachers' instructions are indexical expressions, which requires teachers and children to employ contextually bound interpretive practices to make sense of the instructions.

APPENDIX

Orientations Lessons
First Lesson: Picture drawing, 28 Jan. 10:15-10:30

OL

1:1 SW: *Yes. Let's take our green crayon and make a line at the bottom of your paper. Just take your green crayon and make a green line at the bottom.*

2 Ci: *Like that?*

3 SW: *Yeah.*

4 Di: *Now what are we going to do?*

5 SW: *Now take your orange crayon and make an orange worm under the green line. Pretend that's grass. Just a little wiggle. Here let me show you on this one. An orange worm.*

6 Di: *Hey, can you make it on* ⌈*yours?*
     Je: ⌊*under?*

7 SW: *No, I'm watching you make yours*

8 Je: *Over here*

9 Ci: *Under?*

10 SW: *Listen, I'm going to say it just once. Make an orange worm under the green line*

11 Di: *Like that?*

12 SW: *Beautiful. Ok. We are going to pretend that green line is the grass, ok? Can you pretend that with me? All right, where is the orange worm, Do?*

13 Do: *Right there*

14 SW: *Ok, tell me where he is*

15 Do: *Under the grass*

16 SW: *Ok, now, would you please make um, a, a, little brown seed under the grass.*

17 Ci: *How do you make a little brown seed?*

18 Ri: *Easy. You see. You go like this. Simple. A little circle.*

19 Ci: *Like that?*

20	SW:	*Oh, beautiful*
21	Je:	*Look at mine*
22	Ci:	*Under what?*
23	SW:	*Under the grass.*

OL
2:1	Ri:	*I'm making a thousand seeds: one, two, three//*
		SW: *How many seeds did I tell you to make?*
2	Ci:	*One*
3	SW:	*Make a̲ brown seed and when I say a̲ brown seed that means how many?*
4	many:	*one!*
	Ri:	*eight*
5	SW:	*One. All right. Ri, where is the little seed? Where is the seed?*
6	Ri:	*Under the grass*
7	SW:	*Can you say that in a sentence: The seed is under the grass?*
8	Ri:	*The seed is under the grass seed*
9	SW:	*Where is the worm, Je?*
10	Je:	*Under the grass*
11	SW:	*Can you tell me in a sentence?*
12	Je:	*The the worm is under the grass*
13	SW:	*All right now, I'm going to make, and you can make this too, with your crayon, I'm going to make a tree*
14	Do:	*I am too*
15	Ri:	*I don't know how to make a tree*
16	SW:	*We're not trying to be artists, today, we're just*
		//To: stuck on there?
17	SW:	*To. To. Make a tree*
18	Je:	*Under it? Under it?*
19	SW:	*To, have you done your work?*
20	To:	*No*
21	SW:	*David (Roth) is over at your table, maybe he can help you. You are all making very fine trees. Ok. All right. Now. I'm going to make a little flower and I'm*

131

*going to make a little flower and I'm
going to put the flower under the tree.
I'm going to make a red flower under the
tree. You do it first. I want to watch
where you put it.*

OL

3:1	Ri:	*I don't know how.*
2	SW:	*Make a red flower under the tree.*
3	Ri:	*I don't know how to make flowers.*
4	SW:	*Make a red flower under the tree. Make a red flower under the tree. Ok, let's look at the red flower. Can you tell me where the red flower ⌈ is*
	all:	*⌊ right here, right here Dora?*
5	Do:	*under the tree*
6	SW:	*Tell me in a sentence*
7	Do:	*It's under the tree*
8	SW:	*What's under the tree?*
		⌈ Do: Tell me, the flower...
	Do:	*⌊ The flower*
9	Do:	*The flower is under the tree*
10	SW:	*Where is the red flower, Ri?*
11	Ri:	*Under the tree*
12	SW:	*Can you tell me in a sentence?*
13	Ri:	*The flower is under the tree*
14	SW:	*Ci, where is the red flower?*
15	Ci:	*The red flower is under ⌈ the tree*
	Ri:	*⌊ Hey, that's not red*
16	SW:	*Di, where is the red flower?*
17	Di:	*The red flower*
18	SW:	*The red flower...*
19	Di:	*Is under the tree*
20	SW:	*Now look at the red flower. Is the red flower under the grass?*
21	all:	*⌈ No*
		⌊ Yeah
22	SW:	*Where is the red flower if you want to tell me where it is?*
23	Di:	*Off the grass*

24 SW: *Can we say the red flower is above the grass?*

OL

4:1 Ci: *The red flower is above the grass*
  2 SW: *Je, can you tell me where the red flower is?*
  3 Je: *The red flower...is...by the tree*
  4 SW: *Yes the flower is by the tree. What can we say about it when we talk about the flower and the tree? Where is the red flower in relationship to the grass? What can we say about it when we talk about the flower and the grass? Do you know what? Can you listen to each other now?*
  5 Ri: *Can we make mud under here?*
  6 SW: *Maybe we can make mud under here. Right now it's Je's turn to talk. Ci can you put your crayons on the table?*
     ⌈*Where is the red flower, is it under the*
    Di: ⌊*My name is Mrs. Crayon*
     grass?
  7 Je: *No*
  8 SW: *Where is it*
  9 Je: *On the grass*
 10 SW: ⌈*All right, it's on the grass. Is it*
     above the grass?
     ⌊
    Di: ⌊*My name is Green Grass. Can you talk to me? My name is Green Crayon. I am sticking a crayon in my earphone*
 11 Je: *No*
 12 SW: *Let's do this a minute. Let's make a picture of the sun and let's make the sun//   //above the*
     Ri: *Where, right here?*
     tree. Let's make the sun above the tree. I didn't make much room so it was hard for me to make mine above the tree//
                    Je: *Look*

//All right,
at mine is above the tree
put your crayons down. Put your crayons
down. The sun is under the grass.

13	SW:	*The sun is not under the grass*
15	all:	*no*
16	SW:	*All right, can you tell where the sun is*
	Ci:	*above the grass*
17	SW:	*All right, Ci, tell us where the sun is*
18	Ci:	*It's above the tree*
19	SW:	*All right, Di, can you tell me something* *else that the sun is above. The sun is...*
20	Di:	*Above the ground um ground*
21	SW:	*The sun is...*
22	Di:	*is above the* ⌈ *tree*
	Ci:	⌊ *tree*

OL

5:1	SW:	*All right, can you say it in a sentence* *now? All together?*
2	all:	*The sun is above//*
	SW:	*Let Diana do it* *and say it all of it. The sun* *is* ⌈ *above the tree*
	Di:	⌊ *above the tree*
3	SW:	*Can you say it?*
4	Di:	*The sun is above the tree*
5	SW:	*All right, can you tell me something else* *the sun is above, Ri. We said the sun is* *above the tree. Can you tell me something* *else the sun is above?*
6	Ri:	*I don't know*
7	SW:	*All right, Do, can you try it*
8	Do:	*Try what?*
9	SW:	*Is the sun above something else besides* *the tree?*
10	Do:	*Yeah the line*
11	SW:	*Say it in a sentence*
12	Do:	*The sun is above the line*
13	SW:	*Now listen to me. I'm looking around the* *room and I'm going to try to find some-*

things that are above me, that are up
above me. And I can say...

14   Je: *The ceilin'. The ceiling is up above me.*

15   SW: *Ok, the ceiling is above me. Can you tell*
me something that is above   ⌈ *you.*

      Di: ⌊ *you.*

16   Di: *I know//*

                SW: *Tell us//*

                             Ri: *I know what's*
       above me: a light

17   SW: *Say it in a sentence//*

                          Di: *a garbage can*
//The light...

18   Ri: _____

19   SW: *Ri, Ok, just tell me something that is*
above you and then you can go to the
bathroom.

20   Ri: *The light is above me*

21   SW: *Ok, you are excused. Go through this way.*
Can you tell me something Ci?

OL

6:1   Ci: _____

2   SW: *Those are kind of hard to say. Those are*
acoustical tile. The acoustical tile.
Why don't you just say the tile.

3   Ci: *The tile is above me*

4   SW: *Ok, Do, can you say something that is*
above you

5   Do: *The light is above me*

6   SW: *All right, Di, can you find something*
that's above you?

7   Di: *A table*

8   SW: *Can you tell me something that's above*
you Di?

9   Di: *Table*

10   SW: *Is that above you? What table is above*
you?

11   Di: *It's above*

12   SW: *I can say something//*

                        Di: *What that means?*

//All right, my feet are under the table, aren't they? And I can also say the table is above my feet. It's up higher than my feet. All right, you may go to your seats now. You may take your pictures with you.

Second Lesson: Flannel board, 28 Jan. 10:45-11:00

13 SW: *Ok, I have a green line, and I'm going to take this pink diamond and I'm going to put it above the green line//*

                      Je: *That's*
            //This is the bottom and this is the grass
the top. This is the top. Let me put a um//   *//Maybe I can find*
      Ro: *Triangle*
a//
    Pa: *a triangle? Let me put this up here. This is the sun, Ok? This is above the green line.*

14 Pa: *That's the journey//*

              SW: *Ro, can you put something above? we can call that the journey into the sky//*

            SW: *...choose*
    //Pa: a journey//
something   SW: *and put it above the green line. Ok, Pa, can you find something and put it above the green line?*

OL
7:1 Ro: *It has to be away in the corner*
  2 Pa: *One of these*
  3 SW: *It doesn't matter, you choose something and put it above the green line*
  4 Ro: *There, that's the sun. I moved it.*
  5 Ro: *That's the number. That's the number one*
  6 SW: *Ok, Je, can you find something and put it above the green line?*

7	Ro:	*That's the numeral one*
8	Pa:	*That's the stoplight ya see*
9	Ro:	*Hold it down over there*
10	SW:	*Choose quickly*
11	Ro:	*Hurry up, you are taking our time*
12	SW:	*Ok, all right, can you tell us, Pa, about what you did? What did you do?*
13	Pa:	*I put a one on there*
14	SW:	*Ok, where did you put it?*
15	Pa:	*On there*
16	Je:	*In the middle*
17	SW:	*Where did you put it on there*
18	Je:	*In the middle//*

Ro: *up above//*

Pa: *In*

*//up above
the middle*

19	SW:	*Did I say put a one in the middle, or put something in the middle? What did I tell you to do?*
20	Pa:	*Put anything*
21	SW:	*Where did I tell you to put it?*
22	Pa:	*At the bottom*
23	SW:	*Listen. Ro, can you remember what I said?*
24	Ro:	*Put it above*
25	SW:	*Above what?*
26	Ro:	*The green line*
27	SW:	*All right, Ro, tell us what you did*
28	Ro:	*Put a square aaa Put a square above the green line*

OL

8:1	SW:	*Could you listen to what Ro said? Ok, listen to what Ro said.*
2	Ro:	*I put a um square above a above the green line.*
3	SW:	*Ok, Je, can you tell me what you did?*
4	Je:	*I put a blue triangle above*
5	SW:	*Above what?*
6	Je:	*The green line*

7 SW: *Ok, I put a pink diamond above the green line. Pa, what did you do?*

8 Pa: *I put a green one above the line*

9 Ro: *The green line, not the blue line*

10 SW: *Ok, let's try it again. Um, Ro, put something yellow above the green line. All right, Pa, you put something pink above the green line.*

11 Ro: *I know what else is pink*

12 SW: *Je, put something//   //blue above*
         Ro: *green*
  the green line. Put something blue, do it quickly.

13 Je: *Blue?*

14 Ro: *Yup, blue*

15 SW: *Something light blue*

16 Ro: *That's not light blue*

17 SW: *Blue, light blue. Je, can't you find something? All right Je, tell me what you did.*

18 Je: *I put a blue u:u:n:n//   //square*
         Ro: *square*
  //SW: *square*

19 Ro: *I'm not going to tell you guys*

20 Je: *Above the green line*

21 SW: *Pa, what did you do?*

22 Pa: *I put a pink//   //I mean, no,*
      Je: *yellow*
  what was it?

23 SW: *A pink//*
     Ro: *diamond//*
        Pa: *A pink diamond*

24 SW: *Where?*

OL
 9:1 Pa: *Right by the sun*

  2 SW: *All right, it's by the sun, but where is it?*

  3 Ro: *Up above the line//*
       Je: *The green line*

  4 Pa: *The line*

5	SW:	*Where did I tell you to put it?*
6	Pa:	*Above the...*
7	SW:	*Above the what?*
8	Pa:	*Above the green line*
9	SW:	*All right, Ro, what did you do*
10	Ro:	*Put a yellow rec, I put a yellow rectangle above the green line*
11	SW:	*All right, Now look, this is the sun. This is the sun and this is the grass. I'm going to put an orange, no I'm not going to put an orange, I'm going to put a two under the grass. Ro, would you put something magenta under the grass?*
12	Ro:	*Magenta?*
13	Je:	*A color*
14	SW:	*Put something magenta under the grass. Do you know what color magenta is?*
15	Ro:	*No*
16	SW:	*Ok, Let me show you. This is magenta. You find something this color and put it under the grass.*
17	Pa:	*Where's magenta?*
18	SW:	*All right, ok, Ro, what did you do?*
19	Ro:	*Put magenta under the grass.*
20	SW:	*Ok, maa:a:genta. (Ro: magenta) All right Pa. Would you find something magenta and put it under the grass? Ok, what did you do Pa?*
21	Pa:	*I put a, a a, a ?magenta? under the grass.*
22	SW:	*Magenta what? Is it a circle? (No) Did you put a magenta circle under the grass?*
23	Pa:	*I put a magenta square under the grass.*

OL

10:1	SW:	*All right, This is a um this is blue. Put something blue under the grass, Je. Here Ro, can you wait just a moment. Da and CC, can you go to your seats? Da can you go to your seat?*
2	Ro:	*What's up doc, what's up doc*
3	SW:	*I can't answer your questions because*

139

*I'm trying to help these people while
its their turn. What did you do Je? Je,
what did you do. Listen again: put
something blue under the grass. Ro, come
over here. Je, what did you do?*

4	Je:	*I put a blue...*
5	SW:	*A blue what. Blue*
6	Je:	*A blue...*
7	SW:	*A blue what?*
8	Je:	*A blue rectangle*
9	SW:	*Fine. Now, can you look around the room and see what you can see and tell me about something that is under something else?*
10	Pa:	*Under?*
11	SW:	*Raise your hand when you see something that is under and tell me. Oh good, you are thinking. Stay here Je, stay here.*
12	Pa:	*I know what's under*
13	SW:	*Sit down at the chair. Sit down. Ok, Ro.*
14	Ro:	*Da rug.*
15	SW:	*Ok, tell me about it. The rug is...*
16	Ro:	*On the floor.*
17	Pa:	*Under*
18	SW:	*Under what? What is the rug under?*
19	Pa:	*Under the floor*
20	SW:	*The rug is under the...*
21	Ro:	*floor*
22	Ri:	*I'm finished*
23	SW:	*Is it under the floor?*

OL

11:1	Pa:	*Under the ground*
2	Ri:	*I'm finished Mrs. Wa*
3	SW:	*Is the rug under the ground?*
4	Ri:	*Mrs. W, I'm finished*
5	Pa:	*On the ground*
6	SW:	*Not now Ri. The rug is under, it's on the floor. Is it under the floor? My hand is under the table. Is the rug under the floor? What is the rug under?*
7	Je:	*On the floor*

140

8	Ro:	*It's on the floor*
9	SW:	*It's on the floor, and we could also say it's above the floor, couldn't we? But the rug is under something, too. In some places I can see it's under the...*
10	Ro:	*Cabinet*
11	SW:	*Right*
12	Ro:	*Under the cabinet*
13	SW:	*Ok, say it all by yourself now*
14	Ro:	*The rug is under the cabinet and the tv.*
15	SW:	*All right, Je, do you have something that you can tell us about?*
16	Je:	_____
17	SW:	*Very good, Je you showed me; that you were thinking. Pa can you tell me about something that is under something else?*
18	Ro:	*I want to say up what's up doc*
19	SW:	*Pa, can you tell me something that is under something else?*
20	Pa:	*The boxes*
21	SW:	*What are they under*
22	Pa:	*Under the flat blocks*
23	Ro:	*They are under the wood*
24	SW:	*Ok, the big blocks are under the flat bloc blocks. Can you tell me something something else that is under? Raise your hand when you can tell me something about something else that is under. Pa?*
25	Pa:	*The clay*

OL

12:1	SW:	*Ok, the clay what?*
2	Pa:	*The clay is under the stuff*
3	SW:	*What stuff?*
4	Pa:	*The toys and stuff*
5	SW:	*Ok, Je, can you tell me about something that's under? Ok, come over here so we can hear you now.*
6	Je:	_____
7	SW:	*Ok, Ro, can you tell me?*
8	Ro:	*The tables are on the ground*

9	SW:	*On the ground. What is the table under? Is it under the floor?*
10	Ro:	*On the floor*
11	SW:	*Ok, the table is under something*
12	Ro:	*The ceiling*
13	SW:	*Right. Ok, you may go to your seats*
14	Pa:	*Weeeee*
15	Je:	*How come we didn't color?*
16	SW:	*Because we don't always do the same things the other boys and girls do. Ok, Ro, can you go now? Now we put the chairs under the table, didn't we? Ok, you may put your papers in a nice neat stack and you may get in line for recess.*

Chapter 4
INTELLIGENCE TESTING AS A SOCIAL ACTIVITY[1]

David R. Roth
University of Texas

The Psychological View of Intelligence

Intelligence has primarily been the concern of psychologists rather than sociologists because intelligence is assumed to be an individual rather than a social phenomenon. Within the psychological literature, intelligence is generally approached operationally. Jensen (1969:6) comments that intelligence, like electricity, is easier to measure than define. He states *"that there is no point in arguing...the question of what intelligence really is. The best we can do is to obtain measurements of certain kinds of behavior and look at their relationships to other phenomena, and see if these relations make any kind of sense and order."*

Spearman (1904) found that any and every test involving any kind of complex mental activity correlated positively and substantially with any and every other test involving complex mental activity. He then proposed the existence of a single factor common to all tests of complex mental processes, and called it *g*. Jensen (1969:9) notes that *g* is the nuclear operational definition of intelligence. The higher mental processes of which *g* is the common factor involved *"'the ability to deduce relations and correlates' — that is the ability to be able to see the general from the particular and the particular as an instance of the general."* Thus while intelligence

---

[1]I am grateful for comments made by Courtney Cazden, Aaron Cicourel, Kenneth Leiter, and Hugh Mehan. My wife, Ruth Cohen Roth, has assisted me in more practical and intellectual ways than I could ever acknowledge.

143

is admitted to be only what intelligence tests
measure, psychologists generally assume that innate
mental problem solving ability underlies high performance on IQ tests. The correlary question causes
controversy however. Do those who score low on IQ
tests possess less of this general problem solving
ability, or do they simply possess less of the background knowledge and learned skills presupposed by
the tests? Usually this lack of background knowledge is
accounted for by environmental conditions such as poverty,
lack of parental interest, lack of socialization, etc.
All of these factors have been labeled by the terms
"cultural" or "environmental deprivation" (Coleman, et.
al. 1966; Deutsch, et. al. 1967; Riessman, 1967).

The notion that the environment affects scholastic
performance and performance on IQ tests introduced a
sociological perspective into the study of intelligence.
The direct relationship between socioeconomic status
(SES) and IQ test scores was observed as early as 1912
by William Stern. He found that a group of 10-year-
olds in a low economic status German school showed
exactly the same proficiency on the Binet-Simon tests,
a forerunner of the Stanford-Binet test, as did a
group of 9-year-olds in a high status school. Subsequent studies tend to show the same general results.
There are significant differences in intelligence test
performances of children from differing SES backgrounds.
The higher SES children always obtain the higher scores.

Eells et. al. (1951) summarizes the three main interpretations of this finding. Do the higher test scores
of children from high SES groups reflect genuine superiority in inherited or genetic equipment? Or do high
scores result from a superior environment which has
brought about real superiority of the child's intelligence? Or do they reflect a bias in the test materials
and not any important difference in the children's
intelligence? The nature-nurture dispute crystallized
around the issue whether genetic or environmental
factors best accounted for the disparities in IQ
scores between high and low SES groups. Thorndike
(1968) points out that a great deal of pre-World War II

research focused on either genetic or environmental factors. Genetic research compared IQ scores of identical twins brought up in the same and in different households. IQ scores of children were compared with their natural parents and their foster parents. Heredity or environment were held constant in IQ comparisons. Therefore, any significant difference in IQ score between identical twins brought up in different households were said to be due to environmental factors.

Investigations into the effect of changed environments were also carried out. Children from orphanages were retested after a period of residence in a foster home. Negroes from the South were compared with those migrating to New York City. Klineberg (1944) found that Northern urban Negroes had higher IQ's than Southern Negroes, and that the differences increased with length of residence in the North. Davis (1951) took this as clear evidence of the great influence of school training and other cultural acts upon problem solving. The environmental explanation of group IQ differences appeared to gain very wide acceptance. Thorndike (1968:428) writes: *"At the present time there would be little dissent from the proposition that measured intelligence is a function of the environment to which the individual or group has been exposed, and that some part of the differences between individuals and between groups is attributable to such environmental differences."*

Cultural Bias of Tests

Those who have claimed that IQ tests are culturally biased against the low SES child make one of two environmental arguments. The first is that intelligence is subject to modifications by a stimulating or non-stimulating environment, and that the higher SES environment provides more stimulation. Hence it is understandable that higher SES children score higher on intelligence tests than lower SES children. Havighurst (1951) says factors of middle class life are 'stimulating' to the development of intelligence.

145

However, little research has been carried out in homes to see whether these *"stimulating"* factors were more frequent in middle class rather than lower class homes, and if present, how they affected the development of intelligence. This argument has nonetheless provided the theoretical foundation for countless cultural enrichment programs, such as Head Start. The stimulating-environment proponents acknowledge that while lower SES groups may in fact have lower average intelligence test scores, their intelligence, as measured by tests, may be raised if the environment is suitably altered. They do not dispute the argument that intelligence is measured by an intelligence test.

The second cultural bias argument (Eells, 1951) holds that test items draw a disproportionate amount of material from high SES cultural experiences. Hence observed differences in IQ scores between groups are artifacts dependent upon the specific content of the test item. The cultural experiences which allow the higher SES child to achieve a higher score are exactly those experiences which Havighurst and others take to be the 'stimulating' factors in a middle class environment: trips, books, conversations, etc. Havighurst (Eells, 1951:21) states that: *"...an intelligence test which is to get at the 'real' problem solving ability of children must draw its problems entirely from experiences which are common to all or nearly all of the children to be tested."* Acknowledgment of the *"cultural bias"* of standard IQ tests like the Stanford-Binet encouraged the construction of 'culturally fair' tests which did not rely so heavily upon middle class background experiences, especially the use of words. It was assumed that the lower SES child had less facility with language, and would be penalized by a test that was largely dependent upon verbal skills and verbal symbolism.

After their thorough study of the middle class bias of standard IQ test items, Davis and Eells constructed a "games" test that presented items designed to be familiar to all or almost all American children. In the Raven Progressive Matrices Test, a pattern with

146

a piece missing is presented to the child, and he is
asked to choose one of six pieces to complete the
pattern.

The discouraging part of the quest for a culture
fair test has been that low SES groups do not perform
better on them than they do on the highly verbal
Stanford-Binet type. Shuey (1966) documented that
American Negroes still score one standard deviation
or fifteen IQ points below the average, even when
tested on the Davis-Eells Games Test. This finding
suggests that the cultural bias of test items can not
account for black-white or low SES-high SES score
differences. But Thorndike (1968:425) explains the
persistent difference by noting, *"To the extent that
poor test performance is a function of cultural deprivation, this effect appears to be far reaching...."*
In other words, the cultural or environmental conditions of low SES groups were believed to retard the
development of intelligence, such that any test of
abstract problem solving would yield a lower average
score.

Arthur Jensen's article *"How Much Can We Boost
IQ and Scholastic Achievement"* (1969) interjected a
racial aspect into the IQ and environment controversy.
Jensen claimed that black children had lower IQ levels
than white children even after environmental factors
had been controlled. He also stated that no one had
produced any evidence based on a properly controlled
study to show that representative samples of Negro
and white children could be equalized in intellectual
ability through statistical control of environment
and education. Jensen felt his analysis of existing
data suggested that a genetic rather than an environmental hypothesis might explain the average Negro-
white intelligence score difference.

Problems of Measuring the Environment

Environmental explanations of SES and racial IQ
differences are based upon assumption of important
and measurable differences between high and low SES,
and black and white environments. But environmental

theories of IQ differences are conjectural as long as we do not have direct, anthropological observation of the social processes making up the environmental factor in human development.

The two most popular types of environmental data used by researchers are both indirect. The first is impersonal information on demographic characteristics of families and neighborhoods. The socio-economic status (SES) of families is measured by income, occupation of the father, presence or absence of father in the home, ethnicity of the parents, and education of the parents. This information is obtained through questionnaire interviews with parents and children. The socioeconomic status of neighborhoods is computed from census data or information reported by school administrators.

The second popular type of data is more personal information about the patterns of interaction between children and parents, parents' ideals of childrearing, and parents' hopes for career achievement for their children. This information is also gathered through questionnaire interviews with parents and children, and the contact between the researcher and the families studied lasts only as long as it takes to perform a standard interview. These procedures are rarely designed so the researcher can observe the routine interaction of parents and children, and the social organization of the family and the neighborhood. A few comparative studies of child-rearing practices and intelligence have tried to observe parent-child interaction more directly. For example, Hess and Shipman (1965) observed mother-child interaction in a controlled setting designed for unobtrusive observation by researchers. But neither questionnaire type data or observational data from controlled settings comes very close to an ethnographic account of the everyday patterns of social life or environment of the family.

The greatest source of measurement error in indirect environmental studies is that the researcher's taken for granted expectations about proper child-rearing practices, and his culturally ingrained prejudices about the irresponsibility of black and lower-class parents will be the main basis for interpreting the social relations which underly the data. Data obtained from even the lengthiest questionnaire is so lacking in ethnographic detail that it lends itself to sterotyping, even by well-meaning, liberal social scientists. On the other hand, direct observation in the anthropological tradition produces richly detailed descriptions of social relationships so the researcher is more likely to discover details which do not fit his stereotype of these groups (Becker, 1970).

Comparisons of Black and White Ways of Life

There are two realms of discourse concerned with comparisons of black and white ways of life. One is psychometric, the other cultural. The psychometric research comparing American blacks and whites in terms of intelligence test scores has never come to terms with the research on the properties of the American black subcultures. The work done by social scientists like Dubois (1914) and Dollard (1937) has described the cultural knowledge and social organization of everyday life for black people in America. Such cultural knowledge is no less complicated than the knowledge required of white people. However, this background knowledge has been disregarded in psychometric and social psychological discussions of intelligence and educability.

Research on race, class, intelligence and educability normally views the environment as socioeconomic conditions which affect the life chances of the individual as a member of a group independent of the actor's own knowledge of these conditions (Deutsch, et. al. 1967; Pettigrew, 1964). This ignores the actor's own subjective awareness of his environment, for example the black child's awareness of race prejudice, and the significance of skin color. Researchers do not deny that low SES Negro children are aware of prejudice. In fact anticipation of prejudice is often acknowledged as a source of discouragement and fear for black children, accounting for low motivation in white-dominated schools. But this easy acknowledgment of black children's sensibilities evades the basic question for theories of intelligence — what the black child knows about his social world that involves conceptual abilities unrecognized by tests, and unappreciated by school personnel and social researchers (Baratz and Baratz, 1970).

Ironically, psychometric researchers exploit black children's background knowledge of their environment without appreciating that the children's answers are remarkable examples of intellectual performances. Deutsch's index of cultural deprivation is a typical example of this unthinking exploitation of background knowledge combined with indifference to the unknown properties of everyday life in the black community.[2] A high score on this index is supposed to show deprivation of opportunities in which abstract abilities and a broad world-view might have developed. Deutsch entirely ignores the fact that the children who score high on cultural deprivation are able to give an account of their lives that extends deep into the past. These accounts may well be equivalent in abstractness to that of the children who score low in cultural deprivation.

Language comparisons are one of the most important areas where intelligence research has suffered due to isolation from the cultural realm of discourse.

----

[2]Deutsch's index was based on five questions: how often children eat dinner with their parents, how frequently they had been taken to the museum by their parents, etc. As he expected, Deutsch found that his index correlated inversely with IQ and school achievement for both black and white children independent of class. But this combination of questions is so blatantly based upon the middle-class conception of a good home life, that it provides no information at all about the ways of socializing children that are valued in the black community or the conceptual schemes that black children learn to use in everyday life.

150

Recent work by linguists and sociolinguists on black
dialects has clearly documented these dialects have
all the characteristics definitive of complex language
(Labov, 1969; Stewart, 1970; Baratz, 1970). It seems
evident that the linguistic deprivation corollary of
the cultural deprivation argument has been based upon
linguistic naivete at its worst. Bereiter, Engelmann,
Deutsch and others have claimed that black children are
uncommunicative and illogical relative to white children,
that they are relatively unable to express themselves
clearly because they are unable to plan their use of
language. But folklorists such as Abrahams (1970a,
1970b) and sociolinguists such as Labov (1969, 1970)
and Mitchell-Kernan (1969) have described the elaborate,
traditionalized styles of communicative performance in
black life. Labov's work in particular has challenged
the middle-class complacency of the cultural and
linguistic deprivational arguments. He notes that the
deficit theory does not focus upon the interaction of
the black child with his family or with his peers.
Instead it draws its conclusions from indexes such
as Deutsch's. This evidence is then used to explain
and interpret the large body of tests carried out in
the laboratory and in the school. Labov does not deny
that black children may appear to have little skill in
language in the classroom or in a testing session. He
sees this is a reasonable response to the found or
anticipated hositility in the school. However, Labov's
observations outside of adult-dominated environments
indicate that black children are extremely verbal,
offering much information, eagerly displaying verbal
skills.

The work of folklorists, sociolinguists, anthro-
pologists and sociologists in describing the in-
stitutionalized norms, values and styles of communication in black life has also gone unrecognized by
psychometricians and cultural deprivationists. While
the cultural deprivationists conjecture that noise and
overcrowding in the ghetto reduce the expressions of
love and care, the ethnographically oriented researchers
have reported that ghetto parents, neighbors and relatives

are enthusiastically interested in children (Mitchell-Kernan, 1969; Rainwater, 1970; Stein, 1971; Valentine, 1971).

The Measurement of Intelligence

The current controversy about the effects of race and environment on intelligence prompts a careful reanalysis of the validity of measures of intelligence. The validity problems of environmental and intellectual measurement are conceptually related because they both apply to the phenomenon of social interaction processes. In the environmental case, the processes of socialization occur through the social interaction of the home and school . In the measurement of intelligence, test items are realized through social interaction between the tester and the subject(s).

There are two basic problems of validity in the measurement of intelligence. The first is that the conception of the phenomenon being measured remains vague apart from particular measurement systems associated with particular tests. Educational psychologists, including Jensen, are quite frank in their admission that intelligence is whatever intelligence tests measure.

Given this operationalism, it is appropriate to view the work of Jensen and other psychometricians not as theories of intelligence, but as theories of intelligence testing. Therefore, it is necessary to ascertain the accuracy of standardized tests in registering the subjects' performances on the test.

The second problem of intelligence measurement is whether the testing process is accurately standardized. Standardization of intelligence tests has two meanings, one psychometric, the other sociological. The psychometric connotation is that an individual subject's performance is scored by reference to the standard or mean score of all subjects at his particular age level. The sociological connotation is that the testing process has a standard organization specified by the rules of the test. The sociological type of

standardization — normatively organized interaction
— is a condition of the psychometric type of standardization since it supposedly guarantees that all testers
will uniformly administer the tests to all subjects.
Without such testing uniformity, standardized scoring
would be called into doubt.

Let me further clarify the sociological meaning
of standardization. Sociologists believe that social
interaction will be uniform or standard when actors
comply with norms that specify appropriate ways for
them to behave. The term 'norm' refers to obligatory
standards of conduct and is synonymous with the term
'rule'. Social interaction between testers and subjects, teachers and students, husbands and wives will
be uniform to the degree it is normatively organized.
'Normatively organized interaction' refers to actors'
interactions when organized to conform to obligatory
standards of conduct.

The term 'norm' has another meaning for psychometricians, namely the average score on a test for a
certain population. Sociologists and psychometricians
reading this article can avoid terminological confusion
by remembering that the two different meanings of
standardization correspond to two different meanings
of norm.

An intelligence test is normatively organized
in the sociological sense because it has rules that both
the tester and the subject are obligated to follow. For
example, the peabody Picture Vocabulary Test has a rule
obliging the tester not to pluralize or add articles to
the test words when she says them. If the test word
were *"horse"* the tester should not say *"the horse"* or
"horses." The rule warns that articles or pluralizations
of the test words might be clues for a subject in matching the word with a picture. If the testing process were
organized to conform to this norm, we would expect to
find in a verbatim transcript no cases where the tester
pluralized or added an article to the test word. If we
found such a case, we would expect the tester to have
discounted that item or to have thrown the test out altogether as a non-standard performance.

The Peabody also specifies normative behavior
for the subject. A rule tells the child he should give
an answer on each problem, even if he has to guess.
Therefore, if a child's performance is normatively
organized, we would expect to find that the child has
never refused to answer a problem the tester gave him.
If he resisted, we would expect the tester to have
insisted that he answer, waiting until he did before
going on to another item.

When analyzing intelligence testing as a social
interaction process, both the psychometric and sociological conceptions of norm are relevant. The rule-
connotation of norm is relevant to theories of intelligence in two ways. It is the basis for theories
of environmental influence on intellectual development,
and it is the basis of objective testing procedures.
In the first case, the influence of a child's family
and neighbors on his intellectual development is
assumed to be guided by rules of interaction that are
part of their culture. In the second case, the rules
of the test are supposed to guide testers and subjects
through the test problems in a uniform way, so that
all test scores are comparable. Logically speaking,
the sociological meaning of norm as an obligatory
rule is more basic than the psychometric one since
it produces the procedural uniformity that standardized
measurement requires. Specification of an objective
scoring norm for a type of subject presupposes that
the subjects in the criterion sample and in all subsequent testing conformed to the obligatory rules of
testing procedure.

I am taking the theoretical position that conformity by testers and subjects to particular testing
rules cannot be taken for granted because it is
problematic for actors to achieve perfect conformity
to any rules. In trying to achieve normatively
organized interaction, the actors face a problem of
articulating the meanings of rules with the situations
they are acting in. Matching rules to situations in

action is a variable process, not fully anticipatable in advance (Cicourel, 1973; Garfinkel, 1967). This suggests that the processes of interaction will vary from occasion to occasion even though the outcomes, viewed as products, appear equivalent. If that is true, we should not take for granted that children of equivalent age with equal IQ scores performed the test the same way.[3] The equivalence of the product (the IQ score) does not mean that the processes of interaction between tester and child were equivalent.

The problem of valid recording of test performances becomes apparent when we begin to take the problems of normative conformity into account. If the test participants are involved in defining the meaning of the rules during the course of the interaction, it is not possible to specify in advance what form the interaction will take. Because unanticipated events will routinely occur as both the tester and testees deal with the practicalities of the test, the test design should arrange to record unanticipated as well as standard events.

A standardized intelligence test like the Peabody solves the problem of keeping records by taking for granted that the testing process will follow the rules and by arranging in advance to record only whether a child answered any item correctly or not. In other words, the Peabody, and many other tests, *"solve"* the problem by denying its existence. Because the test record records only standard or anticipated events, the existence of a particular standard test record does not prove that the particular testing process was actually standardized.

From a sociological standpoint, this recording procedure seems naive since it ignores the variations

---

[3]I am not referring to the possibility that children can get different items correct and still be given the same IQ score. I am referring to more general dissimilarities of performances, involving differences in the way testers and children interpret and enact the test rules.

in interaction that follow from the problematic character of rule following. This naivete has drastic implications for the validity of intelligence measurement. If the test recording procedures do not show us whether the test was standardized or unstandardized according to the rules, we can never treat the validity of any test score as a settled matter. As long as the score sheet does not allow us to separate the standard from the non-standard test performances, we can never separate the valid test scores from the invalid ones.

Instead of taking the test scoring record as an adequate summary of what went on in the testing sessions, I have studied the entire testing sessions by means of audio and video tape analysis. By using sound and visual recordings, I was able to record all audible or visible events within the range of the machinery and was not restricted to the events which a formal analysis of the testing rules would lead me to anticipate.

Analysis of the recordings brings the context-bound negotiation of the performance into clear view. It shows us how the children receive the instructions from the tester and establish with the assistance of the tester whether the situations that emerge are the ones they anticipated. The recordings show us how the children discover in the course of the test that the meanings of the test rules and test items are not what they first thought. We see how the tester and child adapt to unanticipated events, such as intruders, bells ringing, and need to go to the bathroom, etc. In some cases we also find the children recognize the test as one they have taken before, and the testers emphasize children's previous experience with tests in explaining what they are to do.

In summary, the testing process as social interaction is defined by both tester and child as an event embedded in a more or less extended history of events that constitutes an environment known to the actors. In this perspective, the relationship of the environment to individual performance is viewed as subjectively meaningful, an unfolding background of events which is taken into account by the actors. Intelligence can thus be viewed as the ability to bring appropriately remembered and anticipated events to bear on the present situation, to link background knowledge to current, unfolding events, judging the reasonableness and logic of courses of action. In other words, intelligence can be viewed as a gloss for the organizing of action in terms of a background of social and individual knowledge.

I was interested in finding out what young black and white children knew about the environment or background of their lives, and what aspects they brought to bear upon their testing activities. At issue were the ways the children negotiated the normative interaction of an intelligence test. I hoped to find that the test scores misrepresented the abilities of all the children, black and white, high IQ and low IQ. By analyzing the audio and video recordings of the testing sessions, I hoped to find that important information about the childrens' organizing and conceptual abilities was lost when the only record of the testing interaction was the test score sheet.[4]

In the next section, I will briefly describe Jensen's theory of intelligence types and then examine transcripts taken from tape recordings of Peabody Picture Vocabulary testing sessions with first grade

---

[4]Some test score sheets, like the Peabody, have a place where the tester is instructed to give any reason why the score may not be a good measure of the child's abilities. This report is insufficient for scientific purposes. When compared with a tape recording, the tester's memory of the test glosses over the temporal ordering of events in the test. Furthermore, annotated entries limit the freedom of interpretation that others may have in deciding how well the test measured the child's performance. The reader of the tester's analysis only has the score sheet as a base point for evaluating the tester's interpretation. Furthermore, the tester's comments do not allow the researcher to recompute the child's IQ.

children from school B. My analyses of the transcripts
will show that Jensen's measurement of intelligence
rests on erroneous assumptions about the relationships
of stimuli-inputs and response-outputs in the interaction process of testing (cf., Mehan, 1971; MacKay,
this volume, who make similar observations about
language development and reading testing, respectively).

Jensen's Input-Output Model of Intelligence

Jensen contends that there are two types of
intelligence, associative and conceptual. In the
development of any individual, associative intelligence
is supposed to emerge first, and conceptual intelligence
second. Jensen hypothesizes that all children develop
associative intelligence more or less equally, but that
there is significant variation in children's development
of conceptual intelligence. The development of these
different intelligence types in each individual is
supposed to be determined largely genetically. Though
Jensen's argument has become notorious as a racial
theory, it has much broader application. The theory
applies as well to differences in intelligence among
white persons as to differences between whites and
blacks. Jensen's theory implies that low-achieving
white children have less conceptual intelligence than
high-achieving white children. I am not denying that
Jensen's writing has been focused on the racial comparison. But it would be inaccurate to reply to his
arguments as though they were nothing more than racial
comparisons.

According to Jensen (1969:111), associative intelligence (Level I) involves a stimulus-input and a
response output which are very similar: *"Level I involves the neural registration and consolidation of
stimulus inputs and the formation of associations.
There is relatively little transformation of the input,
so there is a high correspondence between the forms of
the stimulus input and the form of the response output."*
Associative intelligence can best be measured by such
direct learning tests as digit memory, serial rote
learning and paired associate learning. In general, it

is best to think of associative intelligence as the ability to imitate and memorize. For example, in digit span memory, the child is read a list of numbers in series, and then he is asked to repeat them in the original order from memory. The number of numbers he remembers, and the errors he makes are the basis for an associative intelligence score.

Serial rote learning involves repetition of strings of numbers or words, with the child imitating the strings after each presentation. The number of presentations of the string of symbols before the child is able to do a perfect imitation gives the measure of the level of associative intelligence. The fewer the trials required, the more associative intelligence the child has. Paired-associate learning involves presentation of pairs of words, which may or may not have any semantic or syntactic relation to one another. The child is required to learn which words or symbols are paired. As with serial rote learning, the measure of intelligence is inverse to the number of trials required for learning the associations.

Conceptual intelligence (Level II) involves *"self-initiated elaboration and transformation of the input before it eventuates in an overt response"* (Jensen, 1969:11). Jensen refers to concept learning and problem solving as examples of conceptual intelligence. Standardized intelligence tests which have a high loading of Spearman's *g* are excellent measures of conceptual intelligence. Jensen cites the Peabody, the Raven and the Stanford-Binet as tests of abstract problem solving.

The most important aspect of Jensen's theory of intelligence types is the conceptual unit that he assumes — the input-output pair. An input is nothing more or less than a combination of sensory stimuli presented to the subject, and an output is nothing more than an observable response made by the subject. The typical input and output pair that Jensen appears to have in mind is the question and answer in a test problem. The tester's question to the child constitutes the input to the child, the child's answer the output.

Jensen feels that all tests can be classified in terms
of input-output similarity to determine whether they
are measures of associative or conceptual intelligence.
Therefore it is critical to investigate whether the
input-output unit is a useful device to analyze the
testing situation. Does the input-output unit accurately reflect what goes on in a testing scene, or
does it drastically limit our knowledge of the testing
interaction, and the child's interpretive abilities?

Collection of Materials

A sample of black and white children was tested
at home and at school. All school testing was done
by the same white research assistant who also tested
the white children at home. Home testing of black
children was done by two black testers. The children
were tested both at home and at school to see whether
they would perform better in one situation than the
other. The IQ test philosophy assumes that children's
intelligence is constant at any age, implying that
children would score the same on an IQ test (within
the limits of test reliability) wherever the test was
administered, as long as the rules were followed uniformly and the testing dates were close enough in
time to avoid the effect of children's intellectual
maturation. But recent research in sociolinguistics
and psycholinguistics has demonstrated that variations
in the situations contribute to significant variations
in performance (Cazden, 1970; Labov, 1970). We anticipated that children would do better at home, since
it was more familiar and assuring. We also anticipated
that black children tested by black testers at home
would be more likely to express interpretations of the
test materials from the standpoint of black sub-culture.

All testing sessions were tape-recorded, and the
tapes were transcribed by the testers in order to
maximize the ability of the transcriber to identify
events in the tapes by memory of the testing session.
The testers were encouraged to leave their tape re-
corders on as much as possible while in the home in
order to get more extensive samples of conversation.

160

The main purpose of the transcript analysis will be to show that both black and white children exhibit intelligent, conceptual performances involving background knowledge that is not measured by the recording devices and measurement procedures provided by the standardized test itself. Since these tests are usually assumed to objectify the conditions of scholastic achievement, it will be noteworthy to show that the tests do not record performances in the testing process which have a clear relationship to educational activity. I will show that regardless of test scores, the children performed conceptually in ways that were not recorded by the test. I will also show that the children performed more elaborately cross-referenced interactions than Jensen's theory of intelligence types conceives of. The discussion of correct and incorrect items with the children will indicate that they had abstract understandings of test items far in excess of those indicated by their test scores.

Test Materials

The Peabody Picture Vocabulary Test, as its name makes clear, is a vocabulary test. The score sheet of the Peabody contains 150 words, each corresponding to a particular page of four pictures in the test booklet. The tester reads the stimulus word to the child, and the child is instructed to select from four pictures the one which matches the word. The word and the four pictures are the stimulus inputs to the child. The child can either point to the picture of his choice, or say its number. The indication of his choice is his output. Here is an example of a Peabody item:[5]

----

[5]We have been refused permission to reproduce any of the pictures in the Peabody test.

59____(1) globe $\left[\text{This appears on the scoring sheet with 149 others.}\right]$

picture of a globe of the world	picture of an anchor
1	2
picture of an open pea pod with peas in it	picture of a tassel on the end of a woven cord
3	4

$\left[\text{This is one of 150 pages in separate picture booklet.}\right]$

The number 1 in parentheses before *"globe"* indicates that picture 1 is the correct answer. If the child chooses the correct picture, the tester writes 1 on the line. If the child chooses any other picture, the number of the choice is written in, and a slash mark is made through the numeral *"59"*. When the child picks the wrong picture, we supposedly know that he doesn't recognize the word, or the picture, or that he doesn't know that they go together. This interpretation seems clear cut and useful and is similar to what Mehan (1971) and MacKay (this volume) report about other educational tests. By interpreting the child's mistakes in this simple way, it is possible to measure intelligence by the number of items that he gets right and wrong.

Given the input-output form of the Peabody, it seems reasonable for Jensen to have imagined this intelligence test could be validly analyzed in terms of

cumulative individual pairs of input and output. It
also seems obvious that the Peabody should be classified
as a conceptual test since the input and the output
are dissimilar actions. The input is words and pictures
while the output is pointing to a picture or designating
its number. But such a classification seems unreasonable
as soon as one compares the score sheet record of a
performance on any items with the tape recording of that
performance. Jensen's assumption of an ordered, bounded
input-output pair does not fit the verbatim transcript
of the live testing process.

Analyses of the Performances
     The following is the score sheet record of An's
performance at home on item 59.

59 __4__ (1) globe

The tester was a black female college student who had
tested him before at school and home. This was part
of a testing session at home. An is a black child
who got the lowest over-all IQ score on the Peabody.
He is also the black child who appeared to live in the
most middle-class home. The tester marked An's choice,
picture 4, and then put a slash mark through 59 to indicate that his choice was wrong. Let us analyze the
transcript of item 59 in terms of Jensen's input-output
model. We will assume that anything heard on the tape
recording is also audible to An and the tester.

163

Table 4.1.   Key to Abbreviations and Marks

(p), (bp), (lp)	=	pause, brief pause, long pause
(pf)	=	page of picture booklet flips
(An: ...)	=	a remark interrupting the remark it is embedded in with speaker identified by the first two letters of first name
?...? (or) ?...?	=	alternative tentative versions of section of tape
(...)	=	parenthetical remarks by tester/ transcriber or author, comments about motives of the actors, identifying non-verbal sounds, etc.
(hes)	=	hesitation
(long)	=	previous word was prolonged in articulation

Tester:	*Four* (awful lot of noise in the background) *Um* (prolonged pause) *Globe*	INPUT
Woman:	*Yeah, it's a friend.*	INPUT
An:	*What?*	OUTPUT
Tester:	*Globe.*	INPUT
An:	*?Globe? (or) ?Glub?*	OUTPUT
Tester:	*Globe.*	INPUT
An:	*What's that?* (insistent)	OUTPUT
Tester:	*Don'ch* (hes) *you know what a globe is?* (dubious)	INPUT
Baby:	...(indecipherable)	INPUT
Woman:	*uh huh*	INPUT
Baby	...(indecipherable)	INPUT
Woman:	*Where's Al?*	INPUT
An:	*Four.*	OUTPUT

Clearly the combination of inputs and outputs that occurred during the performance of item 59 was more complicated than the score sheet record indicates, and Jensen's theory can accommodate. This result was representative of all Peabody items. Jensen's unit of analysis for intelligence — the independent pairs of inputs and output — does not fit the testing process. If we take An's last output, *"four"* as a response to the input immediately preceding it, then it must be a response to the question, *"Where's Al?"* Of course it doesn't make sense as an answer to that question. It does make sense as an answer to the testor's previous questions about *"globe."* But if we treat the tester's remark, *"Don'ch* (hes) *you know what a globe is"* as an input paired with An's output *"four,"* we gloss over all the other inputs that An heard but didn't respond to.

An's performance in this transcript section indicates an ability that any teacher would look for in a student: He shows that he can recognize and disregard events around him which are irrelevant to the task at hand.[6] There are indications that An fully knew what was going on around him, even though he did not comment on all these events as they happened. For example, at the end of the session, he asked if he could watch *"Dark Shadows."* An knew all along what was on the television, even though he hadn't mentioned it before. Further along in the test, An made a remark to the tester explaining a picture and referred to his uncle who had just come into the house. I had noticed the entry of a man from the tape, but An did not remark upon it until some minutes later when it became relevant to the problem at hand — explaining the test materials.

This transcript section also casts doubt on a popular aspect of the cultural deprivation argument: that chaos, noise and activity present in the lower class home prevent the child from developing the ability to abstract. This home test session with An

---

[6]Bruner, Goodnow and Austin (1965) and Bourne (1966) view the ability to pay attention to certain events in the situation while ignoring others as a basic constituent of the ability to abstract.

was the noisiest of all our sessions. Many people's voices were distinctly heard; the television was on loud enough in the adjacent room for me to have transcribed whole sentences from the ads, and to have recognized the name of the show from its theme music. If the deprivation argument is correct, all the noise and chaos in An's home should have had a retarding effect upon his conceptual performance. He should have had great difficulty in concentrating on the task at hand, being constantly distracted by the remarks and presence of other persons. Yet the transcript shows that An managed his part in a stream of interaction with varied inputs and outputs which were not obviously bounded or paired. We cannot escape the conclusion that the noisy conditions of An's homelife did not prevent him from performing social interaction in an orderly manner, or from displaying the ability to abstract. Neither can we escape the conclusion that the official test record hides these abilities from us.

The next transcript section is taken from the middle of the school test session with the white tester. Unlike the previous example, An and the tester were alone together in conditions that approximated a formal testing situation. Even so, the testing process was more complex than the test record could show.

1	R:	...On 76,
2	An:	*This one, is this one.*
3	R:	*You better listen first before*
4		*you guess. On that page (76)*
5		*the word is 'scholar',*
6		"scholar." (An is pounding
7		rather energetically.) *An*
8		*I want you to look at the pic-*
9		*tures before you put your*
10		*finger on it.*
11		(An smiles.)
12	An:	*That one?* (pointing)
13	R:	*Scholar? Number three?*
14	An:	*That one.*
15	R:	*Come on.*

I   R begins the routine, but An cuts her off (2), making a

O   wild guess, as though he were no longer concerned with

I   maximizing the accuracy of his choices. R's next output (3-10) is concerned with getting An to do his part right.
It refers back to his guess (2) and forward to his next choice

(O)   output. The parenthetical output (6) is intended to show it embedded in R's output.

O   Here (11) An gives another non-verbal output.

O   On line 12 An begins a cat-and-mouse game with the

I   tester that goes on to line 62. In this game it is the

O   child who takes the initiative rather than the tester. The

I   tester is trying to get An to settle on one picture so they

167

16 An: *That one!* (An keeps pointing
17 to first one picture, then
18 another.)

O — can complete the routine, but An keeps escaping from her grasp. (21, 27, 32-3, 44-5, etc.)

19 R: *Number two?* (A picture of a
matador with a cape.)

I

21 An: *I mean number three.* (A pic-
22 ture of a black Pullman
23 porter)

O

24 R: *Which one do you want?*
25 *Number two or number*
26 *three?*

I — When she tries to get him to choose between the two pictures he has already chosen, he escapes by choosing still another, picture 4 (32-3).

27 An: *Well, I choose number four*
28 (A picture of a man in an
29 academic robe holding a
30 diploma.)

O

31 R: *Number four? Ok*

I — Here (33) An asks R what the stimulus word is, harking all the way back to R's inputs on lines 5-6 and 13.

32 An: *No, I mean number* (pounds
33 the table) *what's its name?*
34 (He keeps tapping his finger
35 on the picture of a soldier

O — Here (32-7) An's output is both verbal and non-verbal, and the fact he is tapping on picture one while asking for the term again suggests to me that he

168

Line	Speaker	Utterance		Commentary
36		carrying a rifle, picture number 1.)		has settled finally on a choice, the only picture he hasn't chosen before.
37				
38	R:	*You tell me what's its name.*	I	R seems to think he is asking for the proper name of picture 1, not the stimulus word,
39	An:	I don't know. (The loud tapping is continuing.)	O	since she refuses to give him the term (38). There wouldn't be any reason not to give him the stimulus word, "scholar," again.
40				
41	R:	*Which one do you want? One, two, three, or four for "scholar."*	I	Finally, on 37–9, R tries to bring the item to a close once and for all, indicating each option by numeral and giving
42				
43	An:	One, two, three, four (under his breath). *I think I'll take scholar.* (He has stopped tapping on the table.)	O	the test word again. It seems she's left no options un-covered; he has to choose once and for all. But An responds with a new game; he turns the tables on her by making her
44				
45				
46				
47	R:	*You got to tell me the picture.*	I	do the guessing while he gives the test word to identify his choice (44–5). He and R keep
48	An:	*Scholar.*	O	insisting on their own versions
49	R:	*Show me the picture.*	I	of the proper game during the next few lines (47–51).

169

50 An: Scholar.
51 R: Show me the picture
52 An: Well, I think I'll take the man
53   who's carrying something. I
54   bet you don't know what it is,
55   the man who is carrying some-
56   thing.
57 R: You bet what?
58 An: I bet you don't know the man
59   who is carrying something.
60 R: What, what do you mean I
61   bet you don't know?
62 An: That one, number one. (All
63   four pictures show men who are
64   carrying something. I guess
65   (An was playing a game to
66   see if I knew which man he meant.)

O
I
O   Finally, on lines 52-6, An
    changes the game again. It's
    a new guessing game. In this
    new game he implicitly classi-
    fies all the pictures on the
    page together as pictures of
    men carrying something. That
    is why this new "choice" is a
    put-on' there's no single
I   answer because the identifica-
O   tion fits all four pictures.

I   R's repeated questions (57,60-1)
    may be authentic requests for
    clarification or a tactic for
    suppressing his newest attack.
O   Finally, on lines 62, An seems
    to relent, identifying picture
    one, and that is the output which
    was recorded as his performance on
    this item.

170

On the score sheet of the Peabody test this whole
event could only be recorded as an incorrect answer
to a standard item. Consequently, the lengthy and
complicated conversation you read above was reduced
to a single input-output pair. Our careful analysis
of the tape shows that An made 5 different types of
choices, 4 of them unserious. First, there was the
blind guess before the tester said *"scholar"* (2);
second, the sequences of changes of mind (12-27);
third, identification of his choice by the test word,
so Ruth had to guess the picture (44-50); and fourth,
identification of the picture by a label covering all
the pictures (52-29). Finally, he let Ruth off the
hook, giving her a serious choice, using a numeral
once again (62).

Theories of intelligence concerned with children's
ability to interpret and transform inputs cannot
justify the use of research methods which systematically make those things invisible to the researcher. In
Jensen's terms, An has shown an incredible level of
conceptual intelligence, given his far-ranging manipulation and transformation of the stimulus input in his
responses. Of course from the standpoint of An's
teacher this kind of fooling around interfered with
An's education and her efforts to teach other children
in the class. In discussing the relationship of
class, ethnicity, IQ and educability, educational
psychologists usually assume that high IQ or abstract
intellectual reasoning ability guarantees school
success, but this ignores the kind of trouble that
some highly intelligent behavior can cause. It takes
intelligence to 'act smart'. Once researchers appreciate the 'pure intelligence' involved in making
trouble in a test or classroom, they may appreciate
how little 'pure' intelligence has to do with educability and school success. Whatever his intelligence,
a kid who acts 'smart' is going to get in trouble in
school unless he has protective sponsorship, whether
it comes from teachers, administrators, counselors, or
parents (Becker, 1970, Cicourel and Kitsuse, 1963).

The next transcript section demonstrates that

the testing recording procedure also misrepresents
the performance of well-behaved, high-IQ children who
are academically successful. Because the score sheet
of the Peabody records the testing performance as a
sequence of isolated items, it obscures the fact
that the children and the testers perceive relationships among items.

1	R:	*On 64, the word is "chef."*	I
2	Pe:	*Four banana.*	O
3	R:	*Four banana. On 66 the word*	
4		*is "construction."*	
5	Pe:	*Three banana.*	O
6	R:	*On 68 the word is*	I
7		*"assistance."*	
8	Pe:	*Four banana again.* (Sounds a	O
		little bored).	
10	R:	*Ok.*	
11	Pe:	*There sure is a lot of four*	
		bananas.	O

Except for Pe's pairing numerals with the word
"banana," his talk seems to conform to Jensen's model.
What are we to make of *"banana"* though? The banana
routine was established on item 64 (1-2). There was
no picture of a banana on that page, so the term is
not merely a labeling response to a picture-stimulus.
(The only banana pictured in the test is on one of
the three examples at the beginning of the book.) As
a transformation of inputs, its relation to any input
in the testing process is completely obscure. His
use of the term with the numeral is formally equivalent to children's verbal routine, *"one potato, two
potato,..."* and he may be following that as a model.
Pe continued using the banana term in this way for
several more items, and then he dropped it. But soon
after that he renewed it, and continued it until the
end of the test, on item 98. In recording this performance, the tester ignored the *"banana"* and simply
recorded Pe's answer in numerical terms. She didn't
explicitly encourage Pe to say *"banana,"* but she

condoned it by repeating it as though she took it for granted as an appropriate part of the answer.

Pe's two remarks, *"Four banana again"* (8) and *"There sure is a lot of four bananas."* (11) are observations about the frequency that he has chosen picture 4 on recent items. This response indicates a retrospective awareness of the testing process that goes beyond the boundaries of the particular item at hand. Such a summary perspective is obviously important from a strategic perspective. It is a rational approach to the problem of doing well on the test. This is another instance of conceptual ability that would be entirely overlooked by the actual test score.

I've taken examples from these two boys' performances because they represent the extremes of the IQ distribution in our sample: An had the lowest IQ on the Peabody in our testing (80) and Pe had the highest (130). But these children are not atypical so far as the complexity of testing performance was concerned. All the children we tested, regardless of IQ, performed in ways which were more complicated than the test record and Jensen's input-output scheme could handle. This fact raises another point: the IQ tests misrepresent the abilities of all children, not just minority group and lower-class people.

Intelligence Test Scores and Educability

By restricting its analysis to the question-answer pair, most conventional research on intelligence testing glosses over abilities that are important constituents of both intelligence and educability. The Peabody procedure yields only a limited piece of information — whether the child knew the word well enough to match it with a picture. But for purposes of teaching, a teacher might want to know the answers to some of the following questions.

1. Could the child identify the picture in terms that were relevant to the word? This would indicate the child could understand the concepts represented by the picture and word.

173

2. Could the child identify the other pictures
on the page? If he could, the teacher might then be
able to explain the concept represented by the test
word and picture by relating it to the child's understanding of the other pictures. If the child had
missed the item, it would reassure the teacher that
the child could conceptualize the other pictures.
If the child's explanations of the other pictures
rivaled the correct concept in complexity, the
teacher would understand that the child was able to
handle complex ideas.

3. Could the child see the things represented
by the pictures? The child's explanation would be
useful to the teacher for at least two reasons. It
would show whether the child could see the pictures
as symbols of things experienced elsewhere in his
environment. It would also allow the teacher to
infer what experiences the child might have had, what
parts of the city he was familiar with, what the
child was interested in, etc. With this knowledge,
the teacher could then devise more interesting
lessons for him.

4. Could the child remember after a period of
time what picture he had chosen for a particular
word, and give an explanation of his choice?
These are useful abilities for learning, because
they mean that the child can remember what he is
doing and has done. Since the continuity of lesson
plans is a serious practical problem for a teacher,
the child's contribution to this continuity by reconstruction from memory is an asset for education.

5. Could the child choose again after being
told that he had been wrong the first time? This
shows whether the child has the self control required
to continue working in the face of failure and do
hypothesis testing strategies that take errors into
account (Bruner, Goodnow and Austin 1965).

6. Could the child pay attention to the test
in the face of distraction? This is important as
far as teaching is concerned because children work

174

in the midst of other children doing other things. If the child is able to pay attention to what is relevant to his own work, he will be able to follow a lesson more efficiently.

These were some of the questions that I wanted to answer in doing my work on the testing process. Accordingly, I tape recorded all testing sessions and elaborated the standard test procedure to allow the child and tester opportunity to converse about the pictures and words. My data indicate that all children tested could routinely perform these and other activities that are so functional for education. This was true regardless of the child's score on the Peabody, and thus indicates that the Peabody scoring system glosses over what the children know about the test materials.

I found that the test words and pictures referred to persons, places and things in their environment that were not intrinsic to the word and pictures themselves. This raises a problem vis-a-vis the idea of test standardization. Standardization requires both that the test be uniformly administered to all children and that the test materials be understood and interpreted uniformly by all the children. But I found that the words and pictures tapped and indexed varied experiences in the children's backgrounds. They recognized the words and pictures as signs representing other things in their experiences. Some children had neither heard the test words nor seen the things represented in the pictures. Some children had never heard some words, nor seen the things represented by the pictures. Some children had only a general sense of certain activities portrayed in the pictures, and others had a very specific sense. Often a picture signified a particular activity or state of affairs to one child and quite another to another child. One signification might be presumed correct by the test and the other taken as incorrect even though it was equally complex and abstract.

I felt strongly that because the correctness or

incorrectness of the children's responses tells you very little about their knowledge and understanding, it is necessary to go beyond the normal testing interrogation, and to go beyond the normal method of recording the testing interaction.

In the following transcript section with An **we** find answers to many of the questions posed above. This section took place immediately after the Peabody test had been carried out according to its regular format. The tester and An are going back over his choices, and the tester is asking An to explain why he chose the way he did. The transcript of the session is on the left. The comments on the right locate the performances which the teacher would be interested in vis-a-vis classroom activities and questions of educability.

The pictures on the page they are discussing show the following objects: (1) a standard home thermostat (2) a bolt with a nut on it (3) a slide projector (4) a fishing reel.

1	An:	*All right.*
2	Tester:	*Ok, we're gonna* (cut-off)
3	An:	*All right, and what's this?*
4	Tester:	*Wait a minute. We're gonna go over some more, Ok?*
5		(Woman in background is still conversing
6		through these last few and subsequent remarks.)
7	An:	*How many more? Eight?*
8	Tester:	*No, not very many more.* (An drums on
9		table during pause here.)
10	Tester:	*Ok, on page 53* (p)
11	An:	*?63?* (or) *?53? what?*
12	Tester:	*The word was rr* (hes) *turn to page*
13		*53, An.* (p) *Come on page.*
14	An:	*?54?* (or) *?64?*
15	Tester:	*Page 53.* (clunk) *On page 53* (bp)
16		*the word was reel.*
17	An:	*Reel.* (prolonged with odd voicing)
18		(p) (sound of man's voice in background)

19		*reel?* (normal voicing)
20	Tester:	*Reel.* (Overlaps An's second *"reel"*
21		above) *D'you remember which you*
22		*picked?*
23	An:	*Wait a minute though?* (really
24		impatient)
25	Tester:	*On page 53.* (Sound of page sliding)
26		*That's not even 53* (scrape of mike with
27		lots of drumming). *The word was reel*
28		(end is drowned by the following)
29	An:	*Oh this one's the one that I picked.*

This shows that he can remember the picture he had chosen (29).

30		(loud)
31	Tester:	*What number's that?*
32	An:	*Um, three.* (p) *Did I?*
33	Tester:	*Uh huh.* (yes) *No! Um*
34	An:	*Yes I did!*
35	Tester:	*Why did you pick that one?*
36	An:	*Well, because you can reel this*
37		*backwards and frontwards.* (Drumming
38		here.)

Having pointed to the picture he had picked, he identifies it by number at tester's request (32). Though he expresses doubt at first, An reasserts that it was three even when she contradicts him (32-4). She apparently sees her error (35). An here reconstructs the reasons for his original choice (36-7). He uses the test word grammati-

cally in a sentence which
fits the normal meaning of
the word, and is also
obliquely relevant to the
picture he chose, a slide projector. In his classroom the
children and teacher use a
projector with film-strips
that are reeled back and
forth. *"Reeling backwards and
frontwards"* is precisely what
reeling is all about.

An identifies the picture by
an incorrect but relevant
label since a projector pro-
jects images from pictures
taken by cameras (41).

Here he elaborates his identification (43-4), making
clear he understands what it's
all about. In his class they
project pictures on walls as
well as on a screen hung on
the walls.

39 Tester: *Well, what would you call the*
40 *picture?*
41 An: *It's a picture camera.*

42 Tester: *A picture camera.*
43 An: *Uh huh. There are lots of things*
44 *that you show up on the wall.*

45	Tester:	*Have you seen those things before?*
46	An:	*Yeah, me an my uncle Will, the ah*
47		*one that just came in.*
48		(drumming. Can hear man's voice
49		in background among the voices
50		of the women) (pause)
51	Tester:	*Can you tell me what the other*
52		*pictures on this page are?* (lots
53		of laughter in distant back-
54		ground)
55	Tester:	*No! On this page, page 53.* (brief
56		pause) *What about the other three*
57		*pictures, what're those?*
58	Man:	*?I guess so?*
59	An:	*This are a termoter.*
60	Tester:	*Therma* (hes)

An does two types of locating: he locates the occasion he saw *"those things"* by reference to another person; then he locates that person for the tester (46-7). With this information, the tester could have questioned either An or the uncle about *"those things."* I'm not sure what things he's referring to as the conversation stands.

Here is an example of noise that An makes no note of, focusing instead on the project at hand (52-3).

An makes no note of this remark either (58).

An again identifies a picture by a wrong but relevant label (59). The picture is of a thermostat, but of course, it

has a visible thermometer in
it. The tester apparently
agrees with him. She corrects
his pronunciation, but not his
label (60). She might have
corrected the latter by telling
him *"thermostat."*

Even the tester has a bit of
trouble pronouncing this word
possibly confusing *"thermostat"*
and *"thermometer"* (67).
This word is lengthier, with
more syllables than *"reel"* but
he can easily say it as soon
as tester says it correctly
(68). He then identifies the
picture of the nut and bolt
by a relevant term, *"screw"*
(69). Finally he gets to the
picture that is supposed to

61	An:	*What is it?* (loud, wondering
62		at his own pronunciation and
63		possibly hearing her hesitant
64		cue. I understood tester's
65		previous remark only after
66		hearing the subsequent remark:)
67	Tester:	*Therma* (hes) *thermometer.*
68	An:	*Yeah, a thermometer, and this is*
69		*a screw and this is a* (brief
70		pause) *a thing that you* (slow-
71		ing down) *a fishing pole!*
72	Tester:	*A fishing pole? I don't see a*
73		*pole on there?* (pause) (laughs)
74		*Ok.*

be labeled "*reel*" and he identifies it incorrectly as far
as the test is concerned but
in an extremely relevant way
as far as we are concerned:
"*fishing pole*" (71). He has
partially mastered the conceptual scheme of which "*reel*"
and the picture are a part.
The tester recognizes this.
She teases him but accepts his
identification as sufficient
when she says, "*Ok*" (72-4).
An isn't satisfied. Goaded
by tester's teasing, he
elaborates the identification,
dropping "*fishing pole*" and
introducing the function of
the reel (75-7).

He ends up with another relevant label, "*hook*"(81-2).
It's not clear whether he
meant to call the picture a
hook or rather to indicate
what was attached to the

75 An: *It's um* (pause with lots of chatter
76   from women in background) *ah, it's*
77   *a thing that you roll up the thread.*
78   (loud)

79 Tester: *Ok, I* (hes) *let's turn...*
80 An: *Whatever you call it, whatever*
81   *you fish with, the hook or some-*
82   *thing. Yea, the hook* (Child cries
83   out loudly in background.)

181

thread. He did not note the equivalence of pictures 3 and 4 (projector and reel) but there is no question he understood the functions of both. He even used the term *"roll up the thread"* correctly although he did not associate it with the word *"reel"* (77).

84 Tester: *On page 55 (pause) (Child or woman:*
85 *Stop! (loud)) Don't skip it, this*
86 *is it.*

1. He identifies the picture that he chose for *"reel"* and properly uses the term as a verb in a sentence. The sentence made use of other words which were appropriate to the activity and object of *"reel."* He also describes the picture of *"reel"* (no. 4) in terms compatible with the conventional meaning of reel as a fishing instrument.

2. An identifies all the other pictures on the page in sensible terms. Even his change of mind about what to call picture 4 was relevant to the object in terms of its social use as an instrument for fishing.

3. An reports that he has seen some of the things pictured although he is not specific in saying where he has seen them. He tells us he saw *"those things"* with his uncle, thus linking the present with the past.

4. An is able to reconstruct his original choice. He correctly identifies which picture he chose even though the tester gets confused and contradicts him. This, too, shows he can link the present with the past. He was able to give clear reasons why he chose picture 3 for *"reel."*

5. An ignores a lot of background noise and identifiable talk that occurs in the course of the discussion of item 58. In the course of this transcript section, he makes a remark about his uncle having come in. This indicates that An was aware of the man's arrival even though he did not comment on it at the time it took place. When he brings it up, it is relevant to the on-going discussion.

The next transcript section is from the same testing occasion. It reflects the tester's interrogation of the child's understanding. After the Peabody test was administered, and the child had been interviewed about his first choices and the other pictures, the tester was to tell the child which items he had missed and ask him if he wanted to choose again.

Then she was supposed to find out the reasons for the new choice. All the children we tested chose again. Many of them justified their answers by identifying possibly relevant properties of the picture. Others simply gave *"guessing"* as the reason for this second choice. But in this session with An, the tester simply went through each of the items he had missed and gave him the right answer. In other words, she apparently thought she was to teach the child the items he had missed. While this reduced the information, An responded with remarks we intended to solicit in the first place.

After missing some items, An was able to follow the tester's explanations of the concept represented by picture and word. He was able to learn the correct association between the two immediately. This suggests clearly that the IQ score obtained on the Peabody does not signify that the items missed, or the items beyond the cut-off point are too abstract or too complicated for An to learn. The child's score on this test is an arbitrary measure of his knowledge. It is not a measure of the limits of his educability at the time of the test.

An took the corrections in a rather jovial way. He sometimes responded by making comments, elaborating the tester's explanations. His clowning in this section is often self-mocking. But the corrections do not make him hostile as a child with a bad scholastic record is 'expected' to respond. His acceptance of criticism shows a teacher could work with him systematically in explaining concepts.

1	Tester:	*No, I just want to show you the*
2		*ones you got* (page flips) *wrong,*
3		*Ok? So you'll know, this'll help*
4		*you* (pause) *Ok, we'll turn to*
5		(hes). *We'll do this really quick.*
6		(Man on TV or in background talking.)
7		*On page 53,* (pause)
8	An:	*I got* (hes)
9	Tester:	*You picked number 3 and that's wrong.*

10 Tester:	(more loud man's talk in background)
11	*The real answer's reel, number four,*
12	*and that's a reel.* (Thumping, pause
13	while the man's voice comes through;
14	then An giggles).

Tester takes for granted that An can distinguish between the two words pronounced the same way, *"reel"* and *"real."* (11)

15 An:	*All right, what else I get wrong?*

He responds by challenging her to show him any others he got wrong. (15)

(Page 55 of the picture booklet shows the following pictures: 1. a beaver on his hind legs gnawing at a tree 2. a hand holding an electric drill without an electric cord; the drill has gone all the way through a board 3. two football players, one with the ball being tackled by the other 4. a girl coasting downhill on a bicycle)

16 Tester:	*Ok, on page 55* (pf) (p) *do you remember*
17	*which one you picked?* (Four or five
18	taps) *That's right.* ("...*football*" —
19	presumably An himself, but voice is sub-
20	dued, maybe even away from mike, not
21	quite sounding like him) *You picked*
22	*number three, an the word is gawing*
23	(sic), *gnawing.* pounding noise) *An'*
24	*this is the answer, number one. Cause*

He apparently indicated his choice by tapping the picture. (17-18) He probably is the one to say "...*football*" (18) because he and the tester are the only ones who can see the book with the picture of the football

185

25 *this is the answer, number one. Cause this*
26 *is a (hes), look An, this is like a beaver,*
27 *and it's gnawing away at the (hes) at the*
28 *tree.* (p) (Sound of theme music from TV
   coming through loud and clear) *Ok?*
30 (pounding irregularly) *Wha'cha call that*
31 *picture?*

players, unless there is someone in the room we don't know about. The strangeness of his voice may be a sign (20-1) that these corrections are bothering him, but it is important to appreciate he is still conversing with the tester. Tester mispronounces *"gnawing."* (23) then corrects herself. She starts to explain that no. 1 is gnawing, but has to ask for his attention (28). She identifies what the animal is, and then uses the word *"gnawing"* (27-8). An is expected to fill in that it means *"chewing."* He is also expected to see that it has wider meaning than just what beavers do to trees.

In turning the page, tester sees picture of gun and decides to let An identify a picture in a successful way (31-2). Picture of gun is on page 56, and was not covered in this session. An identifies it enthusiastically (33).

33 An: *A gun!*

(Page 57 of the picture booklet shows the following pictures: 1. a long view of the wall and a counter top above shelves and cupboards along the length of wall 2. a fireplace with andirons, wood, two small plants on mantel, and a rectangular mirror above it 3. a short flight of stairs with a bannister prominent in the foreground 4. a sink with two legs in front attached to the wall in back; an old-fashioned bathroom sink, with towel rack on side.

34 Tester: *Ok. On page 57 (pf) the word is*
35   *bannister, and you picked number*
36   *four, but the real answer is*
37   *number three.*
38 An: *Aaaaaaaagh!* (loud, mock agony)
39   (sound of thump, as though he
40   had collapsed on the table or
41   floor) (Tester chuckles, An
52   chuckles momentarily with her.)

187

43 Tester: *Come on An* (still good humored)
44 *An* (insistent, but not wheedling
45 or harsh)
46 *Uh huh* (guttural, far from mike,
47 possibly on floor) *?I'm doing*
48 *my quitting?* (or) *?I'm feeling*
49 *like quitting?* (giggles)
50 Tester: *Huh?* (somebody giggles, perhaps
51 second tester) (Someone comes
52 in door to other room.)
53 Tester: *Ok An, this one's bannister be-*
54 *cause this is a* (hes) *part of the*
55 *staircase.*
56 An: *Did I get that one wrong?*
57 Tester: *No, you picked number four, you*
58 *picked the sink.*
59 An: *I know. Di-id I get that one*
60 *wrong.*
61 Tester: *You got that one wrong.*
62 An: *Is this one right?*
63 Tester: *This is the right answer, number*
64 *three, but you picked number*
65 *four.* (Female voices in
66 background saying something
67 about "fresh air") *Ok, on page*
68 *59.* (pf) (pause, with woman

In his act, An has forgotten that tester had told him he was wrong (35-6). She apparently misunderstands his question, thinking he asked if he got it right (57-8).
He deals with her misunderstanding and then reiterates his original question (59-60). Tester then catches on (61). An wants to know for sure if he got item wrong.

69   still talking in background)
70   *You picked number three but the*
71   *real answer's one, this is*
72   *"globe."*

(Page 59 of the picture booklet shows the following pictures: 1. a globe of the world 2. an anchor 3. a pea pod, open, with peas in it 4. a tassel on the end of a cord.)

73 An: *?Hi? globe.*

He pays close enough attention to imitate the word correctly, (73) possibly making it into a mock greeting in response to the tester's remarks *"this is globe"* (71-2) which sounds like an introduction (This is John. - Hi John.)

74 Tester: *A globe. You remember that, ok?*
75 An: *Uh huh.*
76 Tester: *On page 4, I mean on page*
77   *fifty (hes) sixty-one, you picked*
78   *number four.*

189

(Page 61 of the picture booklet shows the following pictures: 1. a hand pulling a card out of a file drawer 2. a workman plastering a wall 3. a traffic cop 4. a middle aged woman brushing her hair before a mirror.)

79	An:	*Three! Number three.* (pounding
80		table)
81	Tester:	*No you said you picked number*
82		*four.*
83	An:	*Yeah! Number four.*

An is still involved in the correction process, even though he has not remembered correctly what he chose for this item, (78-80). He is obviously paying close attention to the problem of reconstruction. He accepts tester's word that he chose 4 (83). Tester explains what filing is (84-7).

84	Tester:	*The answer's number one. This*
85		*person is filing something.* (p)
86		*Filing these cards. You put'em*
87		*in order.*
88	An:	*Maybe* (p) *I* (hes) *I think he sh*
89		(hes) *he might be a dentist!*
90		(p) *What do that say?*

An's response seems relevant, an intelligent elaboration (88-9). He is able to impute a typical identity to person doing filing even though all he can see of person is his hand and cuff.

190

91 Tester: *An...*(gives An's full name)

92 An: *...*(An's last name) (wonderlingly,
93 as though he had never heard it
94 before).

95 Tester: *Don'choo know your name?*

96 An: *No* (couple of thumps)

97 Tester: *Ok. On page 65 An* (p) (pf)

Reference to dentist seems very apt, since dentist keeps track of patients on file cards. A teacher could respond to his answer by discussing how the dentist and others use filing.

Question *"What do that say?"* (90) refers to writing on top of score sheet. It was turned away from An. Probably he is looking for distraction, and teases tester by claiming not to know his own name.

(Page 65 of the picture booklet shows the following pictures: 1. a young woman peeling a bowl of potatoes, while seated on a chair. 2. an elderly woman talking on the phone 3. a surveyor looking through a transit, a piece of paper in his hand 4. a farmer picking corn by hand from a stalk, with a bushel of corn at his feet.)

98 An: *Come on* (whining) *because I*
99 *want to watch "Dark Shadows."*

Expresses impatience (98-100) and for first time

100		(pounds a few times)
101	Tester:	*The answer's number four,*
102		*harvesting, but you picked number*
103		*two.* (bp) *This farmer's harvest-*
104		*ing.* (p)

indicates awareness of what's on the TV. But he still responds in a co-operative way to tester's explanation of *"harvest-ing."* An elaborates her explanation, and correctly fills in when you do it; *"soon as they get ripe."* (105-110)

105	An:	*Corn*
106	Tester:	*He's harvesting corn, that's*
107		*when you go out and gather up*
108		*the crops.*
109	An:	*Uh huh, eh* (hes) *soon as they*
110		*get ripe.*
111	Tester:	*That's right. Kay, on page 67*
112		(pause, with man's voice on TV ad
113		coming on loud and clear) (pf)

(Page 67 of the picture booklet shows the following pictures: 1. a stadium en-closing a playing field 2. a church with two spires 3. an igloo 4. an observatory)

Even after tester moves on to the next page (111)

114	An:	*?I'll try and get ripe up in the*
115		*winter?*

An persists in his elaboration of harvesting, even though he is confused about which season harvesting occurs in. (114-5).

116 Tester: *Na, I think it gets ripe when*
117 *it's warm. The answer is* (p)
118 *number four, observatory. An*
119 *this is like a building where*
120 *they study stuff.*
121 An: I know (hes) that (hes) about
122 was the one that I picked I think.
123 Tester: *...study stars.* (This last phrase
124 by tester was covered by what An
125 was saying above.) *No, you picked*
126 *two.* (An is drumming through this.)
127 *You* (p) *picked the church.* (Drumming)
128 *Ok on page 69* (p) *the answer's*
129 *number two.*

(Page 69 of the picture booklet shows the following pictures: 1. a woman cuddling a baby in her arms. 2. a little boy kneeling and playing with a sort of erector set 3. a woman drinking something from a cup; the cup is at her lips, and the saucer is in her hand at lap level. 4. two boys fighting; the boy on top has one hand on the opponent's neck and the other, in a fist, a few inches from his face; the boy on top has a fierce expression on his face.)

130 Tester: ...*erecting.* (Lots of talk in
131 background along with TV.) *And you*
132 *picked number four.*
133 TV: ...*no obligation...*
134 An: ...*one?*
135 Tester: *"Erecting" ?was? (or) ?is? building,*
136 *"erecting" means (hes) to build*
137 *something up.*
138 TV: *5151 Main Street*
139 Tester: *Ya understand An?*
140 An: (moans)
141 Tester: *Ok, one more. On page 71.*

142 An: *Ok, one.*
143 Tester: *Come on, come on back to the*
144 *table.*
145 An: *One more?* (Calling out, sounds
146 pretty far away.)

An has returned to parody (140).

Apparently this implicit promise to do only one more (141) was an attempt to coax him back to the table which he had left about the time he did the moaning (140)

She had to tell him to return (143-4).

He wants firm commitment that there will be only one more before he returns (145-149).

147	Tester:	*One more and we're finished.*
148	An:	*An ?watch? I can watch "Shadows"?*
149	Tester:	Uh huh.
150	An:	*Shadow* (closer to mike, loud) (bp)
151		*Shadows are dark!* (Mock announce-
152		ment, almost singing)
153	Tester:	*Page 71.*

(Page 71 of the picture booklet shows the following pictures: 1. a piece of meringue pie 2. a covered casserole 3. a barbecue grill with hot dogs cooking on it; smoke is coming from two of the hot dogs 4. an ear of corn with the tassels still on it.)

154	Tester:	*The answer's number two, "casserole"*
155		*An that's a kind of dish.* (Drumming
156		a bit) *And you* (cut off by An
157		saying:)
158	An:	*Did I get that one right?*
159	Tester:	*No, you picked number three,*
160		*"barbecue."*
161	An:	*Barbecue?* (funny voicing) *mmmmm*
162		(silly or dumb sounds)

Tester refers to a picture of a barbecue grill. (159-60). I think An reacts peculiarly (161-2) because barbecue probably means *"rib"* to him, and there aren't any ribs on the grill.

195

			Commentary
163	Tester:	*Barbecue pit -*	The tester appreciates the difference in frames of reference and elaborates the original label to *"barbecue pit"* so that it will fit An's sense of barbecue better (163).
164	An:	*Barbecue* (higher pitched) *weiners*	
165		(lower pitched).	
166	Tester:	*Barbecue pit.*	An elaborates, using barbecue as a verb, and specifies what is being barbecued. (167-170). An corrects the tester about proper labels. Just as he can negotiate how much more work there is to do, he can negotiate correct identification of objects.
167	An:	*Barbecue weiners* (this is	
168		sing-song) *little weiners*	
169		*?didn't?* (or) *?gettin? barbe-*	
170		*cued* (tap) (this is kind of a	
171		song)	
172	Tester:	*Ok An, you can watch the TV now,*	
173		*thank you.*	

Let us consider the general significance of An's mistakes on the Peabody. A common argument about the class or ethnic bias of intelligence tests is that the lower class child has not been exposed to many of the things which the tests refer to. This claim is not borne out by our research. All children we studied could identify most of the Peabody pictures in ways which properly indexed knowledge of the objects and their uses. This is true even of items which should have been the most difficult for the children, the items at the upper limit of their mental capacity. We have seen that An's remarks about harvesting and barbecuing weiners indexed his knowledge of the activities represented by the pictures. We would be very wrong if we took the fact that he missed these items as evidence that he was unfamiliar with the kinds of activities involving these pictures and words. Yet that is the implication of taking the test as a measure of his intellectual capacity. The test is supposed to be a measure of the ability to understand certain relationships. He obviously understands these relationships even if he cannot match the picture and the test word correctly.

Thus far, I have tried to incorporate the context of An's remarks to point to the practical problem of discovering what a child knows. I now want to extract some of his comments about the pictures to show how much farther An's understanding goes beyond the limits presumed by the test.

When An was discussing item 71, *"casserole,"* he was ten items beyond his mental limit according to the rules of the test. As the test takes for granted, An did miss almost all the items beyond his cut-off point. But since he is able to identify almost all the pictures, these misses are a spurious indication of his mental capacity. The tester should have ended the test after item 57, according to the scoring rules for the Peabody. Instead, she took An all the way to item 71. Keep in mind that the Peabody test assumes that these items are beyond his intellectual capacity.

Item 63 - "horror"
An apparently got this item right, picking no.
1.

Picture 1: This shows a woman staring in
fright with her hands raised in reflex action. An
remarked, *"Horror, Oh she's scared!"* When the tester
asked him what was going on in the picture, he replied:
"Oh she so scared, she'll be 'aaaaa, aaa'," mimicing
the woman's cries.

Picture 2: This shows a girl with a large ice
cream cone. When identifying this picture, and
pictures 3 and 4, An remarked that they were *"easy"*
to do. An said, *"She's gonna get ice cream all over
her clothes."*

Picture 3: This shows an older boy or a young
man seated at a table, reading a book. An said,
"He's reading a book."

Picture 4: This shows an infant asleep in bed,
with his head on a pillow. An said, *"He's asleep."*

Item 65 - "harvesting":
An got this wrong, picking picture 2.

Picture 1: This shows a young woman seated on
a chair, peeling potatoes. An identified this as
"peeling potatoes, mother peeling potatoes."

Picture 2: This shows an old woman talking on
the phone. When asked why he chose this one as
"harvesting," An replied, *"cause she's using a phone,
maybe somebody's trying to call her."* A moment later,
when the tester repeated the stimulus word to him, An
interrupted and said *"Granny,"* apparently a more
specific reference to the identity of the old woman,
and also a contrast to the *"Mother,"* in picture 1.

Picture 3: This shows a surveyor looking through

a transit, a kind of telescope. An calls this
"styroscope," which I interpret as an approximation
of *"microscope"* or *"telescope"* or *"stereoscope."*
These are all labels for optical instruments that
produce a special kind of image. His creation of a
non-existent word, *"styroscope,"* makes me think he
recognizes the transit as some kind of optical instrument. I infer that An has conceptualized in some
relevant ways the function of the object in the
picture.

Picture 4: This shows a farmer picking corn
from a stalk, with a basket of corn resting beside
him. When the tester asked An what the man was doing,
he replied, *"Ah um, he's ah picking corn."*

Item 67 - "observatory"
An missed this item, picking picture 2. When
An and the tester returned to this item after the
initial run-through, An told her which picture he
had picked and then said, *"How come I gotta say the
words, that's hard?"* Then the tester changed her
question somewhat. First she asked, *"What's going on
in the pictures,"* and then she switched to, *"jus* (hes)
*can you just tell me what you think about the pictures,
An?"*

Picture 1: This shows an old fashioned sports
stadium with roofed bleachers. An said. *"Um, maybe*
(hes) *I think it's gonna be a* (hes) *football game in
there."*

Picture 2: This shows a Gothic cathedral.

Picture 3: This shows an igloo. An said *"an
um, I think is you can go up in* (hes) *when it snows."*
He made this comment right after talking about the
stadium, before the tester had asked him a specific
question.

Picture 4: This shows an observatory with no
telescope visible, but with roof portals open.

An may have been referring to this picture, or to
picture 2 when he said, *"an uh, this might be the
watch* (hes) *I mean this might be the watch-house."*
The tester asked him, *"The* (hes) *what house?"* An
said, *"The ware house."* The tester asked again,
"the warehouse?" (pause) *"What's that?* (tap)*."*
An replied impatiently *"the warehouse!"* and the
tester said, *"Oh I see."*

I am not sure what An meant by warehouse, and ıd
apparently, the tester was confused too. She seems
to have tapped one of the pictures that she thought
was still unidentified. But An reacted with impatience, as though she tapped the picture which he
had been calling the warehouse all along. *"Warehouse"* doesn't seem associated with either the church
or the observatory, although it does index the category
of building. Remember that An first used the term
"Watch-house" which might have specifically referred
to the picture of the observatory, i.e., a place where
one watches the heavens. Perhaps he switched to
"warehouse" because it was a more familiar word to
him. From this text, there is no way to determine
whether An knows that a warehouse is for storage
purposes. If we had interviewed him more thoroughly,
we might have found that he did know what a warehouse was, and that he knew of one that looked like
either the church or the observatory. The teacher
frequently faces this sort of discovery problem. The
fact that we didn't recognize what An said the first
time through doesn't mean we couldn't find out later.
In this case, it is unfortunate that the tester became confused. When she identified *Picture 4* as a
place where they study the stars, An had nothing to
add.

Item 69 - *"erecting:"*
An got this wrong, choosing picture four.

Picture 1: This shows a mother with a sleeping
infant in her arms. An said, *"an a baby's going*

200

asleep."

Picture 2: This shows a boy assembling something with tinker toys. The object he's working on is a tall, three dimensional framework, with a small rectangular appendage that's on a neck. It's important to visualize the construction to appreciate the relevance of An's identification; see Figure 4.1.

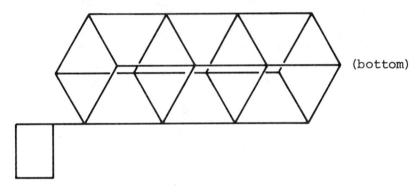

(bottom)

An said, *"he's um building* (hes) *a long giraffe."* This remark shows that he recognized the activity referred to by the word *"erecting." "Building"* is a good synonym for *"erecting."* The phrase *"long giraffe"* shows that An can conceptualize a highly simplified and unrealistic figure as a schematic representation of an object. This is an important aspect of the ability to perform abstractly.

Picture 3: This shows a young woman drinking from a cup with the saucer held in her other hand, resting in her lap. An said *"oh she's drinking coffee."*

Picture 4: This shows two boys down on the ground, fighting. The boy on top has the other boy by the throat. On the previous run-through, An described this picture by saying, *"s'boy be beatin up that little boy,"* and pounded on the table for emphasis. Later when An spied the picture again, he said, *"?When you're? (or) ?He's? really fightin. He's* (hes) *takes him by the neck."* The tester didn't get this, and asked, *"huh? Wha'd ya say?"* An replied, *"I say I say he takes the big boy by his neck, and he goes* (vaguely ferocious noise indicating doing bodily harm.)*"* *"On page 69?",* An teased by saying, *"can* (hes) *can't you see upside down?"*

Item 71 - "casserole"

An got this item wrong, choosing picture 3. The correct answer was picture 2. In telling the tester why he chose picture 3, An gave an elimination procedure. He identified the pictures he didn't choose as well as the one that he did choose. He probably came to this procedure by collapsing the answers to the two anticipated questions together: why he chose the picture he did, and what were the other pictures. This shows that An could catch on to what was expected of him in this procedure during the course of the testing session. He had concept- ualized the typical standpoint that the tester ex- pected him to take toward the test materials. This allowed him to answer the questions before they could be asked. This is an obvious asset for educability. It indicates that An was learning the pattern of interaction with the tester as well as dealing with particular aspects of the test materials.

Picture 1: This shows a piece of custard or meringue pie, without a plate.

Picture 2: This shows a casserole dish.

Picture 3: This shows hot dogs on a portable barbecue grill.

Picture 4: This shows a partially husked ear of corn.

Here is the way An identified the pictures in his elimination procedure:

202

Tester: *Which one did you pick:* (thumping noise, probably An's pointing to a picture) *You picked number 3. Why'd you* (tapping) *pick that one?*

An: *Uh hum, because they makin hot weiners (3) an um there's there's there's the corn with all the leaves (4), an um there's there's there's the pan (2) and there's the pie (1).*

On the first run-through, An had also identified picture 3 as *"barbecuin weiners."* Later in the test, he and the tester had a negotiation about whether the picture should be called *"barbecue"* or *"barbecuin weiners."* As you will recall from the section of the transcript already presented, An won.

These examples do not justify the test cut-off for An as the limit of his mental capacity at the time the test was administered. An can obviously conceptualize these pictures correctly, and he can use vocabulary appropriately to identify them in ways that a tester or teacher could understand. That means that a number of common arguments about why black children do poorly on intelligence tests are contradicted. It is common to say that IQ tests are biased against black and low SES children because they emphasize verbal skills. The Peabody test is often referred to as an excessively verbal test. But An's low score on the Peabody cannot be accounted for by a lack of verbal skills. Although, he didn't use the test words correctly in many cases, he almost always used language correctly to identify all the pictures. There was rarely any question about the pictures he was talking about. *A more reasonable conclusion is that the Peabody test is insufficiently verbal because it limits the child's verbal performance to matching picture and word.* When the child is encouraged to verbalize about the pictures and words, we find that he knows much more than the test score indicates. Because the Peabody limits the child's display of knowledge, we need ways to encourage children to use their elaborative abilities. If the

203

teacher does not do this, she will gain from the test score a very unrealistic picture of the child's knowledge.

A second argument about the bias of the IQ test is that such tests index background experiences characteristic of everyday middle class white life, and not experiences of lower class or minority group children. While this is probably so in some respects, there has as yet been no demonstration of the categories of test items which are familiar and/or unfamiliar to the lower class or minority child.[7] Such a demonstration waits upon a more elaborate description of class and ethnic subcultures than exist. It also raises such serious questions as whether black and white cultures are distinct, overlapping, or the same (Valentine, 1971).

The conclusion supported by this data is that the tests are biased in a double way. They are biased in presupposing background knowledge that is class-restricted. They are also biased because they limit the tester's or teacher's access to the child's background experiences. This second bias works against the white child as well, since the rules of standard procedure restrict the questions that can be asked of any child during a standardized test. To substantiate this second bias, I want now to present transcript sections from An's opposite, Pe, the white child who scored the highest on the test.

Pe's understanding of materials beyond his cut-off point shows that the Peabody does not measure the limits of his mental capacity any more than it did for An. Since this test was supposed to measure their relative mental capacity, An's and Pe's performances beyond their cut-off points cast doubt on the significance of their score difference:

---

[7]While Eells opened this line of research years ago, it has not been pursued and Eells' own results did not achieve improved scores for lower class and minority children relative to middle class white children.

Pe's combined IQ: 133[8]   Pe's age: 7 yrs. 5 mo. 22 days
An's combined IQ: 83   An's age: 8 yrs. 4 mo. 13 days
Difference in IQ points: 50

I am not challenging this difference in IQ scores as
an example of measurement error. I am challenging
it as a fundamental misconception of intelligence.

Pe was as difficult to work with in the testing
situation as An was. He was playful and talkative,
though much less noisy than An, and never defiant.
The main trouble with Pe was how easily he reached
the verge of tears when the testing reached items he
couldn't answer confidently. Asking him to explain
his choices on items he missed was a very delicate
task. The tester couldn't probe as deeply as she
wanted for fear Pe would break down. Nonetheless,
Pe's remarks usually indicated understanding of the
activities involved in the pictures.

Pe worked on the odd Peabody items at home with
a white tester. The same white tester had administered the even items to him at school. In the home
session, Pe's cut-off point was supposed to be item
83. The tester took Pe all the way to item 93, *"rodent."*
He got 93 correct, but he missed all the other items
above his cut-off point. I will present transcript of
his comments on the last two items that he missed, 89
and 91. From a practical standpoint of test management,
these two items are interesting because the tester went
over them after she interrupted the Peabody testing
session by having Pe do some sentence imitations, another test procedure we were interested in. She may
have done this because of confusion about which Peabody
items Pe was supposed to do, or she may have felt that
Pe was suffering so much that she had better switch to
something else, and then come back to the last items
after he had had a more enjoyable experience.

---

[8]See Peabody Testing Results below for origins
of combined IQ and age computation.

Picture 1 shows a young boy
with an arm in a sling and
faintly glum expression.

Picture 2 shows a little girl
crying loudly and sort of
pointing at a glass which has
just hit the floor and broken
(9). Picture 3 shows a woman
crying out in pleasure and
enthusiasm (11) Picture 4
shows a badly scared woman,
her hands up in reflex (13-14).
This is the same picture that
represented "horror" on 63.
Remember An had also indicated
his interpretation by imitating
her cries.

1	Tester:	*On 89 the word was "jubilant." Do*
2		*you remember what you chose?*
3	Pe:	*Yeah. That one.*
4	Tester:	*Number one. And how come you*
5		*chose that one?*
6	Pe:	*I don't know.* (laugh)
7	Tester:	(laugh) *Ok. What are the other*
8		*things pictures of?*
9	Pe:	*Break.*
10	Tester:	*Yeah, number three?*
11	Pe:	*Scream.*
12	Tester:	*And number four?*
13	Pe:	*Ahhhh* (sort of a little scream)
14	Pe:	(laugh)
15	Tester:	*She looks scared, huh?*
16	Pe:	*Scary wary.*
17	Tester:	*Was there anything else on the*
18		*page that could have been* *"jubilant."*
19	Pe:	(p) *No.*
20	Tester:	*How come?*
21	Pe:	*I don't even know what it means!*
22	Tester:	*Well, how do you know then that*
23		*nothing else on the page could*

24		*have been it? How come you de-*
		cided to pick number one?
25	Pe:	*Because it looks like a "jubilant."*
26	Tester:	*Ok (Pe giggles)*
27	Pe:	*What is it?* He asks what the word means
28	Tester:	*"Jubilant" means happy.* and she gives him a synonym
29	Pe:	*Happy?* (27-8)
30	Tester:	*Yeah.*
31	Pe:	*Goes "whoo-who, whoo-who."*
32	Tester:	*Ok. Which one do you think if "jubi-* She gives Pe another change
33		*lant" means happy, which one do you* (32-4)
34		*think it is?*
35	Pe:	*(pointing)* He picks the appropriate
36	Tester:	*Ok. Three. That's a good thing* picture, showing he recognizes
37		*to try. (I am saying this to my-* the emotion labeled *"jubilant"*
38		*self: if you presumably give the* (35).
39		*child a synonym which he knows,*
40		*can he then look at the page and*
41		*give the "right" answer.) Now*
42		*on 91 the word was pursuit. Do*
43		*you remember what you chose?*
44	Pe:	*Pursuit of happiness.* Pe shows he is familiar
		with an appropriate cliche
		(44), perhaps from the
		Declaration of Independence,
		perhaps generated from this

45	Tester:	*Pursuit of happiness. What's that mean?*
46		
47	Pe:	*You have a suitus and you're happy.*
48	Tester:	*Ok. You chose four.*
49	Pe:	*Huh.*
50	Tester:	*Ok. What's number one a picture of?*
51	Pe:	*Love.*
52	Tester:	*And what's number two a picture of?*
53	Pe:	*No one there.*
54	Tester:	*No one there?*
55	Pe:	*(laugh) He's looking at no one.*
56		*(laugh)*
57	Tester:	*What are they doing though?*
58		*(p) What kind of game are they*
59		*playing?*

word and the word "happy" that was relevant to previous item.

He makes a verbal game out of it (47). This nonsense explanation may also signify that he doesn't know the meaning of the cliche even though he has mastered it as a phrase. Picture 1 shows a smiling couple on a special occasion; she wears a corsage, and he is smiling at her (50-1).

This is a reference to picture 3, not 2 (53-6). It shows a man coming down a stairway, looking into the left distance, without anyone else in the picture to be seen. Peter has switched from his one word responses.

Tester refers again to picture 2 — the correct picture of pursuit (57-9). One little

60 Pe: Guns, guns.
61 Tester: And what's number three a picture
62 of?
63 Pe: I don't know.
64 Tester: What's he doing there?
65 Pe: He's playing on an island.
66 Tester: Do you think he got shipwrecked?
67 Pe: No. (laugh)
68 Tester: Why would he be sitting on a
69 little island all by himself
70 then?
71 Pe: Maybe his boat sunk, and he swam
72 over here, on an island.
73 Tester: Do you think he'll have to sit
74 there very long?
75 Pe: Yeah. (p) I don't see no boats
76 ...(p)
77 Tester: You gonna draw a boat in? (Pe
78 has picked up a pencil lying on
79 the table and started to draw.)
80 Now he can get off the island,
81 huh?

boy is running after another, both with toy guns in their hands. Pe recognizes the game this picture indexes (60). Is "pursuit" a more complicated concept than "playing guns?"

Picture 4 shows a castaway sitting on an island (64-81)

Pe indicates he doesn't know what shipwrecked means; he may be teasing given that he laughs, and given that "shipwrecked" seems to me to be such common childhood literary and television fare (66-7).

Without any verbal indication that he is teasing, Pe proceeds to give a perfect interpretation of being shipwrecked; maybe "shipwrecked" is unknown to him (71).

> In response to her questions
> Pe adds an elaboration of
> his own, indexing more about
> the implications of being
> shipwrecked: you stay until
> some other boat comes along
> and picks you up (75-9).

On both items 89 and 91, Pe shows that he can
identify the pictures appropriately from the standpoint of an adult, and elaborate the courses of action
to which the pictures and words refer. There seems
to be no doubt that Pe could have learned the correct
identification of word and picture of these items the
very same day that he missed them. In the case of
"jubilant," this is precisely what happened.

It has been frequently suggested in the literature
on testing, intelligence, and race that the black and
low SES children do relatively poorly because the
testing situation, the testing materials, and the tester
are relatively unfamiliar and threatening. If we assume
that the home is more familiar to the child than the
school, and a tester of his own race is more familiar
than a tester of another race, and that taking a test
a second time makes it more familiar than taking it
the first time, then we might expect all these children
to score higher on the home sessions after the test
had been done at school. Only the black children had
testers of a different race in the two sites; the
other sources of familiarity (the home and the second
session) would still bolster the home score. These
assumptions were not borne out (Table 4.2). There was
a tendency for the children to reach the cut-off point
on the test earlier at home than at school. Four out
of eight dropped three or more item-pairs from school
to home. Only one child went up more than three
item-pairs from school to home: H (child's name)
went up six item pairs.

Table 4.2

Changes in Scores from School to
Home Ordered from Positive to
Negative Change

Raw score		Mental age		Intelligence quotient	
He	+10	He	+19	He	+17
Mi	0	Mi	0	Mi	0
Ri	- 2	Pe	- 3	Ro	- 8
Pe	- 2	Ri	- 4	Su	-10
Ro	- 4	Ro	- 9	An	-10
Su	- 6	Su	-11	Ri	-13
An	- 6	An	-12	Pe	-17
Bo	-10	Bo	-19	Bo	-26

For each type of score, we see that only one
child showed a score increase from school to home
trial. I would not say on the basis of this evidence
that familiarity is irrelevant to test performance.
I would argue however that familiarity does not have
the unidirectional relationship to test performance
that is usually taken for granted by researchers on
both sides of the nature-nurture controversy (Shuey,
1966).

In Table 4.3, we can see that the two ethnic
groups are quite evenly distributed for all variables
except chronological age.

Table 4.3

Students Ranked by Age, Combined Raw Score,
Mental Age, and Intelligence Quotient[a]

Combined raw score		Combined mental age		Combined IQ		Birth date	
An(B)	56	An(B)	6-2	An(B)	83	An(B)	1-19-62
Su(B)	59[c]	Su(B)	6-8[c]	Bo(W)	88-90[b]	He(W)	5-10-62
Bo(W)	59-60[b]	Bo(W)	6-8/6-10[b]	Su(B)	88[c]	Mi(B)	2-6-62
Ri(W)	62	Ri(W)	7-3	He(W)	93	Su(B)	6-24-62
He(W)	62	He(W)	7-3	Mi(B)	95	Ri(W)	12-19-62
Mi(B)	63	Mi(B)	7-5	Ri(W)	102	Bo(W)	1-3-63
Ro(B)	68[c]	Ro(B)	8-4[c]	Ro(B)	114[c]	Pe(W)	1-3-63
Pe(W)	78	Pe(W)	10-4	Pe(W)	133	Ro(B)	2-3-63

[a] B = black;   W = white

[b] Minimum and maximum estimates

[c] Underestimation based upon arbitrary ceiling since no cut-off point is establishable

212

As the scores in Table 4.3 indicate, the small number of black children studied do not show the marked difference in test performance relative to white children that theories of genetic and cultural differences address. This does not mean, however, that our study compared atypical samples of black and white children. There are three reasons for this. First, ethnic and class differences in test scores are recognized to be cumulative. Jensen's theory of the developmental ordering of intelligence types is intended to account for this fact. In light of the principle of cumulative deficit, the similarity in our group of first grade children is to be expected. Second, we are interested in showing that the Peabody Test underestimates and otherwise misrepresents the performances of children of all backgrounds, whether or not they do well on the test. Usually test bias is viewed as a threat only to black or low SES children. The standard intelligence test's compatibility to the abilities of the white, middle class child is taken for granted. But models of intelligence that fit the case of high achievers do influence models of low achievers' intelligence, so rigorous analysis of the performances of all children is relevant to issues of intelligence, environment and heredity.

Third, we have some evidence that our sample of black children has scholastic and familial histories which fit the stereotype of the black child who is expected to suffer cultural deprivation and do poorly in school.

Three of the black children in our sample had been in Junior First, a remedial first grade program, instead of being promoted directly from kindergarten to first grade. Only one white child, He, had been in Junior First. Ri, another white child, would have gone into Junior First if his parents had not insisted on full promotion. After his placement in the regular first grade, Ri's parents and his new teacher developed an enthusiastic homework program to help him keep up or catch up with the other students. Three of the black children were quite a few months older than three of the white children. An, Mi, and Su were falling behind, because of their age, even if their test scores as first graders didn't show it. All four black children showed the 'classic' matriarchal family pattern to some degree, not having natural fathers in their homes. The natural fathers of all the white children lived in the home. Two of the white children lived in upper middle class homes. One white child lived in a trailer, and another lived in a lower middle class home. One of the black children lived in a decrepit house; another lived in an extremely small, decrepit duplex; the third lived in a lower class home; and the fourth lived in a very new, large house. In our study of the classroom, we were less interested in the socio-economic status of our subjects as studied by sociologists than we were in the picture of their status and family history that the school staff and children themselves had. The point is that all the black children showed roughly various aspects of the environmental pathologies that are at issue in the nature-nurture controversy regarding race and intelligence.

It would be a mistake to imagine that the black children were being prepared for failure in the classroom. The details I have mentioned above are selected because they fit the stereotype of failure maintained by the cultural and hereditary deprivationists. There are other details which run counter to that stereotype. Our time in the classroom uncovered activities not normally taken into account by Jensen and the deprivationists. For example, An, the black child with the lowest Peabody score, lived in a large, new house which seemed to be middle class in its amenities. He also showed great verbosity in the testing session. Yet his progress in the classroom was deteriorating as far as the teacher was concerned, and he showed the cumulative deficit which is supposed to be associated with low SES. Other counter-examples to the low SES, black stereotype were apparent. Mi and Ro, the younger black children, were in the highest reading group, along with Pe and Bo, both white boys. Ri,

a white boy, and An, a black boy, were together in
the lowest reading group during most of the period of
observation. An had dropped down from the middle
reading group early in our research phase, and he was
ultimately sub-categorized within the low group as
one of the three lowest. Su, a black girl, and He,
a white girl, were in the middle reading group together. From our observations, the teacher's judgments about the standings of the black children in
no way suggested their uneducability; instead she
emphasized the progress they made. The teacher considered Ro an exceptional student, Mi a bright child
who was somewhat immature, and Su a hard worker and
a good student, even though she was not a rapid
learner. As for An, she told me late in the year that
she was really sure he could take care of himself and
would turn out all right even though she hadn't
figured out how to motivate him to be a good student.

SUMMARY
    The difficulties of managing a focused con-
versation make it hard to establish the child's
knowledge. It is unreasonable to expect that a tester
or teacher can maintain a strictly standardized procedure while probing children's unstandardized background knowledge and while managing the children's
feelings. Theories of intelligence which ignore the
negotiated features of intelligence measurement ignore
very relevant issues concerning educability.
    Conventional testing theory conceives of the
interaction between tester or teacher and child in
terms of strictly standardized and isolated pairs of
questions and answers. But such standardized routines
are not effective in probing children's background
knowledge. The adult has to adapt to the unexpected
aspects of the children's answers. The children also
have to adapt to the adults' actions. A conception of
intelligence as standardized input-output pairs is
useless because it neglects the irregularity and continuity of the interaction process. The ideas of
mental ability, background knowledge, and educability

require a general theory of social or communicative competence which covers children's abilities to act in complex social situations (Cicourel, 1973: 42-99).

The conception of children's intelligence in terms of measurably limited capacity is not justified by our intelligence test data. Instead of being a measure of the children's intrinsic capacity, the test cut-off point on the Peabody imposes arbitrary limits on our knowledge of the children's abilities.[8] This is true of the lowest-scoring black child and the highest-scoring white child, as well as all the children in between. This means that both the geneticists and the environmentalists are wrong in treating the IQ tests as measures of children's intellectual capacities. Furthermore, if IQ tests are incompatible with the teaching processes, then it would be unfounded to attribute relative success in school of black and white children to measured mental ability, even if test scores and school achievement are highly correlated.

The questions posed about the children's test performance on earlier pages of this chapter aren't meant to be prescriptive. Teachers will have many other questions which their experience shows are relevant to educability in general and to certain students in particular. It is unlikely that standardized intelligence tests will answer these questions very directly. Whatever their questions, teachers should seek answers themselves by going over the tests with their students, to obtain the information

---

[8] The Peabody test is partially validated by its correlation with large-scale tests like the Stanford-Binet and the Wechsler tests (WISC and WAIS). The spuriousness of the Peabody calls these bench-mark tests into question. We will of course have to analyze these base tests before we can make final judgements.

they need. I am not recommending that teachers prepare their students for intelligence or achievement
tests. I am recommending that teachers follow-up
any testing of their students by re-administering the
tests themselves, using all their experience and skill
to assess and bring out the student's understanding
of the test materials. This information can then be
used by the teacher to advise parents realistically
and to challenge unqualified evaluations of their own
teaching and their student's abilities based upon test
results.

Chapter 5
STANDARDIZED TESTS: OBJECTIVE/OBJECTIFIED MEASURES OF "COMPETENCE"

Robert MacKay
University of Toronto

In the literature of Zen Buddhism there is an anecdote of a master who handed a fan tó a disciple, asking, 'What is this?' The disciple handed it back and said, 'A fan.' The master frowned in disapproval and handed the fan to a second disciple with the same question. Without a word, the disciple took the fan, scratched his back with it, and opening it, placed a flower on it and handed it back to the master. The latter smiled in approval.

> (Wienpahl, 1970:22)

This paper is concerned with the production of knowledge about students' capacities and skills. Knowledge about students is produced, collected, and interpreted from a wide variety of sources but my interest is only in knowledge about students produced from *standardized* tests. Standardized tests are instruments which are intended to produce objective information. It is important to note that this form of knowledge is a necessary part of any large bureaucracy of which schools are among the most refined and proliferated examples.

Tests are administered to groups of students. The completed papers are computer marked and a small gummed printout containing some figures is duly peeled and pasted into each student's file. The score becomes then a fact about the student. It constitutes a 'report' of the child's competence (Cf. Goslin's 1965 use of the term absolute validity) to any reader of the file.

Criticisms of standardized tests usually revolve

around the handicaps that slow workers, culturally different, and culturally disadvantaged students face. While these criticisms are important, my analysis focuses on the relationship between the idealized conception of testing which grounds the validity of any empirically obtained results (i.e., any student's score) and the social organization attendant to standardization in the classroom.

ORIENTATION

Since the basic way in which one experiences entitites is in being concerned with them, the structures of ones' world are the necessary conditions for the possibility of ones' experience. From the standpoint of Being and Time, these structures are manifest in all ones' dealings with the object of ones' concern, but in his natural attitudes a man's very concern with the objects of his concern focuses his attention away from the structure of that concern itself.

(Erickson, 1970, 90)

Attention must be directed therefore to "the structure of the concern itself" — the test and testing situation. This is a shift from preoccupation with the practical difficulties in administering tests and improving items to examining how tests produce knowledge about students and what this knowledge means; i.e., the basis of that knowledge.

Standardized tests rest upon a theory of learning (exclusive of a theory of social organization) which does not accord with any empirical situation. The theory of testing assumes explicitly that the test takes place in a non-contextual social setting with a non-contextual cognitive orientation. Yet, clearly, the processes of teaching and learning are integrated socially organized activities. Tests imply that meaning is a given in the world and that individuals passively receive stimuli and then mechanistically respond.

To experience something as something is to
experience and interpret that something in terms of
one's world. Had one no world, one would have no
cognitive experience at all. Thus one's world serves
as a necessary condition for the possibility of anyone's experience.

(Erickson, 1970, 92)

Proceeding from the latter perspective the
analysis suggests that objective standardized tests
are an impossibility and decisions based upon the
results of such tests (often) invalid and capricious.
My analysis is of *Form 12A of the Cooperative Primary
Reading Test* focusing particularly on how the Grade
One students to whom it was administered arrived at
answers to test questions (i.e., how they decided
which ones were correct). The test is used by the
California State Board of Education to assess the
effectiveness of school reading programs. This test
first was administered in California in 1970.

As soon as teachers became aware that the test
was to be administered they began preparing lessons
similar in format to the test to instruct their
students in the form of the test. A pre-test was
provided which was administered the day before the
actual test.

After the children had taken the test I went
over it with them, asking them to read the stimulus
word or sentence and to tell me why they had chosen
the answer they had marked. The interviews were audio
tape recorded and later transcribed.

In this chapter, the answers and reasons which
the children gave me for their choices are contrasted
with the test constructors' designation of correct
answers. What is of interest is whether or not the
students linked the stimulus and the answer in the
same way the test constructor *assumed* was *the* correct
way and the implications of alternate linkings. The
testing situation is compared to the routine classroom situation to see if the test measures those skills
that the students use and develop in interaction with

the teacher. The *Manual* (p. 7) states that such
skills are measured by the test. The results of the
study suggest that the test and test results cannot
be understood except by analyzing them within the
social context of which they were an integral part.

ROUTINE CLASSROOM ACTIVITY
*Teaching and Learning Within the Context. of the
Classroom.*

Emphasis on formal lessons and lesson plans in
schools suggests that teaching is conceived of as information flow from teacher to student. Ideally
lessons are logically organized and coherently presented. Metaphorically the big pitcher fills the
little cups.[1] Teaching is the presentation of information. Learning is the reflection of the
teacher's activities at least in an informational
and attitudinal sense. In this chapter, teaching
and learning are studied as socially organized
activities.

When the social organization of teaching and
learning are considered, the teacher is recognized
as an integral part of the child's competence and
the child an integral part of the teacher's.[2] The
teacher's competence as a teacher is known by the
students' abilities to demonstrate their memory for
information, to answer questions, and to follow
rules (i.e., to maintain order in the classroom).
This is usually formulated as what the teacher knows
about what the child has learned. Childrens' correct
answers to questions reflexively provide the teacher

---

[1] See Paulo Freire (1970) for one recent discussion of this view of education.

[2] This point takes on particular importance in
the testing situation because test results are
assumed to have an independent status.

with information that teaching is going well. Con-
cretely teachers and students are each others resources. On particular occasions the demonstration
of teaching/learning depends upon the right question
being asked for which the correct answer can be
given. This may mean reformulating the question
until the 'correct' answer is given (sometimes by
the teacher cf. Mehan, Chapter 3).

The following excerpt from a lesson about the
story, *Chicken Little*, demonstrates this relationship between teaching and learning. The children
are sitting in a semi-circle around the teacher near
the front blackboard.

Teacher:	*How did he* (the fox) *know that he could trick them?*
Student:	*I know he told...*
Teacher:	*Re*
Re:	*...them a story*
Teacher:	*Yes but some animals might have said 'I'm not going to believe you, I'm going away.' How did he know it would be easy to trick these animals?*
Student:	*Because...*
Student:	*Because they're not very bright.*
Teacher:	*How do you know they're not very bright?*
Student:	*Because sometimes foxes...*
Teacher:	*How did he know they weren't smart enough?*
Student:	*By the way they believed in Chicken Little.*
Teacher:	*They believed him, did they go out and check it out to see if it was true?*
Class:	*Nooo*
Teacher:	*You know, did Chicken Little tell them what he thought was the truth?*
Class:	(variously) *No/Yes*
Teacher:	*Remember he said he saw it 'with my eyes' — did he?*
Class:	*No, no.*
Teacher:	*I heard it with my ears?*
Class:	*Yes/No*

222

Teacher: *He might have heard it. He probably heard it and he said, 'apiece of it fell on my tail,' — could he have believed that?*
Class: *Yes/No*
Teacher: *So what was the one part that he told them that was not true?*
Student: *A piece of it.*
Student: *He saw it with his eyes.*
Teacher: *Did he really? Do you think if he had taken time to see it with his eyes how would the story have been different in the end?*
Student: *If ( ) hadn't eyes ( ) wouldn't have believed him.*
Teacher: *What if he had used his eyes and looked behind him — what would he have seen?*
Student: *Acorn.*[3]

(Transcription of audio portion of a videotape.)

This segment illustrates how the teacher guides the students to the answers that are relevant to the lesson by reformulating the questions until the correct answers are given. What is interesting is that 'incorrect' answers are ignored. This assumes either that students are able to tell at the end what the correct answer was to a question formulated some minutes before or that it does not matter.

Assumptions About Learning in the Lesson Format
In this lesson of *Chicken Little* The teacher

---

[3] I have come to see Chicken Little as a metaphorical tester who, depending upon indicators rather than using his eyes, identified an acorn as a piece of sky. Oak trees from acorns but what from a piece of sky?

was introducing the students to the *concept*[4] of sequencing. The teacher told the story of *Chicken Little* with the aid of a flannel board. The children then read the story out loud with the teacher and were assigned the task of arranging sentences from the story in the proper order. During the telling of the story and during the reading the teacher asked various children to repeat the order of the characters' appearance in the story. The children also repeated the order of events in unison (e.g., *"I saw it with my eyes, I heard it with my ears, and a piece of it fell on my tail"*). It is implied that the telling, the reading and the doing of the story brought the children to an understanding of the concept of sequencing. Paradigmatically, the teacher gives information, repeats it, reformulates it, elaborates its, relates it to previous information, and asks questions all of which is assumed to lead to learning on the part of the students.

This model makes the following assumptions about the capabilities of students:

Hearing/Reading: Student as Linguistic Analyst (Life as Hermeneutics). Whether specified or not, all teaching methods are based on particular models of human cognition, of the way that persons learn. A central aspect of teaching is the model that teachers hold of those they instruct. This lesson assumes a model of the student as a hearer/reader who not only pays close attention to each and every word the teacher says, but also is able to discriminate clearly between relevant and irrelevant utterances.

---

[4]There is a distinction here between knowing how to sequence or knowing about sequencing. The students are able to relate everyday events in sequence, they know the sequence for performing everyday activities but they do not know the word which labels all like processes.

During one lesson the teacher makes this explicit.

Teacher: *I'll count to four. You'll be ready for*
the directions on this page. One, two,
three, four. If the picture begins with
s, l, sl, you'll write those two letters
in the box. If the picture does not begin
with the sl sound, you'll leave it alone.
I'll read the pictures, say them after me.
I will tell you only once. This is the
time to listen, this is the time to learn
the name of the picture.

(Transcription of audio portion of videotape.
Emphasis added.)

Thus, using close listening ability the student
is given only a few seconds to learn the gist of a
45 minutes lesson. Near the end of the sequencing
lesson, described above, the teacher while reading
aloud the sentences of the worksheet in the correct
order says (with no emphasis in her voice):

Teacher: *This is called sequencing. It's important*
to know the order things happened.

(Transcription of audio portion of a videotape.)

Here in a few seconds the teacher has explained
what the children have been doing, given a definition,
and pointed to its importance (relevance). The
teacher has thus assumed that the student is able to
ignore the offhanded character of the utterance and
see that it is central (crucial) to 'the whole
activity.' The student is expected to listen to and
understand the teacher's *every word*. This is clearly
impossible. Apart from the fact that children do
not always pay attention to the lesson, a close look
at any transcript will reveal that much of what is
said is not immediately understandable and in the
course of conversation unclear utterances are often

allowed to pass (see Garfinkel, 1967, for a discussion
of this property of interaction). Conversations proceed regularly in the absence of complete understanding. What is meant becomes clear as the interaction
unfolds. In the classroom, students often ask what
they are supposed to do when they return to their seats
after a lesson and ask either another student or the
teacher. Close listening is not required in the classroom

  2. Remembering: Memory. Teachers also assume
that students are competent rememberers, that they
will remember important information from day to day;
i.e., 'learn' this information. The teacher relies on
the students' ability to listen closely (i.e., not
ordinarily) to 'find' the important information to
remember. This assumption is evident in the following utterance.

Teacher: *Now watch carefully when you do this. Try
and remember exactly what happened in the
story. You'll see it again tomorrow and
I'll ask you to paste it.*

(Transcription of audio portion of videotape.)

While a close listening would allow the student to
find the important information, it would also have
produced confusion for *"tomorrow"* was Saturday. No
one commented — it was let pass.
  The teacher relies on memory when teaching is
seen as the accretion of information in logical order.
In addition, memory as a display of knowledge becomes
an index of the student's comprehension and competence as well as a reflection of the teacher's
ability and competence.

  3. Relevance/Relationships as Obvious. In
the daily classroom situation the teacher is constantly
providing students with information about the correct
interpretation of the ambiguous situations. Tacitly
the teacher is orienting to the fact that consensual

meaning is available only through the process of
interaction. This is important to note, since test
constructors assume that meaning is given unambiguously
in the world. The teacher provides enough information
so that exercises can be interpreted in only one way
(if the student is listening and is willing to comply).
The reduction of ambiguity is accomplished by pro-
posing *the* overriding rule or schema of interpretation
for the particular situation. The following audio
transcription demonstrates this strategy. This segment comes from a morning assignment. The children
are sitting in a semi-circle of chairs around the
teacher near the front blackboard.

Teacher: *Would you look at the first picture please.
It is a picture of a...*
Class: *Bed, bed, bed*
Teacher: *You will spell the word bed. All of the
pictures on this page are spelled with a
sha, with an eh sound. Like an eh or the
ell sound. Let me read the pictures to
you. Bed, nest.*
Class: *Nest.*
Teacher: *Let, ten, James is going to choose a book
from the library that is by him and David's
going to do the same, ten, tent.*
Class: *Tent.*
Teacher: *Elf.*
Class: *Elf.*
Teacher: *Wet.*
Class: *Wet.*
Teacher: *Hen.*
Class: *Hen.*
Teacher: *Steps.*
Class: *Steps.*
Teacher: *Sets.*
Class: *Sets.*
Teacher: *These are stars, but it's also a picture of
a set, of three jointed to a set of two to
make a set.*
Student: *Should you, should you write the word?*

Teacher: *I beg your pardon. To make a new set of five. Are there any questions about this?*

Figure 5.1 is a reproduction of the ambiguous item.

Set _____

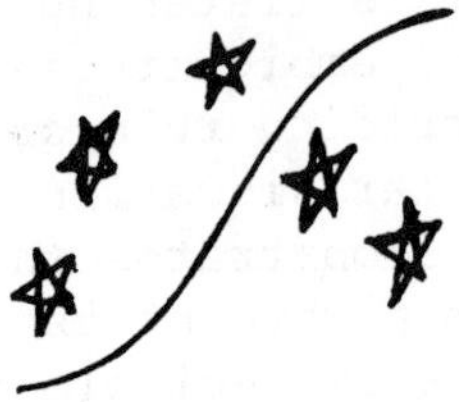

FIGURE 5.1

The teacher acknowledges the ambiguity and indicates tacitly (even subtly) that the important feature to orient to is words with an *"eh"* sound. This frame of reference grounds the correctness of answers. The teacher routinely provides the *initial* frame of reference. It is just this initial frame of reference that the test does not provide (indeed the test's possibility rests on *not* providing it) which creates the problems to be discussed in subsequent sections.

It is interesting to note that with respect to the state-wide reading test the teacher and students had many 'problems' understanding the frame of reference. In this lesson prior to the administration of the statewide test, the teacher 'taught' the children to 'figure out' the answer by sounding the initial and final letters and if still not sure to guess. The teacher used this excerpt to instruct the students in the form of the test and her actions foreshadow the somewhat arbitrary nature of the frame of reference in these tests.

Teacher: *What did you notice about this word and that picture?*
Child: *They're the same.*
Teacher: *It was exactly the same this time; this is the word "truck" and that is a truck. This says rain but did you see the rain?*

228

Class: *No, no.*
Teacher: *Sometimes it will be the exact word and
          the exact picture. Sometimes it'll just
          be things that* go together.

(Emphasis added.)

The teacher's statement that the frame of reference
will be *"things that go together"* indicates her
necessary reliance upon the tester's frame of reference of *"things that go together."* The teacher's
remark implies the arbitrary character of labelling
such linkings as correct.

In summary, the teacher displays correct
teaching through the use of the strategies of instructing, framing, rewording, repeating, connecting, elaborating, warning (*"remember"*), acknowledging
correct answers, asking questions, and giving the
correct answer. These *methods create knowledge as
publicly available.* Knowledge is socially displayed
and hence learnable by any student.

LEARNING AS AN ACTIVITY
On the other hand students must socially
(publicly) display that the available knowledge has
been learned. The student may display his knowledge
to the teacher by answering questions correctly, by
guessing correctly, by chaining answers to other
students' answers (i.e., repeating an earlier answer),
by looking attentive, and working quickly. In
addition to the students' use of each other and the
teacher as resources for the discovery of what is
being done or what has been done each student can
apply individually conceived schemes of interpretation
to make the same discoveries. While the teacher
assumes the lesson is needed to achieve her objectives
it may not even be necessary for certain students to
carry on in the classroom.

Students typically operate in an environment
that is rich in possibilities for solving problems,
resolving ambiguity, and finding correct answers

(see above). The test situation makes inaccessible
the teaching/learning process of the classroom and
places the child in a literally strange world — a
world devoid of its essential feature — sociality.

THE TESTING SITUATION

In the testing situation all the cues available
to the student in daily classroom activities become
unavailable. The test closes the sources of information and feed-back the child ordinarily relies upon
to guide his activities. Tests attempt to minimize
the amount of information available. The teacher
cannot help and other children are sitting too far
away to be observed. The deliberately created ambiguity means that the student must decide his own
solution to the frame of reference identification
problem.

THE TEST ITSELF

In this section I discuss how standardized
tests administered to groups of students make available knowledge about individual student's abilities.
The testing manual for the primary reading tests
states that the test yield one score based on the
total number of correct responses.

While my analysis suggests what knowledge is/is
not gained about students from standardized tests, it
has nothing to do with the validity of the tests as
conceived by persons engaged in this form of measurement. For a discussion of the validity of this test
using the criteria developed by educational testers
please refer to the last section of this chapter.

What is Known.

For the tester, what the child knows is dependent upon marks being placed in a square: The
instructions are somewhat ambiguous, stating that
"any reasonable mark" even if not a clearly written
"X" should be counted as adequate. The marks (in
the squares) are translated into a raw score which
(and with the aid of the tables in the Manual) can be

compared with other scores (percentile, stainine, grade equivalent). Comparison is possible because of the existence of national norms, which validate the relative score of any student. Probabalistic determinations of normality are thus the grounds for absolute statements about students' abilities.

What is literally known are raw scores. What is asserted to be known is measurement of abilities:

> *"This is a test of ability to read words, sentences, paragraphs and longer passages with understanding"* (Manual, p. 6).

> *"One of the major purposes of the test series is to provide teachers with measures of children's concepts and skills that relate closely to their work in the class- room"* (Manual, p. 7).

The skills are classified as:

1. Comprehension (concrete and abstract).
   (a) Identify an illustrative instance.
   (b) Identify an associated object or instance.
2. Extraction.
3. Interpretation, Evaluation and Inference (Manual, p. 14).

The instructions with respect to the student reduce to making sure that only one box is marked in each square and that no help is given to the student in solving an item. These skills can be known to have been measured if the proper procedures are follow- ed as outlined in the *Manual* in the directions for Administering, Scoring and Interpreting the Test. Cognitive measures, then, are guaranteed by procedural rules guiding practical activities such as marking one square per line, using an X, not allowing cheating, etc. The weakness of this behavioralist assumption that performance can be equated with competence will be demonstrated later.

   How What is Known is Accomplished: Assumptions in Testing About the Relationship Between Stimulus and Response: Behavioralist Theory of Meaning.
Figure 5.2 is the second practice example from the test with the instructions read aloud by the teacher.

"Now look at the second row of boxes on the page. Read the sentence in the arrow. Then make a big X on the box that goes best with it. Did you mark the picture of the car? The arrow says I went for a ride. The box with the car goes best with it." (Make sure everyone marked the box correctly) (Manual, p. 6).

FIGURE 5.2

   This example illustrates the central and yet the weakest assumption in the test. Why does the picture of the car go with the sentence *"I went for a ride"* — well, because it does. The link between the two is 'explained' by asserting that it is the correct link. *It is obvious.* The answers are correct because they are *obviously* correct. Note that the final instruction for the teacher again indicates the way in which procedure guarantees the use of the correct skill (i.e., correct answer *equals* correct skill).

Relevance or Relationships as Obvious. I would like to question the obviousness of this example to demonstrate that it is simply the test constructor's correct answer. It is necessarily (if arbitrarily) correct for the test results to be valid within their own framework. *"I went for a ride"* is a linguistic description of a past action implying that the speaker is presently doing something else. Consequently pictures one or two or three could be correct. *"I* went *for a ride, but now I am swimming/ walking."* *"I* went *for a ride in that car."* If I chose box one I would be wrong even though I am correct. Warranted disagreement is wrong even when it is demonstrated that a student can read the sentence and demonstrate the skills needed to link the sentence to the picture, even though this is what the test claims to be measuring.

The obvious relationship between the stimulus and response is simply the test constructor's way of making the link. Only one answer can be correct or else the test could not measure what it claims. Correct answers allow assertions about reading ability and the display of skills, wrong answers the absence of these.

The assumption of one correct answer is based on the test constructor's faith that he and the students share a common symbolic environment in which objects have only one meaning which is apparent to all. In this perspective meaning is given not negotiated and built up over the course of interaction.

This perspective (see Cicourel, 1973; Garfinkel, 1967; Schutz, 1964) contrasts with the one suggested throughout this book which holds that meaning is built up *in contexts* on *the basis of judgments* about the objects and situation at hand. Sacks (forthcoming) has proposed an analytic solution to the problem of identification which, in the test, is accomplished by linking stimulus and answer. He proposes a solution to how persons categorize any population. Once a first person is identified then other persons are drawn from the same categorization device. For example, if a person is identified as a mother, a man in the same population would be designated father, uncle, etc., from the device 'family,' not male from the device

'sex' or adult from the device 'stage of life.'
Sacks terms this the consistency rule. There is,
however, no principled solution to the problem of
identifying the first person. This is presumably
done on the basis of the identifier's perception of
the situation and interests in it. The tester assumes
that the first person (object) identification problem
is not only solveable but solved. Interpretation is
not part of the test. The data in the next section
suggest that it is in part because there is no
principled solution to the identification problem
that the tester's claims to be measuring reading and
cognitive abilities are faulty.

The test constructor and the teacher make
similar assumptions about students with respect to
their abilities as speakers/hearers/readers and rememberers. The teacher, however, recognizes the
ambiguity of identifying the first object in a
population of objects and routinely provides the
students with the 'correct' frame of reference (recall the earlier example of 'set' and 'stars').

The interest in educational testing is in
'correct' measurement but not in assessing individual
abilities or needs even though educational philosophy
stresses individual differences. The reliance on a
probability based theory produces a conception of
the student as disembodied, passively responding to
stimuli (C.f., Wrong, 1961). The teacher remarked in
an interview about the test after scoring it,
*"Statistically this is a good curve but the children
aren't statistics."*

The test simplifies the complex problem of
measurement of students' abilities. Borrowing assumptions from a branch of mathematics (probability)
allows testers to bring closure to questions about
any student's abilities. Following the procedural
rules of the test produces a *fact* about a student.
The fact is the raw score and its mathematical
normative transformation of percentile, stanine and
grade equivalent but *not* ability.

BEST ANSWER: INTERFACE BETWEEN ANALYST AND OBJECT
    The instructions contain the hint of the
ambiguity encountered in determining correct answers.

> *You are going to work quietly and do all
> the rest of the book by yourself. In each
> row, read what is in the arrow. Then mark
> the box that goes* best *with it. Mark just
> one* box *in each row*   (Manual, p. 6; emphasis
> added).

This suggests that the child is to weigh,
evaluate and interpret the relative merits of each
possibility and then decide which is best. I have
previously shown that this can not be assumed in
this form of measurement. The ambiguity encountered
in determing correct answers reflects a defect in
testing assumptions. The test demands that the child
be both analyst and dope.

STUDENT AS ANALYST OR CULTURAL DOPE
    This section deals with *how* students produce
answers to test items within constraints which are
structurally present. One of the constraints was
the fact that the fastest readers had only been exposed to between 46-58% of the words in class. This,
plus the teacher's advice to the children to guess,
transforms the test into a guessing game. For the
students, another point of reference for doing the
test was the teacher's instructions to identify the
beginning and ending sounds of words not known. The
test, however, was constructed such that the children
following those instructions would get wrong answers.
Several test items were built upon the ambiguity of
words that sound the same. The teacher's instructions
lead the students into the tricks of the test. An
example of this is Item 4 (mail) which some students
following the instructions found to be the boy.
(See Figure 5.3.)

FIGURE 5.3

When the teacher is straightforward the test depends
upon questions which are tricks. Tests, then, can
be conceptualized as *tricks as practice* and *knowledge as puzzles*. The test requires the student to
apperceive the stimulus and possible answers in the
same way as the test constructor. The test constructor assumes that by searching back and forth
between the stimulus and the possible answers the
only correct answer will pop out of the environment
or into the child's mind.

It is important to recall that students in
their daily classroom activities are encouraged to
make up contexts, ascribe human motives to animals,
etc., and yet the tester assumes that the boundaries
of the test are constituted by the stimulus and
answers. Students are attuned to filling in and nobody tells them that this is inappropriate; i.e.,
nobody teaches them about the special features of
tests and how to write them.

The following are one child's accounts of four
items. The excerpts are taken from a transcript of
an audiotaped interview I had with the child outside
the classroom after the test. The purpose of these
excerpts is to demonstrate *how* answers were produced
and how this compared to the tester's assumptions about
the test measuring certain abilities.

236

FIGURE 5.4

ITEM 6: PETS
Author: *Whh what does this one say?*
Student: *Bir bu let me see birds*
Author: *Ok. What's this a picture of here?*
Student: *A cat*
Author: *This one*
Student: *A bird*
Author: *And what's this one?*
Student: *A tree, a flower, a ball, a doll.*
Author: *Right, Ok, so why did you X out this one?*
         (She had X'ed out the picture showing the
         cat and the bird.)
Student: *'Cause it tells you to X it out.*
Author: *Why is that 'cause...*
Student: *That's the name of it.*

This is an example of a 'correct' answer that
was produced in a 'wrong' way. The student could not
read the stimulus word but could link a word to an
object. The student does identify an illustrative
instance which is what the item is designed to 'test'
(the categorization of Item 6, Manual, p. 14). Given
the correct answer the tester would be forced to assume
that the student could read the word — pets. Test
results provide misinformation in this instance.
Although the child's answer is correct, what might be
valuable for the teacher to know is unretrievable

from this type of test.

FIGURE 5.5

Item 9:   BAKE
Author: *Ya, Ok. What does this one say?*
Student: *Bark*
Author: *Right, Ok. What, what's this a picture of here?*
Student: *A girl*
Author: *Ya and what's this a picture of here?*
Student: *Some cookies.*
Author: *And this one?*
Student: *A dog barking.*
Author: *How can you tell he's barking?*
Student: *Because look at 'cause there's these lines that tell you he's barking.*
Author: *Ok, why didn't you X out this one — the cookies?*
Student: *Because cookies start with "C" and that's not a "C."*

In this case, the student does not read the stimulus word correctly and marks the *"wrong"* answer. While the tester would assume in this instance that the student could not read the word this only reduces the form to a *trivial test of vocabulary*. More interesting is the students' demonstration of being able to link a word and a picture and demonstrate its correctness. I see this in the passage

238

How can you tell he's barking? — Because look at 'cause there's these lines that tell you he's barking.' The fact that the student does not identify an abstract associated object (Manual, p. 14) does not indicate the student is unable to perform that kind of identification.

The bird built his own house

FIGURE 5.6

Item 18:   THE BIRD BUILT HIS OWN HOUSE

Author: *Ok. What about this one, this looks like an interesting one.*

Student: *The bird b baby baby bel ba net*

Author: *Well, let's skip that one. Do you know this word?*

Student: *Owl.*

Author: *Do you know this word?*

Student: *Home.*

Author: *Ya, OK. What's this a picture of here?*

Student: *A tree.*

Author: *Ya and this one...*

Student: *A bird home.*

Author: *And this one.*

Student: *A nest.*

Author: *Right. Why did you circle that one or X that one I should say?*

Student: *'Cause a bird, an owl...some owl...a owl can live in a nest too sometimes.*

Author: *Ya, why didn't you circle this one?*

Student: *What, that one?*

Author: *Yes.*
Student: *The there not there's not ain't no things there to keep 'em warm.*
Author: *Umm, what about this one?*
Student: *A bird, a bird some bird, some umm--owls are big--they can't fit in the hole.*

In this item the student marked the correct answer but the reasoning would be incorrect, I assume, from the point of view of the test constructor. The student displays the correct skill — identifying an illustrative instance (Manual, p. 14) but does not know one word. The complexity of what the student is able to do is not recoverable from the test.

...The cat has been out in the rain again.

FIGURE 5.7

Item 19: MOTHER SAID, "THE CAT HAS BEEN OUT IN THE RAIN AGAIN!"

Author: *Ok. Do you know what this one says?*
Student: *Mother said the cat the cat (shrinks sh shr shr)*
Author: *Let's skip over that one do you know this one?*
Student: *B. No.*
Author: *This one?*
Student: *Out in the rain.*
Author: *Right, Ok. What's this a picture of?*
Student: *The coat is (wret) the coat is (wret).*
Author: *The coat is what?*
Student: *The coat is (wret).*
Author: *Wet, oh, good. Ok.*

Student: *The cat is playing with the ball all up the yard.*

Author: *Ya, and this one?*

Student: *It's snowing.*

Author: *Snowing?*

Student: *Yep, there's a door and...*

Author: *Do you know what these are?*

Student: *Ss...Sprinkles.*

Author: *Why did you X out this one?*

Student: *Because it's raining on it or it's pouring down like rain.*

This example is of particular interest. The constructor designated Number 3 to be the correct answer. What for the test constructor was a door surrounded by wall covered with dotted wallpaper seems to have become for the child the exterior of a house with the dots seen as snow flakes. Given this as the perception of picture Number 3, there was no way this could be the 'correct' answer. Yet the transcript indicates that the student is able to display reading and inference abilities. The test constructor suggests Item 19 measures interpretation, evaluation and inference skills (Manual, p. 14).

The student consistently follows what is taught in the classroom. Classroom and cognitive skills are displayed in the answers to the questions — right and wrong. For instance the student is able to guess at words by sounding initial consonants (encouraged by the teacher), to elaborate meaning, and to argue the connection between stimulus and answer. Students exhibit the skills the test claims to be measuring but receive credit in unknown and unknowable ways. That is, scores do not allow for the reconstruction of the process which is *all* that is of interest to the teacher. The students see many correct linkings between stimulus and answer — the test constructor only sees one.

The fact that objects have open horizons of meanings and that perceptions vary suggest that test items are always and irremediably ambiguous. Words and pictures can exist in multiple frames of reference

241

and within those frameworks answers have their own logic and sense. Different interpretations of objects can only be evaluated within the frame of reference, but tests do not and cannot provide the information necessary to understand the answers in relation to the question except by fiat. Test constructors imply that the findings of Gestalt psychology are fallacious and insist that perception only occurs one way or it is wrong.

Since items cannot be constructed so that they are context free I suggest that standardized tests *only obscure* students' capabilities. Nevertheless tests are understood by most teachers to be objective, to belong to a higher reality. Tests are administered as a corrective for their own necessarily subjective knowledge of the students. If the test results do not correspond with the teacher's ranking, it is the teacher's ranking which is at fault and the teacher feels at fault. In this class, some students who were in the high reading group scored low and vice versa. The teacher was upset and could not explain the discrepancies. When I suggested administering another similar test to find out if the results would be the same, the suggestion was welcomed. The results of the second test ranked the children in the same order as had the teacher in her reading groups, and the teacher was relieved.

TEST VALIDITY

I have shown how obtaining the 'correct' answer depends on the child's correct identification of a frame of reference that corresponds to the frame of reference the test constructor had in mind. (This necessitates getting into the constructor's mind to do the test — a 'skill' all successful students learn.) I have shown that students in choosing other answers demonstrate the abilities the test 'claims' to measure. It follows, then, that tests of this sort cannot be valid due to the nature of the assumptions.

242

However, I include this section to suggest
that even according to the criteria for validity
accepted by educational testers, the test is a poor
test. Authors of books on achievement tests and
testing (e.g., Thomas, 1960, and Gronlund, 1965)
stress the necessity of the following points for
tests to be valid.
1. The clarity of directions.
2. Standardization of the testing situation.
3. Keeping time accurately.
Form 12A of the cooperative Primary Reading
Test was inadequate with respect to all three points.
The instructions (given below) were very ambiguous.
The teacher was the first to recognize this and used
her own instructions to begin the test. She instructed
the children in the same way that she usually did when
directing them to work at their seats because presumably the children would understand this routine
more clearly. I offer the instructions as printed
below to illustrate the ambiguity.

INSTRUCTIONS TO BE READ TO THE CHILDREN:
We are going to find out how well you can
read. Teachers administering Form 12A say:
Open your book to page 24, the page with the
cat at the top. Look at the first row of
boxes on the page. Read the word in the
arrow. Which box goes best with it? See
how the box with the bird has been marked.
The word in the arrow is fly. *The picture*
of the bird goes best with it. Now look at
the second row of boxes on the page. Read
the sentence in the arrow. Then make a big
X on the box that goes best with it. (Make
sure everyone marked the box correctly.) *You*
are going to work quietly and do all the rest
of the book by yourself. In each row, read
what is in the arrow. Then mark the box that
goes best with it. Mark just one *box in each*
row. When you get to the bottom of a page, go
right on to the next page. Sometimes you will

*see a story between two arrows. When you do,
be sure to read it carefully. Keep going
until you come to the policemen. Then close
your book and put your pencil down. Sit
quietly until everyone is finished. Now go to
the next row or boxes, the one with number one
by it. In each row, read what is in the arrow
and mark the box that goes best with it. All
right, begin!*

I mention briefly two other points. The test
was not standardized in many ways but two of the most
obvious failures are the form of administration and
the amount of time involved. Some teachers administered the test in two sessions, one session on each
of two days, others gave it all at one sitting. The
amount of time given to complete the test varied considerably with the particular class.

The ambiguity of test items raises further
questions about the validity of the test. Item 18
is one example of what I am referring to. The
stimulus sentence is *"The bird built his own house"*
followed by pictures of (1) a twig; (2) a birdhouse;
and (3) a nest. According to the national norms in
the Manual the distribution of answers was: (1) 5%;
(2) 59%; and (3) 35%. Number 3 (the nest) was the
correct answer. If the relevant skill being measured
is understood to be *"Identifying an illustrative
instance"* then the choice of 2 or 3 seems warrantable.
Indeed most children seem to have thought Number 2 to
be *most* reasonable. The teacher commented on this in
an interview after the test was administered:

*"I saw somebody read the whole thing to him-
self 'The bird build his own' and they checked
the bird house because you build a bird house
and bird built and his own house — the word
house throws them so bird built his own house,
well in fairy stories quite often a rabbit
builds his his own house there's no reasons
why in make-believe bunny rabbits talking that*

*a bird couldn't his own house Monkeys do it we
just read a story where monkeys didn't want to
build their house. To them house is misleading
if it said the bird built its own nest they
would have checked that."*

Perhaps birds do build birdhouses in Walt Disney
cartoons and that is the frame of reference the child
uses. The test constructor's power is to enforce
narrow normative conceptions.

A more extreme example is provided by item 38.
The stimulus paragraph is:

> *"Here is a story Tom wrote: John came to
> our school in April. He and his sister had
> just moved here. He is a lot of fun. He
> knows many new games."*
>
> *The question is: "Which would be the best
> name for Tom's story?" The possible answers
> are: (1) John and his Sister; (2) My School;
> and (3) New Boy.*

To insist that Number 3 is correct seems to be absurd.
How can a creative act such as naming a story be
normatively decided? The distribution of answers may
be taken as evidence for the ambiguity produced by
the question: (1) 28%; (2) 35%; and (3) 32%.

I have tried to indicate here that the test
fails within its own frame of reference because of
lack of clear instructions, lack of standardization,
lack of accurate time keeping and most importantly
ambiguity in many of the items.

RESULTS AND THEIR USE

Test results are placed in the child's folder
on a small piece of white tape which contains the
following information:

S/70	CPR 1	GRO 1
	READ	
RS	17	
GP	1.5	

245

(Note: The child's name does not appear on the tape.)

This indicates that this child has marked seventeen boxes designated as correct by the test constructor. This raw score is transformed by reference to national norms to a Grade Equivalent of Grade One, fifth month. Since this test was administered in the ninth month of Grade One it can be inferred that this child was demonstrating reading and related skills (as defined by the test) which a 'normal' child would be demonstrating in the fifth month of Grade One. This is *all* the knowledge the test makes available. What use can be made of these scores? The teachers only had the tests for one day after the administration of the test and this mitigated against an item by item analysis of each child's test which the Manual (p. 7) suggests as useful. The results of the test came back after the end of the school year so the results had no application in that year.

Some studies (Cicourel and Kitsuse, 1963; Keddie, 1971; Leiter, 1971) suggest that test scores are often used to warrant teachers/administrators already existing expectation of students. The result is a kind of self-fulfilling prophecy (Rosenthal and Jacobson, 1968). Organizationally what results is official or unofficial closed tracks. Polemically I would suggest that the powerful pronouncement of science sanctifies common-sense prejudice and legitimizes the production of persons whose qualifications (or lack of them) block them from anything but menial or semi-skilled jobs. But it is a vicious circle since the objective test started from these prejudiced beliefs about the world. The tests are used by test constructors, teachers, administrators and politicians to support their own beliefs and value

systems. The rationale for these beliefs and values
is in part based upon 'normal'/'correct' ways of linking objects. In *use* measures of performance relative
to some unexplicated standard (usually face validity,
i.e., constructor's common sense view of the world)
become an objective measure of competence that have a
determinative impact on students' lives.

James Coleman (who implicitly subscribes to
the tests' assumptions) describes the results of
testing.

> *What they (achievement tests) measure are the
> skills which are among the most important in
> our society for getting a good job and moving
> up to a better one, and for full participation
> in an increasingly technical world. Con-
> sequently, a pupil's test results at the end
> of public school provide a good measure of the
> range of opportunities open to him as he
> finishes school — a wide range of jobs or
> colleges if these skills (reading, writing,
> calculating and problem solving) are very high;
> a very narrow range that includes only the most
> menial jobs if the skills are very low*
> (Coleman, 1969: 164).

Coleman's analysis of achievement tests only
describes how they are used and in the process tacitly
sanctions their present use. I have attempted to
show that an analysis of what knowledge tests make
available and how that knowledge is made available
may bear no relationship either to the students'
performance or competence. Yet hanging on this thin
thread is the entire occupational and status structure
of society.

247

Chapter 6
TESTS AND EXPERIMENTS WITH CHILDREN[1]

Kenneth Jennings and Sybillyn Jennings[2]
University of California, San Diego

From the standpoint of formal scientific method
within the natural sciences, the relations between
the researcher and his topic are, in principle, irrelevant. The applicability of that standard to the
social sciences has been doubted and remains in
question (e.g., Bantock, 1961; Schutz, 1962).
Ordinarily, we take for granted the differences between children and adults. But when child behavior
is the topic of formal investigation the differences
between children and adults are neither clear nor
irrelevant.

In discussions about the applicability of the
canons of natural science to the study of human behavior, a major point at issue is the status of commonsense reasoning (Nagel, 1961; Schutz, 1962). The
model of investigation which has emerged from the
natural sciences is based on reactions to defects of
common sense and naive perception. In the place of
common sense, science has developed the concept of
method with its conditions of clear formulation,

[1] Without the aid of the administrators, teachers,
and students of the local school, we would have had no
laboratory, no equipment, and no subjects; we are grateful for their help. Our thanks to Courtney Cazden for
her thoughtful consideration of an earlier version of
this paper and to Carol and Bud Mehan for their help.
Especially, we thank our friend, Cass, and her family
for their patient teacherin'.

[2] The study reported was conducted while S.
Jennings held a U.S. Public Health Service predoctoral
fellowship in psychology, University of California,
Santa Barbara.

relevant evidence, and rational inference. Where
common sense is vague, method is explicit; where
common sense is forgetful, method has or makes a
record; where common sense is distractable, method
fixes its attention firmly, and so on.

The relation between commensense reasoning and
scientific rationality has been the central topic in
ethnomethodology (Cicourel, 1964; Garfinkel, 1960;
Schutz, 1964; Zimmerman and Pollner, 1970). The
general point is that scientific rationality is not
in conflict with commonsense reasoning but that
scientific rationality is embedded in commonsense
reasoning. The dependence of scientific rationality
on commonsense reasoning is usually demonstrated
through an examination of scientific method as a social
activity (see especially, Cicourel, 1964). Method
provides a solid enough ground for the enterprise of
scientific understanding, ideally conceived as hypothesis, design, procedure, and results, but when method
is enacted the underlying commonsense reasoning is
clearly visible. Focusing on the researcher's actual
behavior shows that the world of commonsense experience
and understanding the researcher shares with his subject is a greater resource than his ideal and explicit
methods.

This relation between commensense reasoning and
scientific rationality becomes even more critical
when our task is discovering what the child knows and
assessing what the child can do. Not only does the
researcher face the normal problems of inferring
knowledge from behavior, but, in the case of studying
the child, he tries in his research to make up for
the resource of common sense he has lost in turning
from the study of adults to the study of children.
Our reasoning here is that each technique contains
within it, as grounds for its successful implementation,
an image of the child which is conceptually prior to
any specific theoretical issue the technique is used
to explore. Our effort in this paper is to develop
the image of the child caught in our adult techniques.

The view that scientific method rests on commonsense reasoning leads to the recognition that, in

addition to the more or less explicit theoretical
model of the subject under study, the researcher's
practices also support a 'model' of the subject.
The explicit theoretical model is much studied, but
presently there is no model of the subject based on
the researcher's activities. (For treatments of
implicit models of actors in social science research see Cicourel, 1964; Garfinkel, 1967; Schutz,
1962.) One important reason for this omission has
been pointed out by Cicourel (1964;1968). The
actions of the researcher and subject are coded in
categories derived from the theoretical model, and
research results are reported in these pre-coded
categorizations. Thus, the actual activities of the
researcher and subject cannot be seen, much less
studied, through the reported results. The reported
results are simply not intended to describe 'what
happened.' To retrieve the dimensions of the actual
interactional behavior of subject and researcher, it
is necessary to go beneath the reported results and
idealized descriptions of research methods.

THE TESTING ICEBERG

Testing is used extensively in our schools to
assess what students know.[3] Considered as a technique for gaining knowledge about children, testing
falls heir to the problem of method at issue: How
do the differences between adults and children influence our methods for discovering what children
know and what they are like?

Adults construct and administer tests to children,
and children receive scores on a test which summarize
their performance in relation to some larger sample.

---

[3] Educational testing is analyzed as a social activity in Chapters 4 and 5; see also Mehan, 1971. Other
educational encounters, e.g., the placement interview
analyzed in Chapter 2 and the lesson analyzed in Chapers
3 and 7 exemplify the issues discussed here with regard
to experimentation.

Typically, the score a child achieves is assumed to be a function of the ability described by the test items (problems or tasks). The validity of the test items is judged in terms of the theoretical derivation of these items from the ability under test (see Farnham-Diggory, 1972).

But there is more to the test than its idealized description as a set of problems. The test must be administered. In order to administer the test, the tester has to assume that the child is able to enter into and move through the testing occasion — the child has to be 'testable.' These abilities, which are assumed by the tester and are attributed to the child, are partly evident in the formal, and again idealized, instructions for administering the test. However, the instructions for administering a test, as might be given in the test manual, are not complete as MacKay demonstrates in Chapter 5. That is, they cannot be taken as accurate directions for what the tester will do or as an accurate record of what the tester actually did. The tester's practices in administering the test — both explicit and tacit — constitute the method. Our approach is to search back through the grounds of the tester's actions to find those aspects of the child's abilities which the test score does not, and is not intended to, index, but which, nevertheless, are assumed by the tester and attributed to the child.

How are abilities inferred from the tester's method to be related to the abilities under test (described by the test items)? Think, for instance, what it could mean to fail or achieve the lowest possible score on a test. From our perspective it takes ability on the part of the child and work on the part of the tester even to be able to fail. These abilities are hidden in the tester's attributions which are hidden in the tester's method. And the method lies beneath the child's score and the formal description of the tester's actions.

Describing the tester's actions by 'He administered Test A to Child 2' and describing the child's performance

251

by his score on Test A is like judging an iceberg by its tip. The testing iceberg we've been sketching is shown in Figure 6.1.

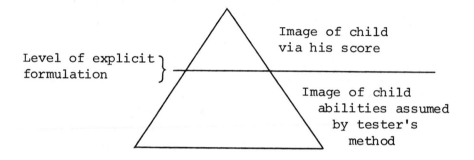

FIGURE 6.1. The Testing Iceberg.

The score provides an image of the child in terms of the theory or model of ability which is the target of the test. But, presently, we have no model of the child as a participant in the production of the testing occasion. The only access we have to a model of these abilities is through the tester's methods, and these are not retrievable from the score. They are only partly discoverable in the formal administration procedure. This means we have to go beneath the score as a summary of a complicated and only partially formulated interaction and attempt to describe the behavior of the test participants. Without studying the dimensions of the interaction we cannot learn how the behaviors of the participants fit together in the unfolding time of the test. Particularly, we do not know how the actions of one participant influence the actions of the other and how this interaction may contribute to the score or profile in ways not catalogued by the formal testing theory and procedure.

Tests, in comparison to experiments, are rather weak in their explicit methodological formulations of the interactional occasion. Emphasis, instead, is

placed on the sensibility of the particular items,
the standardization sample and procedure, and general
criticisms of appropriateness of the techniques, for
example, using verbal instructions on a test designed
to assess non-verbal abilities. Since our tack is to
examine the adult's actions formulated as expressions
of method, we have turned to a technique which openly
emphasizes design and procedure — the experiment.
We elect to view the reported results of an experiment,
like those of a test, as mainly the outcome of the
researcher's skills. Experimentation includes quite
explicit discussion of the researcher's construction
and manipulation of the experimental occasion and,
therefore, it is a fairer object for analysis. At
the level of our interests, experimentation is the
prototype for testing. Tests share the general logic
of experiments so that if we demonstrate the researcher's
reliance on abilities of the child not under examination
in the experiment, we can presume a similar relation
holds between the ability a test claims to measure and
the abilities required to take the test (for a discussion
of the differentiation of abilities from a different
theoretical perspective, but akin to the distinction
we are making here, see Flavell, 1971).

Our study of experimentation affords a precise
analysis of the researcher's construction and manipulation of the experiment as a social occasion. This
analysis allows us to attend the abilities of the
child assumed by the researcher's methods; i.e., to
characterize the images of the child which lie beneath
the level of explicit formulation pictured in Figure
6.1. In Figure 6.2 the researcher's construction
of the experiment is displayed in its functional
segments.

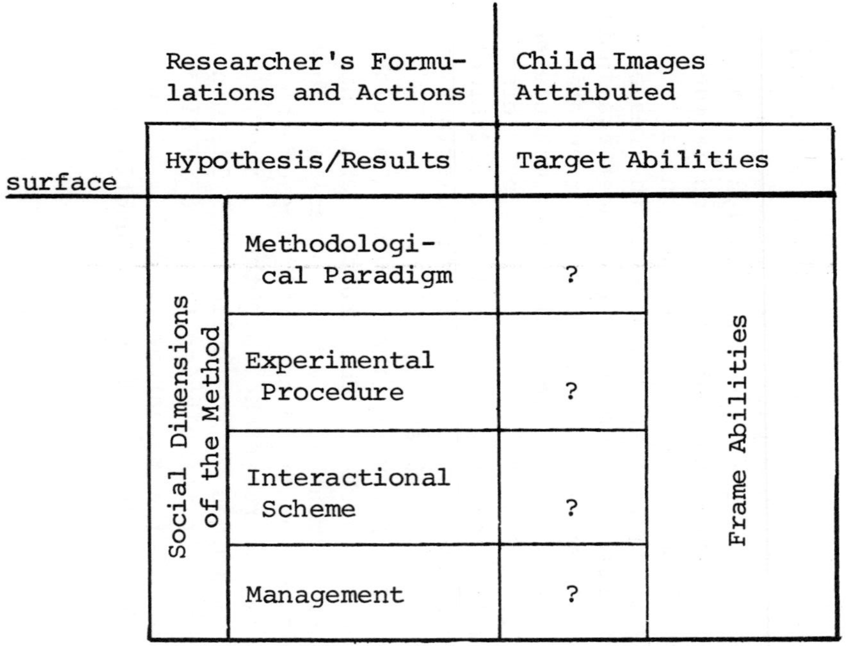

Researcher's Formu- lations and Actions	Child Images Attributed
Hypothesis/Results	Target Abilities

	Frame Abilities
Methodologi- cal Paradigm	?
Experimental Procedure	?
Interactional Scheme	?
Management	?

Social Dimensions
of the Method

surface

FIGURE 6.2. An Analytical Model of Experimentation

EXPERIMENTATION

What we know and what we can learn about experimentation as a social phenomenon is intimately tied to the posibility of sharing the experimental participants' understanding of the experimental occasion. We might study experimentation by adopting the attitude of a subject, ignorant of the experimenter's intent and design and from that viewpoint describe the experiment. Generally, however, the subject is not required to describe his participation, nor does he produce an account of what happens. More usually, experimentation is studied through the perspective of the experimental researcher because he describes what he plans to do and what happens during the experiment. Access to the subject's perspective is indirect through the experimental researcher's accounts of the occasion. The possibility of sharing and the need to share the researcher's viewpoint through his descriptions form both our resource and our limitation.

When the experimental subjects are children, we don't have the option of choosing our perspective, as we might in the case of adult subjects. What can be known about experimentation as a social phenomenon when the experiment includes children is even more dependent on sharing the researcher's attitude, available in his descriptions of the experiment.

We begin our analysis of the social dimensions of experimentation by discussing the notion of experimental control. Concern for control is based on the realization that a person's behavior does not necessarily show directly what the person intends, what he sees, what he remembers, what he knows, or the like. Because the behavior is not directly connected to its grounds, multiple interpretations may be offered in explanation. Control as a restriction on our inferences about behavior is augmented by a sense of control as a style of action or behavioral manipulation. Through the sense of control as behavioral manipulation, the researcher claims to gain access to the grounds of the subject's behavior. The researcher constructs a situation, e.g., an experiment, in which he constrains and manipulates the subject's actions so that the grounds of those actions can be inferred. Control as behavioral manipulation attempts to reach the workings of the system under study.

The experimenter makes elaborate plans for the manipulation of the subject's behavior. These plans are based on two assumptions. Prior to the actual investigation, the researcher assumes he has a viable, though implicit, model of the subject's acts which can be used as a guide for his own actions. The model must support the researcher's need to manipulate the grounds of the subject's behavior, hence the model must formulate those grounds as though they were available to the researcher. In this sense the demands of control force upon the researcher a behavioristic model of the actor — the grounds of action are external to the actor. Secondly, the researcher assumes that he knows how the properties or parameters of situations can and will influence the behavior of subjects. This knowledge allows him to place these properties directly and determinately under his control.

A critical problem emerges from these assumptions. If their conditions are met, then there is no need to proceed, the human sciences are complete. If they are not met, the researcher's theoretical knowledge of the subject's acts and the structure of situations must, in principle, be incomplete. Thus his theory cannot suffice as a basis for his actions. The assumptions are not met perfectly. The main reason for their incompleteness is that the subject himself is an environment of his own actions, and the subject as environment cannot be manipulated from the outside.

Since the researcher is interested in controlling the grounds of action he must employ a method which leaves the subject intact and which influences those subjective aspects of behavior not directly manipulable by changes in physical setting. The researcher is left with the problem of meaning. His method must treat the subject's actions as subjectively meaningful whether or not the theory under direct examination is concerned

256

with meaning or the subject's perspective.

The researcher's task, then, extends beyond the mere modification of a physical setting. He must proceed as if the grounds of the subject's behavior were problems. The researcher must find solutions to these problems which he can then transmit to the subject. The researcher specifies the tasks the subject is to perform. If there is more than one task, he may state priorities or sequences for accomplishing the alternative or subordinate tasks. Ordinarily, he establishes sets of techniques and implements which can and must be employed in carrying out the tasks. He is concerned with both the temporal and spatial boundaries of the action as well as the objects, events, and territories which are irrelevant to the subject or are prohibited.

Beyond direct concern with these features, the researcher must find ways to make irrelevant the subject's normal interests in the world. He must induce the subject to adopt not only the explicitly offered conditions of action but also to suspend the connections between his acts in this situation and those outside it. To accomplish this, the researcher needs a special kind of interaction framework, something like a 'game' or 'drama.' Whether or not the researcher offers his enterprise to the subject with these specific labels, it is useful to apply these analogues in analyzing the framework which the researcher has to establish as the social structure of his experiment. Games (and plays) are special events and special times bounded away from the demands and consequences of daily life (Garfinkel, 1963 and analysis by K. Jennings, 1972). Within them reality seems to be transformed; the status of objects and actions is somehow changed, and symbolic linkages and regular sequences of behavior are altered. It is within the sense of the recognizedly special or the non-ordinary that the researcher can presume to tell subjects what to do and how to do it. Otherwise the researcher's apparatus and instructions are either irrelevant or noticeably strange.

The general issues are the same when children serve as subjects in experiments. However, in meeting the differences between children and ourselves, specifically the problematic status of the child's variety of common sense, we may put an even greater burden on technique. We may require our methods to be more powerful than our explicit knowledge allows. Or, for some purposes, we may disregard the differences between children and adults. We then presume that for some conditions of the experiment the child will act as we would. We put ourselves in the position of transmitting a world to the child which we specify and describe from our adult attitudes and reasoning.

SOCIAL DIMENSIONS OF EXPERIMENTATION

We will analyze the social dimensions of experimentation using materials gathered in our study of eight children (between five and six years of age) drawn from a kindergarten class in School A. Two children, a boy and a girl, participated as subjects in each of the four experimental sessions. These sessions were conducted in the school auditorium; they lasted about 20 minutes and were videorecorded. The recording was monitored and observations of the sessions were made by A. Cicourel. K. Jennings operated the camera, and S. Jennings read the stimulus items. [See Cicourel, 1973, for a discussion of the general theoretical attitude underlying this work, S. Jennings, 1968 for a description of the initial psycholinguistic experiment and 1969 for analysis based on the joint study, and K. Jennings, 1972 for a report of the dual studies within Cicourel's theoretical frame.] We will describe each of the segments of the 'iceberg' in Figure 6.2 proceeding top to bottom.

Hypothesis/Results. The question which formed the experimental hypothesis concerned the influence of "surface" arrangement on the underlying or "deep" logic of sentences (Chomsky, 1965, Katz and Postal, 1964) The distinction between surface and deep structure can

258

be illustrated by the following two sentences:

The girl tickles the boy.
The boy is tickled by the girl.

In both instances *the girl* is the deep structure
subject of the sentence although in the second
sentence the noun in the normal surface subject
position is *the boy*. We examined a group of sentence
forms, related in their underlying or deep structure
(meaning), though displaying different surface dis-
tributions of the constituents (the various noun and
verb phrases, prepositions, etc., specifically, the
direct and indirect objects, as their arrangement was
influenced by ordering transformations [consult
Chomsky, 1957, for a definition of "transformation"]).
For example, the arrangements of the phrases in the
following two sentences differ:

The boy throws the girl the basket.
The boy throws the basket to the girl.

These differences in form are considered to reflect
alternate surface realizations of the same original
deep structure. These surface realizations are derived from their shared deep structure by a history
of linguistic transformations resulting in the
particular order of constituents observed.

In this experiment we asked whether children
comprehended equally well sentences which essentially
meant 'the same thing' despite differences in their
surface structure. Generally, the results of the
experiment showed that surface arrangement influenced
comprehension. The description and linguistic
analyses of the subjects' behavior and the experimental
results built upon them are not relevant to our topic
here and will not, therefore, be reported.

Methodological Paradigm. The methodological
paradigm employed was a "comprehension technique"
(see Fraser, Bellugi,

and Brown, 1963 and Slobin, 1967 for discussion of comprehension techniques). Generally, the assumption of
comprehension techniques is that the subject will consult his linguistic rule system (grammar) to interpret the input sentence. The received language
event (i.e., the linguistic input embedded in the
larger stimulus situation) will be decoded using the
grammar and then encoded in the interpretive system.
In our case the interpretive system was action. A
sentence was read to a pair of subjects, a boy and
a girl, and they were instructed to carry out the
action indicated in the sentence, e.g., *The girl gives
the balloon to the boy*. Comprehension of the sentence
was inferred from the action which resulted and the
consistency of each subject's responses across four
instances of each sentence type (each pair received
64 sentence presentations).

Experimental Procedure. The experimental procedure required that the subjects be instructed verbally
in the actional roles they were to 'play' across all the
sentences; e.g., the girl was to be *the girl* of the
sentences. They were told they would have to do what
the boy (or girl) of the sentence did in the sentences
read; e.g., *the boy* gives *the book to the girl*. They
were familiarized with the objects to be used in performing the sentences, and they were shown where to
stand vis-à-vis the other experimental participants
and the camera equipment. They were promised they would
see themselves on the television monitor after the
session. The subjects were given no training. They
received three practice sentences. An outline of the
ideal procedure follows:

1. Check out subjects' familiarity with the
    objects and try to make them comfortable.
2. Show subjects where to stand and tell them
    about the camera and other persons.
3. Read the instructions.
4. Give the practice sentences.

5. Present the stimulus sentences.
6. Take a break (if needed).
7. Thank subjects and show them their pictures on the monitor.

Ideally, the subjects were to respond by listening to the stimulus sentences. For each sentence they were to decide who was to perform the action. One child was to choose himself as actor, one as recipient of the action. The child who chose himself as actor was to select the appropriate object from the display table and perform the action. The child who received the object was to replace it on the table.

This description, brief though it is, is quite like typical reports of experimental work. In light of our analytical framework, we want to reflect upon the abilities of the child implicit in the experimental hypothesis, paradigm, and procedure. The experimental hypothesis, method, and procedure make assumptions about what the subject is like, what the subject can and cannot do, and what it takes on the part of the researcher to get the subject to do what it is that he can do. This is one sense of the statement that the methods we use to study children themselves provide a picture of what the child knows.

Within psychology, considerations about what a particular technique or procedure requires in regard to subject characteristics belong to experimental design. These considerations have no theoretical status and are seldom reported in their entirety. They are referred to in statements like 'pilot work has shown,' 'the procedure was adapted for three-year-olds,' etc.

The list which follows is not ordered, nor is it complete, but it should give the reader an idea of how the child can be characterized by the method employed.

1. The subject can recognize and attend an auditory input.

261

2. The subject can hold (remember) the auditory input long enough to provide some reading (interpretation) of it.
3. The subject can move; the action responses are in his repertoire.
4. The subject can treat a sentence as a command to act.
5. The subject knows that objects and actions have names.
6. The subject can identify and distinguish the categories *"actor," "action,"* and *"object"* in the auditory input.
7. The subject has some linguistic rule system for interpreting the auditory input.
8. The subject does not need to learn to respond to a sentence as a direction to act.
9. The subject's abilities hold across the entire session.

Interactional Scheme. The researcher has to establish for and with the subjects the 'who, what, where, when, why, and how' of performing the experimental task. These functions follow a sequence of phases visible in the researcher's activities:

A. The researcher identifies *who* is to participate.
B. He tells them *why* they are to participate.
C. He shows them *where* they are to perform and *what* they are to use in their performance.
D. He tells them *what* they are to do.
E. He gives them practice in *how* to do it.
F. He tells them to do it.
G. He tells them to stop doing it.

The ideal experimental procedure (p. 261) covers most of the functions listed in sequence above. However, the experimental procedure is formulated in terms of the ideal design rather than in terms of the experimental subject and the researcher's problems in

getting the child to act like a subject in an experiment. The sequence of functions is interactional
just because it takes into account the subject's
motivations and actions, idealized though they may be.
We now present illustrations from the study conducted
which led to this sequence of functions, which forms,
in turn, the basis for the construct — interactional
scheme. (Not all phases will be illustrated in detail
and no phase will be described completely. The
materials used are drawn from a transcript of the four
experimental sessions. The construction of this transcript and its relation to the phase analysis are described in detail in K. Jennings, 1972.)

Phase A: Recruitment of the subjects was made
by proxy through the kindergarten teacher. The teacher
selected who was to participate in the experiment.

Phase B: The first subject pair was brought to
the school auditorium by their teacher. Introductions
were made as follows:

Syb: *Hello, I'm Sybillyn, won't you come in?*
Mrs. Kelly: *This is Donald and this is Susan.*
Syb: *Hello Donald and Susan. You want to come*
here where we're gonna play a little
game? You wanna take off your coats?
Why don't you just come right over here
where we've got everything set up.

When the children arrived at the scene of the
experiment, the researcher initiated her intercourse
with them as if a new set of grounds were in effect,
transforming whatever grounds for their participation
had been stated by their teacher (the function of
Phase A). The researcher's talk cannot be seen as an
announcement of an existing state of affairs. Although the researcher announced [*"...where we're*
gonna play a little game..."], she also attempted by
her talk to invoke, affirm, and reaffirm a commitment
to an order of activities and participation which had

not yet been experienced, explicated, or given. The researcher has to draw the children into an occasion which contains for them they know not what. This second phase signals the beginning of the attempted transformation from the world of everyday affairs into the special reality of the experimental design.

Regardless of the children's state when they arrived on the scene, the researcher attributed to them the status of hesitant 'volunteer.' Specifying the category of the next occurrence as a game did not, even in the eyes of the researcher, seem to suffice as a transport into the experiment. The researcher asked the children to move into the experimental scene ["...*why don't you just come right over here*..."] as though by physically getting the children into the experiment the researcher could accomplish their entry into the theoretical frame. After the children had taken this first step, the researcher could then identify the other players and pieces of the game.

Until the researcher can motivate the children to participate in the game, i.e., to be subjects, the experiment cannot proceed. The children are to do what the researcher says because they have been selected as players in the researcher's game.

Phase C: The researcher continued to set up the pieces for the game by familiarizing the children with the other players, starting positions, etc. The following excerpt is taken from the session with the same subject pair:

Syb: *...I think that's good, and look, see Ken with the funny earphones on? He's our television man today, and then, when we're finished, you can see yourselves on TV. And Dr. Cicourel's seeing if the picture comes up (?) all right, and so what we want is for you guys to stand like maybe here and here (the positions are pointed out and Donald and Susan directed to them). Ken, can you see us at all?*

These statements indicate the importance of 'placedness' for what is still to come. As adults at any rate, we recognize that a remark like [cf. p. 262 "...*we've got everything set up...*"] signals that something has been done to an otherwise normal and perhaps even familiar setting. Further, what has been done is under the control of the persons who have done it, the researchers. The auditorium is not, at least in this corner, its old, familiar self.

Vivian and Gordo

Aaron: *You guys just stand right here. Here you go. Right here, Ok.*

Syb: *This is sorta the girl's place to stand and that's the boy's place to stand, and I'm gonna read you both some sentences, Ok?*

Dora and Miguel

Syb: *...Now, Dora, could you stand right here? We want to be sure you have — to get you in focus on the camera. And, Miguel, can you stand by Dora. Now, cameraman, can you see?*

The researcher focuses the subjects' attention on where things are and where they are to stand. Certain objects are singled out for special mention thereby creating the principal set of intersubjectively normal referents and relevances for the next phase. This talk of the researcher establishes normal places or home territories. The movement space, direction of orientation, categories and location of relevant objects, and the role categories of the other participants are established and assigned.

In these sessions the researcher does not specifically restrict the setting of the activity by telling the children *not* to do something or *only* to do something, and though such restrictions are possible and are used elsewhere they cannot completely delimit the arena of action. Buried deep in the attributed presuppositions about the child is the idea that the enterprise is located and held within the physical bounds of the conversation which creates it. Whatever activity is offered or commanded in later phases and expected on the basis of the introductory phases is constrained by the confines of normal talk. For example, the researcher presumes that the children will not perform the sentence *The boy shows the girl the book* by the boy carrying the book to the stage of the auditorium behind him out of camera range and the girl walking to the stage to receive it from him.

During this phase the researcher pointed out the objects which the children were to manipulate in their performances. An example follows:

Donald and Susan

Syb:	*Is there anything you see you don't know what it is? What's this?*
Susan:	*Basket.*
Syb:	*Yes. Do you know what this silly thing is?*
Donald:	*Mouse.*
Syb:	*Yeah, that's good. 'N that?*
Susan (?):	*A bear.*
Syb:	*Ok, what's this?*
Donald:	*A orange.*
Syb:	*Do you like oranges? (He shakes head affirmatively.) Yeah. Do you know what this is?*

. . . . . .

Syb:	*And what's this thing down there?*
Donald:	*Re-eraser.*

. . . . . .

Mrs. Kelly:	*And did they name that?*
Syb:	*Oh yeah, they didn't name that one.*
Mrs. Kelly:	*Honey, did you name that, right there?*
Syb:	*This? What's this?*
Donald/Susan:	*Paper.*

Through this procedure the researcher established the word-object references to be shared by the experimental participants and invoked the references which would be sanctioned during the experiment.

The point of such naming, from the perspective
of the formal experimental procedure, is to ensure
that the children know the names which will be read
in the sentences and that they have no trouble in
connecting these names to the objects on the display
table. Responses, from the viewpoint of the experimental hypothesis, are to be assigned a grammatical,
not a lexical, source. But still the word-object connections must be normalized and this takes social
time. Some examples from two of the other sessions
follow:

Miguel and Dora

Syb: *What's this one?*
Miguel: *A stick.*
Syb: *A stick?*
Dora: *Chalk.*
Miguel: *Chalk.*
Syb: *Chalk. That's right. See you could write
with...*

Gordo and Vivian

Syb: *See if you can find a picture (looking at
the book* The Yellow Submarine*).*
Vivian: *Remember when the man told him not to push
the buttons, and he (went ahead) (?) and he
flew out?*
Syb: *Let's see if we can find it. Oh, here they're
in the ocean.*

It is hard to tell whether such linking to the
outside world is an instruction regarding the
relevance of the subjects' knowledge of the objects
acquired in other situations, part of making the
children comfortable, or whether it is just so much
talk.

When a child gave a name for an object which
was different from the one pre-selected by the researcher she often quickly and forcefully offered hers
as not only a, but *the*, substitute.

Dora and Miguel

Syb:	*And what's this?*
Dora:	*Money.*
Syb:	*Money, it's a penny.*
Miguel:	*A penny.*
Syb:	*A penny, and what's this?*
. . . . . .	
Syb:	*A book. What's this?*
Miguel:	*A bunny rabbit.*
Syb:	*Well, a ah it could be a bunny rabbit. This is supposed to be a little toy mouse, see his whiskers...*
Miguel:	*A mouse.*
Miguel/Dora:	*A mouse.*
Syb:	*And his tail; what's this?*

If the child's offering was an accepted alternative like rock for stone, the researcher stated that she tried to remember to adopt the child's name for the object in the stimulus presentations which followed, and in fact, if she could do it quickly enough, she changed the entry on her stimulus cards.

The child is not just being given a name for an object; he is being instructed in the appropriate-in-this-occasion name and designation of the object. When the objects are named, they are labeled and referred to without any mention that only some of the objects are toys. Some are real and some, though real, are small in comparison with the size of the other objects. In this sense, it is not just the appropriateness of reference labels which is being checked and confirmed or changed. Typical uses, activities, and relations to other objects and activities are being made relevant or "corpused" (Zimmerman and Pollner, 1970) for that occasion by the naming.

Phase D: Having familiarized the subjects with the objects to be used and where they are to begin the play, the researcher next tells them what they are to do. In this phase the subjects are given the rules of play.

Donald and Susan

Syb: *Now, Susan, I want you to pretend that you're the girl. D'ya think you could do that? And, Donald, can you pretend that you're the boy. And I'm gonna read some sentences to you, and if the girl's supposed to do something in the sentence, then you do it, Susan. And if it says the boy's supposed to do something, then you do it, Donald. And so let's just try this out.*

Matt and Ellen

Syb: *Now, I want, Ellen, I want you to pretend that you're the girl and do everything I say the girl does in the sentences I'm gonna read. And, Matt, you pretend you're the boy, and you do everything I say the boy does. Now that sounds pretty easy, doesn't it?...*

The instructions assert the legitimacy of the imbalance of power in the determination of relevant talk, action, and frame manipulation by stating that the researcher's 'wanting' is a sufficient ground for compliance by others. The children are instructed that they do not have any motivational basis for their actions other than that offered by the researcher. This is not expressed explicitly, still the children are requested to do only what is theirs as *the boy* and *the girl* to do. This loss of power is marked by the researcher's making the occasion 'unreal' and 'inconsequential' in terms of normal ethical considerations. Specifically, to request the children to pretend is to lead them into a frame of objects, relations, and actions which, though still not entirely known, will be 'safe'.

Just as the researcher knows the starting positions and the pieces (Phase C), she also knows the moves. The world of the experiment is closed, finite, and simple.

269

Phase E: The beginning of this phase is visible in what follows the examples from Phase D.

Donald and Susan

Syb: ... *And so let's just try this out.*
THE BOY JUMPS HIGH IN THE AIR
Yeah, that's pretty good. Maybe we should tie your shoes so you can jump higher. Can you do it? D'ya want me to do it for you?

The notion of practice is rather critical in the evolving interaction. The practice presentations are the first occasions wherein the children are allowed to try to integrate the various instructions with the scene parameters. In this experiment, practice is almost completely a frame check-out. It is not intended in any way to improve an already adequate performance. Quasi-stimulus items are presented both to connect the children's understanding to the scheme of objects and actions and to test and evaluate the nature of that connection.

The training stimuli are designed to be easier than the normal stimuli and thus are seen to be even more transparent. It is assumed that the actions produced in response to the sample stimuli reflect the subjects' comprehension of the instructed experimental frame rather than their grammars. By their failure to respond appropriately to these stimuli, the subjects can indicate that they do not understand an entire social occasion. During the practice items, the researcher may find it necessary to intervene in some way to aid the subjects, for example, by restating the sentence, transforming it, or expanding instructions and identifications given earlier. These examples are taken from each of the remaining pairs:

Miguel and Dora

Syb: THE BOY JUMPS AS HIGH AS HE CAN
      Can you jump high, Miguel? Let's see you jump,
      aah, that's good.

Gordo and Vivian

Syb: THE GIRL WAVES HER HAND AT THE CAMERA
      Right.

Matt and Ellen

Syb: *...Now, let's see, I'll just give a sample to*
      see if we understand, and if you don't under-
      stand something, you just ask me, Ok? Ok.

      THE BOY JUMPS AS HIGH AS HE CAN

      Very good.

It is easy to see that the researcher was not interested only in the children's abilities to translate the syntactic structure of these stimuli into correct action. Nor was she only interested in the particular linguistic competence that that action might indicate. Rather, here the concern was to discover whether or not the whole instructional paradigm had been successful and to make sure that the children were rewarded for having appropriately employed their own occasion-assembling abilities along with the specific instructions to create their responses. The researcher's affirmation of the correctness of the subjects' actions locks them into the required interpretive scheme.

Phase F: The sixth phase, constituted by the actual trials, is the most strongly and most completely pre-organized phase of the entire session. Finally, the subjects are 'doing it'. The stimulus items typed on cards and arranged according to a

271

modified random order for presentation are read aloud
one-by-one to the subject pair. The researcher awaits
the subjects' corresponding activities which constitute the data. Ideally, this phase would include
only the reading of the stimulus sentences and the
children's movements in response. However, the behavior observed showed that the prior planning and
its execution in Phases A through E had not been
complete. The plan essentially failed to achieve its
goals of event organization and action control. We
will discuss this failure and the researcher's work
in attempting to patch up the plan for action in the
section on situation management.

Phase G: This seventh phase terminates the
trials and the experimental occasion. Typically, the
subjects are told that their work is completed, that
they accomplished it well, that their help and
participation has been appreciated, and that they
were well-behaved. The major function of this ter-
mination work is to re-invoke the world of commonsense reasoning and the children's everyday activities.
The suspension of this world, requested at the beginning of the experimental occasion, must itself be
suspended. Energies must be released, and the tensions
which supported the structure of the experiment's
special reality relaxed. The researcher did not only
abandon the pretend world of the experiment, she
seemed to re-establish the viability of the normal
world.

Gordo and Vivian

Syb: *The boy would give it to you. Ok. That's very*
good. You've helped us a great deal, and you
tell Mrs. Kelly...(end tape)

Donald and Susan

Syb: *That's good, you did very well. We appreciate*
your helping us.

272

Miguel and Dora

Syb: *Oh, that was very good. Thank you so much for helping us. You did a very nice job. You were very good children.*

Matt and Ellen

Syb: *Very good. That was just excellent. Thank you very much for helping us.*
Aaron: *That was very good. Come over here, gang.*
Syb: *We'll show you your pictures.*

The overall judgment of *"very good,"* the notion of *"help,"* and the direction to *"tell the teacher"* are essentially directions that the life world which was left behind to enter the experiment-game continues to embed the experiment as its ground. These pleasantries return the control of the children's behavior to its normal place and its usual structuring — the children themselves, the school, and, of course, the teacher.

Allowing the children to view their performances was part of the original agreement. Along with the other cooling-out techniques, this second part of the contracted performance signals that the thing has come to an end. The last phase reflexively terminates the acting out frame both by announcement and by a complete change of the researcher's style of movement and talk. The fragile experimental occasion has been completed. The game is over.

Situation Management. Despite care in planning and executing the design, the work intended to be done prior to the actual trials was not completed within its assigned phase. This work, then, runs over into the actual trials. In our study, subject responses which were not sensibly correct or incorrect led the researcher to intervene. Similarly, any action on the part of the researcher, other than reading the stimulus sentences, seems to be in response to the incomplete construction of the experimental frame.

The researcher repaired misunderstandings due, apparently, to reference.

Matt and Ellen

Syb: THE GIRL TOSSES THE BOY THE BOX
Ellen: *I don't know what you mean.*
Syb: *By 'toss'? You know how to throw it.*
Ellen: *Oh.*
Syb: *Yeah, 'toss' is like throw, just a light throw. There we go. Ok, you can put it back.*
. . . . . .
Syb: THE GIRL IS HANDED THE STONE BY THE BOY
Ellen: *What's a stone?*
Syb: *The rock.*
Ellen: *Oh.*

The researcher did not remark about the child's questioning; she responded without hesitation, indicating that both she and the child were attentively checking the stimulus sentences and responses for correctable difficulties.

Miguel and Dora

Syb: THE GIRL IS PATTED BY THE BOY
(No response from the subjects.)
Who does that?
Miguel: *The boy.*
Syb: *Ok, can you pat? Want me to read it again?*
THE GIRL IS PATTED BY THE BOY
'Pat' 's just like touching, like you pat a dog. What would you do?

Aaron: *Show us what you'd do, Miguel.*
Syb: *Come here; I'll pat you. There, now you*
          pat, Miguel; now, what would you do?
Miguel: *Pat.*
Syb: *Ok, very good, that's just right. Now here's*
          another one.

In these excerpts the work done by naming in Phase C
is continued. Differences in word meaning and word-
action linkages are being cleared away. These differences might interfere with the subject's demonstration of his syntactic understanding. Additionally,
we can see in these excerpts that the everyday world
is an immediately available resource for all participants. The experimental reality is not sufficient
in itself to solve the problems which arise within it.
The world in which questions are asked and answered
lies just outside the world of the experiment with
its stimuli and responses.

    The researcher intervened to provide necessary,
but previously unstated, behavioral instructions.

Donald and Susan

Syb: THE BALLOON IS TOSSED TO THE GIRL BY THE BOY
          Susan, want to put the balloon back?
          TO THE GIRL IS SHOWN THE BOOK BY THE BOY
          'At's very good. You can put that back now.

Matt and Ellen

Syb: THE BOY HANDS THE GIRL THE SPOON
          Very good, Matt. That's just the way. And,
          Ellen, you can put it back when you're
          finished.
Ellen: *Oh.*
Syb: *That's Ok, you don't have to wait for me to*
          say to put it back (?), Ok.

    These excerpts show that the instructions
(Phase D) did not make clear what the subject was to

do with the object after he received it. Instead of
explicitly telling the children to replace the object
on the table after it had been transferred, the researcher waited until the child was holding the object
and did not know what to do with it. At that point
the instructions were amended on the spot. Additions
were not made at just any point during the session.
The child must have asked and/or the object must have
been transferred. One child had to be left holding
the object at the end of the enactment. The researcher
counted on the temporal occurrence of the physical
acitivity to make a slot for the instruction *"put it
back."*

The researcher cautioned the children to *"listen
carefully, now."* Sometimes she read a sentence over
again. Along with this re-motivation (Phase B), the
researcher asked the children questions she thought
they could answer easily. The easy questions seemed
to be an attempt on her part to increase the children's
interest in the experiment (Phase A) and also to take
off the pressure and monotony of the required sequence
of presentation and response.

Gordo and Vivian

Syb:	THE BALLOON IS SHOWN THE BOY BY THE GIRL *Very good. What color balloon is that?*
Vivian:	*Orange.*
Gordo:	*Orange.*
Syb:	*Ok.*

The researcher managed accidents like the following:

Gordo and Vivian

Syb:	THE BOX IS TOSSED TO THE BOY BY THE GIRL *Oh, crash!*
Gordo:	*She didn't (can't) (?) catch it.*
Syb:	*No, she didn't catch it. Ok, you can put the things back when you're finished....*

*(Gordo replaces the box on the display
table. In doing this he knocks the
chalk with his elbow, and the chalk
falls to the floor.)*

*Oh (?), crash, the chalk broke. That's
fine, we'll just have two pieces of
chalk, and (?) now listen to this.*

The children are not to be blamed for accidents that
occur during the special reality of the experiment.
If Gordo upsets the chalk in replacing the box, then
it is the researcher's job to patch up the hole he
has made in the experimental fabric.

The interactional scheme the researcher uses
and his situation management also provide a picture
of what the child knows. They give a picture
of the child's abilities to participate as a subject
in the experiment. The researcher, through his interactional scheme, presumes that the child can enter
and remain in the experimental frame — that he can
play the researcher's game. Without assigning these
'frame abilities' to the child, the experimental
occasion cannot support the assumptions about the
subject's abilities which are implicit in the experimental design. If the child cannot be brought
into the experimental frame, then, obviously, there
is no way to examine the abilities which are the
target of the investigation.

The interactional scheme and the researcher's
management of the situation require that the child
will be able to adopt an experimental attitude. What
this constitutes is not entirely clear, but the following analytic features seem to be included:

1. The child must be able to appreciate and
manage shifts of the "constitutive accents" (Garfinkel,
1963) of events and activities, e.g., across both
idealized boundaries of the situation — internal
and external.

2. The child must be able to appreciate and
employ the differential connectedness of statements

to events and the subsequent consequences for his own
actions, e.g., greetings in contrast with instructions
in contrast with stimuli, etc.

   3.   The child must be able to theorize about or
'see behind' the researcher's statements to their
intent.

   4.   The child must be able to manipulate the
saliency of objects and activities and their labels
to conform to the demands of others.

   5.   The child must be able to distinguish
segments of talk which may have different functions
or intents.

   6.   The child must be able to instance and
embody a specific unit (and with respect to the stimuli,
a sentence) given as an implicit command locating himself in its labeling system and determining his
possible action.

   7.   The child must be able to translate into
consequential activities for himself statements not
directly referring to him; e.g., the girl must be
quiet and stand still if the stimulus is *the boy
jumps high.*

   It is not clear whether, at some level, the
frame abilities are the same as or different from
the abilities under test. Our analytical scheme
formulates the frame abilities as logically prior to
the target abilities being investigated. The researcher's interactional scheme establishes a connection between the frame and target abilities. The
researcher's interactional scheme is important because
through it he works to connect the ideal experimental
design to the real occasioned interchanges of the
experiment. It is this link which permits the researcher to interpret the data collected during the
experimental occasion in terms of the ideal design
and its hypotheses.

Children's Social Skills
   Through the examples above the children have
remained in the background, appearing as the more or

less compliasant objects of the researcher's intended manipulations. We have taken the researcher's perspective in constructing, executing, and managing the experimental reality in order to understand what is required of the child to participate. At no time did the researcher begin the entire sequence of phase functions again. Instead, she corrected those aspects of the experimental frame she imagined proved troublesome for the children. These corrections indicate her assumption that the children can see the links between her talk and her behavior. Failure in a particular instance does not undermine the presumption of such a skill in another instance, even if that very skill must be employed by the child if he is to comprehend the correction. The discussion might be summarized by saying that we have been looking for a way to distinguish error from creative participation.

Even in the constrained circumstances of the experiment, the participants have to be ready for 'troubles' — accidents, interruptions, inattention, mistakes — everything which enters our interchanges with each other at other times. Now we turn to an examination of the children's behavior during the experiment to see as directly as possible how they work at the game.

The children do not always act out the sentence read. They have more than one response mode to choose from, and the experiment has not constrained their choice of response completely.

Donald and Susan

Syb: THE BOY HUGS THE GIRL
Donald: *I don't want to do that.*
Syb: *Ok.*

Gordo and Vivian

Syb: THE BOY HANDS THE GIRL THE SPOON
Gordo: *Where's the spoon?*

279

Syb: *Have to look for it. Do you see it?*
Gordo: *Yeah.*
Vivian: *Right there.*
Syb: *He sees it. Good.*

The child's refusal to respond or his delay in responding throws the burden of the interaction back on the researcher. In this sense, a refusal can be seen as an instance of manipulation. Refusals elicit more information and time from the adult. In the example from the session with Gordo and Vivian above, we are tempted to see that each participant knows that knowledge is distributed unevenly among the participants. Vivian aids Gordo by teaming up with him to solve the problem of responding to the sentence. The researcher also gets caught up in this joint enterprise of helping Gordo find the spoon so that he can hand it to Vivian.

In addition to attending to the stimulus sentence and the behavior of partner and researcher, the children also seem to monitor their own behavior in relation to the stimulus items and the behavior of the other participants. In the example of the chalk breaking discussed in an earlier section, Gordo comments about Vivian's failure to catch the box he has thrown. He shows that he accurately observes what happens, that he knows how to describe what happens in words, and that he knows when and if he can relate his description.

In the example which follows the monitoring is extended to the researcher's performance. Gordo checks the researcher's reading of the item. This follows the preceding excerpt about 'the spoon'.

Gordo and Vivian

Syb: *He sees it. Good.*
Gordo: *I thought you said, 'the sponge'.*
Syb: *'The sponge', (laughter). No. Ok, I'll try to say it more clearly.*

280

Whether Gordo was embarrassed by the team effort it took to locate the spoon and is, therefore, explaining his troubles in understanding which item the researcher had intended or not, he shows that he is putting the action of the others together in relation to his own. He is actively involved in constructing the experimental occasion.

The peak of such monitoring was reached in the following interchange.

Gordo and Vivian

Syb: THE GIRL HANDS THE PENCIL TO THE BOY
Gordo: *We've done these (things) (?) already.*
Syb: *You've done them already? Yeah, you have done some of them more than once.*

Gordo's attending pays off in his historical linking of actions across the experimental occasion. He uses what information he can gain to make the occasion sensible, and to direct it in ways of interest to himself. The excerpt continues.

Gordo and Vivian

Syb: THE BOY GIVES THE GIRL THE TRUCK
        Is that a different one?
Gordo: *(What about the)(?) basket?*

The researcher tries to respond to Gordo's observation asking him to check *"the truck"* against the sentences he has heard. It takes a bit longer for her to substitute Gordo's suggestion of *"the basket"* for whatever was written on the stimulus card.

Gordo and Vivian

Syb: *Oh, I don't know.*
        TO THE GIRL IS TOSSED THE BOAT BY THE BOY
        The basket? Oh, I'm sorry.

281

Gordo is persistent. He points out the basket once again. On the penultimate stimulus presentation, the researcher makes the substitution,

Gordo and Vivian

Syb: THE BASKET IS GIVEN TO THE BOY BY THE GIRL

thus complying with Gordo's firm suggestion.

Our interpretations of the children's expressions rest on the belief that they are actively engaged in organizing the experimental scene and that their activities extend beyond (both forward and backward) any stimulus episode. It would seem that this assumption is implicit in establishing the frame and giving instructions and/or training prior to the actual trials. The activities prompted initially are to remain in effect across the entire session.

But even though the examples suggest that the children are constructing and modeling their own behavior and the occasioned requirements, we have the sense that the past being consulted is not the entire sequence of the session. The child pieces together his action like a sequence of one-trial generalizations.

Experiments, as we have seen, suppress the subject's expression of what he observes and how he might reason in the setting in ways other than those prescribed by the researcher. This is one reason why it is so difficult to catch a glimpse of the subject. Experiments constrain the subject's responses in specified and pre-organized ways. In our experiment the children were supposed to move. We might use the children's movement responses to illustrate their reasoning, but first we would have to translate these responses into words, and they would be our words, not the children's. Talk remains the pre-eminent medium for displaying and conveying knowledge. We wondered what might happen if we allowed the child to move and talk for himself. The examples above suggest that the subjects are continually rasoning along within the experimental occasion. However, their reasoning is only occasionally visible due to our constraints.

In subsequent work, we videorecorded a pilot study session we conducted with a child four and one-half years of age. We recorded the session in the familiar surroundings of our home. The child was not at all hesitant to speak, and the session, which lasted about three hours with lunch and play in-between, was improvised on planned tasks and materials.

We were interested in the child's responses to some tasks we had developed to investigate the pictorial representation of action sequences and their verbal description. Only parts of the session had been pre-planned, thus the tasks were not presented within a strict experimental frame. We had worked with the child on other occasions across a two year period, and she was familiar with some of the procedures, materials, and the camera equipment.

In the interchange presented below, which occurred at the end of the session, Cass was asked to describe a set of seven cards. The cards, reproduced in Figure 6.3, were black ink drawings on 2½ in. poster-board squares. They were spread out in a line in front of Cass and Syb on a 20 × 25 in. masonite board. The cards are described in six separate *askings and tellings*. These askings and tellings constitute the interchange. We will present the descriptions in the order in which they occurred although we have inserted analysis and discussion of the materials in-between as a guide to the reader.

FIGURE 6.3.   The Set of Cards

The first description occurred in the following way:

I.

Syb: *Ok, let's look at this last one.*
Cass: *They have all cars, right?*
Syb: *Yeah. You can start here and tell me what this story is. (Syb points to Card 1 in Figure 6.3, the first card on the left in the single row of seven cards.)*
Cass: *(Cass points to Card 1) First the girl has — Once upon a time there was a girl who had a car. His brother gave it to her. (Cass points to the second picture in the sequence, Card 2), and then the sister gave it to the brother and then (Cass points to Card 3), and then the brother gave it to the sister?*

Cass seems to be using the cards to evoke and document her story. Her telling should alert us to the contrast between the set of cards which, read as a sequence, produces a single action; i.e., viewed from Card 1 to Card 7, the car is transferred from the girl to the boy, and the set of cards which, read individually, produce tellings about the beginning or the ending of a transaction which itself is not shown, (except for Card 4); e.g., Card 2 can show 'The sister will give the car to the brother' or 'The brother gave the car to the sister'.

We might wonder how Cass interprets Syb's *"start here"* accompanied by Syb's pointing to the first card on the left. Is this taken as an instruction to point to the card Syb is pointing to, to look at that card, or to talk about that card? *"Telling a story"* is as ambiguous. We note in Cass' speech, connectives like *"and"* and *"and then."* She also uses *"first"* and *"once upon a time."* She produces present and past tense forms. These features in adult speech signal things like sequences and stories, but we must be wary of what they indicate in the child's talk.

Cass' use of the language connectors seems to have had its taken-for-granted effect on Syb. Syb credits Cass with telling stories. Syb's suggestion of giving the figures names seems to be directed to focusing Cass' attention on the picture set as one story about David, Michelle, and the car.

Within the negotiation of the naming which follows there is an interesting occurrence. Syb does not try to correct Cass' statement that her brother, Eric, calls himself *"Davin."* But she normalizes Cass' pronunciation to "David."

II.

Syb: *Why don't you make them be the same people in every picture? Who will we call him? Max? (Syb points to the figure of the boy in Card 1.)*

Cass: *No, Davi (n).*

Syb: *David?*

Cass: *That's what my brother's name is. He say Davi (n).*

Syb: *Instead of Eric. (Cass' brother is named Eric.)*

Cass: *Yeah.*

Syb: *Ok. And what's this girl gonna be? (Syb points to the figure of the girl in Card 1.)*

Cass: *Um.*

Syb: *What's her name gonna be? David and (intonational slot)?*

Cass: *David and Michelle.*

Syb: *Michelle. (Later we learned from Cass' mother that Michelle [sometimes pronounced /nasel/] was the name of a girl in the neighborhood whom Cass admired.) Ok, here's David and here's Michelle and they're in every single picture, and I want you to tell me what happens to the car.*

"You can start here and tell me what this story is"

has been transformed to the seemingly more explicit
instruction above. But the instruction is still unclear. Is Cass to include each picture in describing
a single action or is she to treat each picture as a
separate occurrence? Focusing on the names of the
figures may have cost far more than it was worth in
that the individuality of the cards has been emphasized. It is as likely, given Cass' next remarks,
that the instruction made little difference.

Cass: *Ok. Whenever... when (she points as indicated*
       by the arrow in Card 2, Figure 6.3).
Syb: *Start here. (Syb points over Cass' pointing*
       to Card 1.)
Cass: *Ok, and then I'll tell you something after*
       this.
Syb: *Ok.*

Across the session Cass and Syb took turns performing the various tasks. Syb would ask Cass to do
something, then it would be Cass' turn to ask Syb something or to try out on Syb the particular task which
she had just been given. Cass captured this aspect
of the session when she told us on the way home *"you*
were teacherin' me and I was teacherin' you." The
child operates in the adult structure of conversational
sequencing (Sacks, forthcoming), and the researcher
relies on the child's knowledge of that structure to
establish and maintain the presentational sequence of
the task frame.

Cass' remark functions both as a response to
Syb's direction and as an interruption. Syb may not
have noticed the interruption and simply feared that
Cass was going to start telling the story at the second
rather than the first card. In that case, *"start*
here" is directed more to Cass' action than to her
words.

Cass than expands her interruption, and in this
she displays expertise in the occasional structure
which she and Syb have been using — Syb asks Cass;
Cass asks Syb. The words of the exchange are un-
remarkable, yet they point to the nearly mechanical

way in which our structures of exchange compel us to
listen to each other (see, in addition to Sacks, forthcoming, the use of the notion of "exchange" by Piaget
and Inhelder, 1969 and Bruner, 1968, and the employ-
ment of question/answer sequences by Brown, 1968).
Cass has as much control of this conversational sequencing as the adult, no matter her understanding
of sequence on the level of pictorial representation
and verbal description of an abstractly depicted exchange.

Cass' maneuvering of *her* telling is even more
impressive. Following Syb's *"Ok,"* Cass runs through
the cards left to right, pointing to the card indicated in brackets at the end of each statement.

III.

Cass: *Then Michelle had this*   [1]
And she gave it to the brother   [2]
And she gave it to the brother   [3]
The brother gave it to the sister [3]
But they both were, they both were
they were saying 'gimme, gimme,
gimme'.   [4]
And then the boy got it   [5]
And then the boy got it   [6]
And still the boy got it   [7]

Again we might point out in passing that it is
far from clear that Cass is responding to the cards
read as a sequence. Rather she seems to describe
each card individually; she describes a single card
twice and later, as we will see, she omits a card.
She has not given up *"brother"* for *"David(n),"* but
then we might imagine they are both names for brother
Eric so easily substitutable.

Having answered Syb's request, Cass claims her
turn:

IV.

Cass: *But I'll tell you the way that it could go.*

288

Syb: *Ok.*

Cass: *See, what about whenever you see that (Cass points as indicated by the arrow on Card 2, Figure 6.3), we'll put it out. We'll take 'em out when you see those little lines (Cass points to Card 3) through. We'll take 'em out and put it up there. Like this, see, there's a line, put it up there. (Cass removes Card 2 from the row of seven cards and places it above the row on the masonite surface.)*

And there's not giving it so put that there (Cass slides Card 1 into the space which Card 2 had occupied).

And there's a line, put it up (Cass places Card 3 above the row of cards and next to Card 2). Move that there (Cass slides Card 1 over from position two to fill the space left by Card 3).

And there's no line there, so we'll still ...(utterance not distinguishable) (Cass leaves Card 4 in place).

And a little teensy line, put it up there (Cass moves Card 5 out of line and above).

And then a line there, put it up there (Cass moves Card 6 out of line).

And no (unclear), and a sorta big line there, (Cass places Card 7 above).

See and those a only two (Cass pats Cards 1 and 4) that don't have any lines.

Our task required that the child have more than one way of viewing the set of pictures. We were concerned that the child was able to distinguish the

pictures visually, and we checked Cass' differentiations
by a match-to-sample procedure.[4] But we did not
expect, nor were we prepared for, this particular
viewing of the set of cards.

   At least to some extent, Cass seemed to join
in our presumdd ways of viewing. We recognized that
she was offering a different viewing here, but we
had no way of understanding it because we simply had
not planned for it ahead of time. Our attitude de-
pended on our setting and delimiting the probable set
of viewings, and when Cass offered us one that was
not in that set, one we had not even dreamed was a
possibility, we had no way of telling what was going
on.

Syb: *I don't see the lines, Cassie.*
Cass: *I'll show you. (Cass picks up Card 5 and
       holds it for Syb to see.) See, the lines
       that go through there.*

[Ken now enters from his position behind the camera.]

Syb: *(to Ken) I don't see any lines. (Ken picks
      up Card 5 which Cass has just put down. Cass
      picks up Card 3.)*
Cass: *They go through there. See. It's between.
       See, they're open spaces, see. (Cass is
       demonstrating with Card 3.) (Syb picks up
       Card 7; Ken puts down Card 5; Cass puts down
       Card 3.) That's not open spaces [We cannot
       tell if Cass is or is not referring to Card
       7 which Syb is holding.]*

---

[4]On the match-to-sample procedure, Cass
failed to correctly distinguish Cards 2 and 3. Although she correctly distinguished Cards 5 and 6,
as she chose the matching card, she said that both
pictures were *"giving."* This raises further questions
about the influence of her verbal descriptions on her
visual discriminations.

We didn't understand, but we understood far
less than we thought at the time. First, Syb couldn't
get a reading for *"line."* Her set is obvious — there
was no line where Cass was pointing; the lines were
the figures in black ink. Note, that Cass was able
to find other words, words that we adults might better
understand, to explain what it was she saw. We cannot help but recognize her talent for our game.
She will help us; she will explain; she will show us.
At the deepest levels our adult abilities are what
the child is developing, and Cass seems the most
diligent of understudies.

The difference between *"lines"* and *"open spaces"*
is greater than the difference mentioned earlier between *"stone"* and *"rock."* Ken quickly applies the
transformation from 'lines between' to 'open spaces
between the figures, and sets out to check his
interpretation:

Ken: *Ok. (Ken points to Card 4), does this, this*
doesn't have any open spaces, does it?
Cass: *Unuh (She shakes her head negatively).*
Ken: *Does this (Ken points to Card 1) have any?*
Cass: *No.*

Syb, who has finally reached the interpretation of
open spaces between the figures, is again confused.
Ken accepts Cass' statement, and proceeds.

Syb: *It doesn't?*
Ken: *Oh, Ok, but this does (He refers to Card 3.*
Cards 2 and 4 are all that remain of the
original row, the rest are scattered above
that row)?
Cass: *Uh huh (She nods affirmatively), there's*
open spaces there.
Ken: *And what about this? (Ken now points to*
Card 2 for Cass to judge. The reader can
imagine the picture recorded by the un-
manned camera.)

291

Cass: *Open spaces.*
Ken: *And this (He points to Card 5)?*
Cass: *Open spaces.*
Ken: *What about this (He points to Card 7)?*
Cass: *No, that not.*

Here we encounter another level of our failure to understand. Our best guess (hindsight, etc.) is that *"lines"* and *"open spaces"* did not refer simply to the white space between the figures. In Cass' telling of the *"lines,"* she separated Cards 1 and 4 from the rest. Card 4 remained *("there's no line there")* and Card 1 remained *("and there's not giving it")*. We have only Cass' syntax to go on, a fragile clue at best, but her judgment of Card 7 seems to be made on grounds other than white space between the figures. *"That not"* recalls her earlier description of Card 1 *("there's not giving it")*. Minimally, there is a disparity between her original judgment that Card 7 has *"a sorta big line there"* and the judgment given here *"that not."*

Ken proceeds, normalizing her statement to *"that doesn't."*

Ken: *No, that doesn't (Ken slides Card 7 down to the row with Card 1 and Card 4). What about this (He points to Card 6)?*
Cass: *Un uh, no, that doesn't have any. (Cass places Card 6 in the row with Cards 1, 4, and 7.)*

(Ken then takes Card 6 out of the row, sliding it back up with Cards 2, 3, and 5.)
Ken: *Well now, can you tell me, can you tell me what these are (Ken is pointing to Card 6 as he moves Cards 5 and 6 next to Cards 2 and 3)?*
Cass: *The lines, well, see (Cass points to Card 6) there's lines that go through there, through there (Cass points to Card 5), and through there, that's between (Cass points to Card 2). (Cass, as she points, traces 'the line' with*

292

her finger.)

Our interpretation of *"open spaces"* prevails and absorbs Cass', whatever hers was or could become.

Ken: *Ok, but can we do 'between' here? (Ken refers to Card 7 in the original row.)*

Cass: *Yeah.*

Ken: *Well, then, this one goes up here (Ken places Card 7 above). Can we do 'between' here (Ken points to Card 1)?*

Cass: *Yeah. (Ken places Card 1 above.)*

Ken: *Ok, can we do 'between' here (Ken points to Card 4)?*

Cass: *No.*

Ken: *Ok. Ok, (to Syb) it doesn't make any difference. (Card 4 stands alone in the original row.)*

With the problem raised by Cass' *"lines"* negotiated and *'solved'*, Ken returns to the camera and Syb to the planned viewings after some further interchange about the cards.

V.

Syb: *Now, Cassie, let's start from the beginning, and I want you to tell me the story of what happens to the car. (Syb, as she talks, arranges the cards left to right in a row, but this time from Card 7 to Card 1.)*

Cass: *Well.*

Syb: *Start here (Syb points to Card 7, the first card on the left).*

Cass: *David has the car (Cass slides Card 7, first in order beginning from the left, out of line).*

Syb: *Ok.*

Cass: *Davin giving it to Michelle (Cass points to Card 6, second in order from left to right.)*

Syb: *Ok.*

Cass: *And Michelle gots it right here (Cass slides*

Card 4 out of the row, having by-passed Card 5).
And then (Cass points to Card 3) Michelle's giving it to Davin.
But (Cass looks ahead to Card 2), no one (?) Davin didn't get it, so (Cass picks up Card 1 and slides it out of line), Michelle gots the car.

VI.

Syb: *Ok, Ok, now, start at this si- end, Cassie (Syb puts the cards back in one row Card 7 on the left, Card 1 on the right). Start over here (Syb points to Card 1 at the right end). Now tell me what happens to the car.*

Cass: *That Michelle gots it. Michelle gots it. And Michelle's holding it, but it a little sharp 'cause she's holding it like this (Cass gestures to show that the car is being held away from the body, see Card 2).*

Syb: *Oh, away from her (commenting on Cass' gesture). There? Oh. Then what happens?*

Cass: *Then she (pause) got (pause) she gots the car (Cass is referring to Card 2, second in order from the right) and then (she refers to Card 3, third in order from the right) Davin and Davin gets in it, but (Cass points to Card 4), then they both got it and (Cass picks up Card 5), Davin gots it now and (Cass puts down Card 5 and picks up Card 6) Davin gots still gots it (Cass puts down Card 6) and (Cass picks up Card 7, the first card on the left) Davin gots it at the beginning.*

Cass' descriptions seem clear. Yet, after reviewing them, we are not at all sure how to coordinate the verbal features of the description with her responses indicating her understanding of the visual features. It seems that what we can see as a single event pictured by

seven cards does not match Cass' conception. (See
the contrast between the adult's meaning and the
child's meaning discussed throughout this volume.)
And we are thrown back once more on the need to
isolate and examine even more systematically the
multiple interpretations which are possible.

SOME CONSEQUENCES FOR TESTING

Researchers, including ourselves, turn to
experimentation in the first place as a means for
discovering what the child knows because they
believe the child's abilities lead him to assemble
events differently from them. By analyzing a situation
according to some theoretical scheme, we can dis-
assemble the event and re-assemble it systematically
piece by piece for ourselves and the child. We try
to incorporate the extensions we think the child
requires so that his version of the event will be more
nearly like our own. We try to make it clearer, to
recode it in ways closer to the child's language, to
focus the child's attention, to aid his memory, to
make up for limited motor control in his responses,
and to simplify and direct courses of action so that
the child does not have to coordinate his activities
or direct them on his own, etc.

But our re-assembly of the event, no matter
our care in rational analysis and procedural design,
will still be insufficient. It will require the
child to reach out for and manipulate as he can the
information we can offer. Our re-assembly counts on
the child's spontaneous entrance into and action
during the event; i.e., 'What does this look like to
you'? And we have no simple and explicit way to turn
off the child's spontaneous generation of action and
thought.

In this we rely on method. But we cannot tell
the child, as we can the adult, the grounds for
responding and assume that, once told, the child, like
the adult, will limit his action, molding it to the
experimental conditions. Any attempt on our part to
manipulate the activity the child subject produces

may lead him to revise his actions in ways that outstrip our methods and their implicit assumptions.

Experimentation is a formal and complex technique for gaining knowledge. The simplicity and clarity of its reported outcomes are attained by a lengthy chain of inferences from adult activities to the child's skills. The child's expression, be it action or words, has to be suppressed and manipulated because it is beyond the grasp of our conscious reasoning. We engage in experimentation in order to bring the child's expression within our explicit understanding and reflection. This does not remove the complexities, it only redistributes them.

In a different context, Holt (1967) speaks to similar difficulties by pointing out some limitations on practical approaches to understanding what the child knows.

> Now, if it were possible for us to look into the minds of children and see what gaps in their mental models most needed filling, a good case could be made for giving them the information needed to fill them. But this is not possible. We cannot find out what children's mental models are like, where they are distorted, where incomplete. We cannot make direct contact with a child's understanding of the world. Why not? First, because to a very considerable extent he is unaware of his own understanding. Secondly, because he hasn't the skill to put his understanding into words, least of all words that he could be sure would mean to us what they mean to him. Thirdly, because we haven't time. Words are not only clumsy; they are extraordinarily slow (Holt, 1967:188).

In experiments we try to take on the burden of the time it takes to know the child. That time is measured in interactional exchanges; it is social time. In our techniques we work to make up for the

ambiguities of our symbol system. By explicit reflection on our techniques and questions we try to
bring our ignorance and understanding of what the
child knows under our control. As Holt says, our
contact with the child's "understanding of the world"
is not direct. Yet that indirectness itself aids our
knowledge of the differences between adults and
children.

In our discussion of experimentation, we have
been juggling contrasting views of the child: those
implicit in the formal hypothesis and comprehension
paradigm used to investigate the child's linguistic
skills, those implicit in the researcher's interactional
scheme, its execution and management, and those which
we can see in observing the children's behavior. These
views have lead us to distinguish two kinds of ability:
target abilities and frame abilities (cf. Figure 6.2),
Both these abilities would be required to model the
behavior of the children we observed during the experimental occasion and Cass' behavior in the pilot
study session. We presume that tests, like experiments,
provide such views of the child and his abilities.

Our analysis has shown that at each conceptual
and actional level of experimentation (cf. Figure 6.2).
there is an implicit image of the child to which
abilities or characterizations are assigned. These
images may not coincide across the levels of con-
ceptualization and action. Our separation of target
and frame abilities may seem arbitrary, especially
given the presuppositional style of analysis. However, these ability types are artifacts which result
from accepting the functional breakdown of experimentation as a viable and adequate characterization
of the actual experimental enterprise. We have shown
in our own work that, at every level, theoretical and
methodological presuppositions are inter-mixed. This
mixing, despite our attempts at distinction, seriously
qualifies the claims any technique can support. From
our perspective, an adequate social theory of methods,
including the use of specially constructed occasions
such as experiments and tests, cannot be based on the

conceptual or real separation of functions.

Yet conceptually within experimentation and both conceptually and actually within testing, the functions of theory, method, procedure, execution, and interpretation are separated and treated serially. The outcomes of experiments and tests are reported as inferences from the subject's behavior as a function of some subset of these divisions, e.g., per cent of error as a function of training. Even a strict operationism omits the behavioral interchange which occurs between subject and researcher in the experimental or testing occasion. Our analysis of the researcher's interactional scheme, his patchwork, and the child's active contribution, even beyond our attributions, force the recognition of the significance of the experiment as a social occasion.

As researchers we are responsible for all aspects of our study (hypothesis, method, procedure, execution, interaction, observation, analysis, interpretation, and report). Our awareness of the incompleteness of our model of experimentation arises from our attempts to integrate these views of the child's abilities and our formal techniques for providing evidence. Ideally, all of the normative demands and accountability fall to the investigator. By engaging in experimentation, we can follow the transformation of a question into a design and, through a procedure, into action. As a social practice, this characterizes how experimentation works.

This is not the case with testing as it is practiced in the schools. There, the conceptual structure of testing is organizationally reified. The design functions are separated and distributed across different people. The test constructor is responsible for theory, but is not involved in the interpretation of individual performances. The test administrator is less responsible for the theory behind the particular items than he is for the interpretation of an individual's performance on the test. Judgments made about children's abilities based on their performances on tests proceed as though the divisions of function were clear, each producing a similar image of the child and his abilities. But these images are not necessarily the same, and none of these images shows the child as a participant in an interactional occasion. And since no one researcher is responsible for the diverse functions of the testing enterprise, *he* cannot even rely on his commonsense reasoning to integrate the various images of the child which obtain at these levels.

Testing is social in two ways: First, it is an occasion of interaction between the tester and the child. Second, it is an interaction between the tester and the other persons involved in the ramified division of labor in the testing enterprise. The tester must manage the potentially diverse images of the child implicit in the contributions of his collaborators, and he must integrate them with the image of the child which emerges from his direct interaction with the subject. Subsequently, the tester must communicate these integrated images to the teacher who is responsible for implementing an instructional program influenced by them.

The separation of the conceptual and social functions of testing promotes a fragmented picture of the child and his abilities. The fragments of this picture have to be pieced back together by the teacher, but the teacher doesn't have access to the grounds on which these fragments were produced in the first place. Unless the functions of testing are reincorporated into an enterprise of understanding which includes the teacher, testing will remain in its bureaucratically empty objectivity.

299

Chapter 7
SOME BASIC THEORETICAL ISSUES IN
THE ASSESSMENT OF THE CHILD'S PERFORMANCE IN
TESTING AND CLASSROOM SETTINGS

Aaron V. Cicourel[1]
University of California, San Diego

Our academic claims to knowledge about the
child's performance under testing and classroom conditions seldom include insightful reports of teachers
who have written about their experiences (e.g. Holt,
1964; Kohl, 1967; Kozol, 1967). Instead, we usually
rely on more formal discussions by educational psychologists who depend on the development and administration of a variety of tests to support their
claims about the child's abilities. There tends to
be a controversial discrepancy between what the
teachers-as-indirect-researchers of their own settings
tell us, and what we read about the child's performance
on tests given under presumedly controlled conditions.
    A central problem in education is the failure to
compare information provided by the test with the information provided by the child's behavior in the
classroom. The omission of this comparison is dependent upon our definition of the term 'information'.
Teachers and testers are usually talking about different
aspects and contexts of the child's performance. In
each case the language used by the teacher and tester
points to information about the child not directly
available to the reader. And, depending on the
educational audience, the reader is expected to imagine
or reconstruct 'typical' classroom or testing settings
to understand what is being said. In this chapter, I

    [1]I wish to thank Courtney Cazden, Sybillyn
Jennings, Hugh Mehan and Martha Ramos for their very
helpful comments and suggestions.

want to raise some theoretical and practical issues
about classroom and testing settings by linking these
issues to the teacher and tester's unfamiliarity with
some recent developments in the study of cognitive
processes. The theoretical framework is based on the
notion of interactional competence. The notion of
interactional competence implies the idea of social
and psychological cognitive processes or interpretive
abilities.

INTERPRETIVE ABILITIES

The acquisition of interpretive abilities enables
a member to create cultural and normative sense in
on-going settings and to make judgments about the meaning of information, thus helping him to decide what is
'normal', 'bizarre', 'threatening', 'humorous', etc.
The child's acquisition of language and cognitive
processes is central for gradually comprehending adult
conceptions of social norms. Sociologists often fail
to specify what cognitive processes and language use
are necessary for producing and understanding normative
behavior. How adults understand norms or rules, e.g.,
a rule of law, is not clear in the sociological
literature. Normative rules are like prescriptive
and proscriptive recipes for deciding what is socially
acceptable and unacceptable behavior. How children
acquire this ability to articulate an experienced
social setting with his or her understanding and
memory of abstract rules or norms is even less clear.
The child's ability to deal with everyday social
organization as a system of norms or rules presupposes
a language system, and language in turn presupposes
cognitive processes integral to the development of a
sense of social structure (Cicourel, 1973). Social
and psychological cognitive processes must be acquired
to articulate immediate experiences with normative
rules governing formal language use, legal codes,
implicit social activities like rules of etiquette,
games, and kinship relationships.

A central problem in the education of children
is that we know little about the child's acquisition

of social and psychological cognitive processes and
often attribute adult social competence to him while
evaluating his intellectual growth. It is difficult
to specify what we assume to be the child's known
and 'obvious' social knowledge. For example, we
often assume a child understands the difference between what is animate and inanimate when he is playing
with toys and infants. As another example, when telling a child to be careful when crossing the street,
we assume he or she can link a general rule about
looking both ways with the immediate setting where
delicate judgments about the velocity of moving
vehicles and the child's ability to run 'fast' are
problematic. We are often forced to presume the
child has interpretive abilities which enable him to
comprehend instructions about a routine task or intellectual activity despite our ignorance of his information processing capabilities. We need independent
research on the child's acquisition of social and
psychological cognitive processes at different stages
of development to understand how we are to construct
and monitor our teaching and evaluative techniques.
The following brief discussion of these cognitive
processes outlines the cognitive resources the child
must acquire for converting information from the
setting and from his memory into instructions on how
to generate socially acceptable behavior and accounts.
I begin by describing four broad aspects of social
cognitive processes that are part of normal communication between two or more native participants in
routine social interaction.

    1. In two or multi-party communication within
a physical space permitting face-to-face contact,
participants must assume that they share the same
social setting and are receiving the same information
available to all, regardless of their own personal
or cultural background and regardless of how they are
spatially distributed. If a standardized native
orientation to the setting and to the language employed
is assumed by all participants, then various appearances
and utterances must be treated as 'obvious' despite a

recognition that differences exist and are being communicated in subtle ways. The central point is that the participants view the scene as containing intelligible and recognizable features they know in common and can take for granted as essentially the 'same' (see Cicourel, 1973 for further elaboration and references). Children must acquire the ability to receive, recognize, and then process information in socially acceptable ways so that emergent activities can be handled routinely and meaningful cultural responses can be produced. Participants cannot continually call into question each other's appearances or motives, nor can they insist on the clarification of all terms employed.

I am not addressing but would include the normative constraints of who speaks first, or what topics are considered socially acceptable, or how the exchange is terminated. The basic issue here is that the participants must assume they are oriented to the 'same' environment of objects despite cultural differences and despite their ability to use a particular dialect or standardized language. If participants cannot make the assumption that they are exposed to the same environment of objects, then their interaction will be difficult at best, and different or 'odd' subroutines may emerge for sustaining or terminating the exchange. For present purposes, this means that when the teacher or tester makes this reciprocity assumption a basis for evaluating the child's performance, a serious constraint is placed on the child. But the teacher or tester's evaluation of the child's performance does not usually include an examination of the constraints of the setting as possibly experienced by the child. The child may view the task or language used as strange yet provide a response the adult interprets as fitting the framework of the test or lesson.

2. In particular social settings, normal forms of appearance, language use or behavior are constructed by the actor. The participants expect that each possesses a *"normal"* (taken for granted) repertoire

of possible appearances, behaviors and utterances
that can be contextually organized. The actor's
ability to normalize cultural or normative discrepancies is essential for creating classes of objects and events to sustain social interaction and
thus provides him with instructions for unwittingly
or deliberately evaluating the setting.

Does the teacher and tester presume that the
task being given the child is 'obvious'? If we have
reason to believe that the child's perspective con-
verts the information available into instructions and
knowledge that are not consonant with the teacher's
conception of the activity, then the constraints perceived by the child become central for assessing the
child's performance. This is especially a problem
because the verbal information used by the teacher
does not displace the same or similar visual, acoustical
and memory information the child is able to imagine or
recall when he hears the verbal forms used by the
teacher. For example, Mehan's (1971) work on testing
revealed how the tester's adult conception of "things
that can fly" was different from the child's conception. The child recognized that birds can fly,
but also felt that Walt Disney's "Dumbo" the elephant
could "fly." Hence, adults' and children's normal
forms cannot be equated and treated as obvious displays of the *"same"* social reality.

3. The child must possess the ability to go
beyond the information given and recognize that general
appearances, movements, utterances and gestures imply
additional meanings. The child makes use of truncated
utterances to force an organization on various perceived fragments as in figure-ground experiments. The
central feature here is the ability to fill in appropriate information where contextually relevant, linking
present informational resources to prior experience,
while projecting the consequences of present attributions of meaning into a future state. For example,
within a particular lesson the teacher presumes the
children can link her urging them to "tell me where
it is," to an earlier part of the lesson where the

location of objects was demonstrated visually, even though no mention was made previously or presently that what she wants is for them to create descriptive sentences about the location of the objects. The child must learn to fill in information from existing wholes or fragments, and then retrospectively and prospectively to link the information to past and possible future objects or events. This ability is necessary if the child is to link idealized normative rules about language and social meanings with contextually bound settings and information and then render these settings and information socially acceptable and meaningful. The hallmark of normal social competence is the reflexive linking of selectively attended information to what is stored in memory so that the socially emerging context can be handled routinely. Understanding the child's ability to use these interpretive abilities at different stages of development is essential if the information presented by teacher or tester is to be commensurate with the child's competence.

4. The previous three properties are necessary if the child is to articulate present, past, and future settings that are experienced or imagined with more general cultural or normative rules or conceptions. Interactional settings always generate emergent features that require subtle negotiation with tacit normative rules. Tacit normative rules deal with what the participants must decide are socially acceptable displays of language use, posture, physical distance, emotion, etiquette, wrong-doing, and the like. These tacit rules are organized by more idealized and often explicit legal, linguistic, bureaucratic or tribal rules. Many of the displays the participants must attend to are visible but are not easily linked to more idealized rules because their relevance for the social setting remains tacit features of the scene (Cf: Goffman, 1959). The actor's ability to create an articulation between idealized rules and particular information from an immediate setting and to assume that others are creating the 'same' types of articulations (as others are

305

presumed to be assuming of the actor), is central to
the idea of interactional competence and performance.
That tacitly acknowledged understandings can be transferred nonverbally is especially important for any
interpretation of children's behavior. The possession
of interactional competence (and hence some level of
pre-adult cognitive processes) by the child can be independent of his ability to use standardized language.
Our evaluation of the child's intellectual competence
and educational performance should not be tied to an
adult's conception of how these abilities should be
expressed, but linked to the child's psychological
and sociological cognitive processes.

LANGUAGE COMPETENCE

In designing our research we sought a development approach that would reveal the kinds of speaking
and listening knowledge the child possessed prior to
his school experience, as well as reveal what he or
she was capable of learning in the classroom. We
wanted to underscore the importance of social interactional factors in speaking and listening that are
not usually included in studies of the child's linguistic competence. Our first concern, therefore, was
to devise ways in which we could assess the child's
language competence in this broader sense. Recent
work in developmental psycholinguistics seemed ap-
plicable here because of the claim that the child had
control of his native language early in his life, and
by offering methods whereby the child's knowledge of
his language was presumed accessible. We directed our
attention to how children make sense of some sentence
types (for example, *Yolanda shows Michael the picture;
Max hands a book to Ernie*) that would be considered
'obvious' to a teacher and which developmental psycholinguists would consider central to the child's normal
language acquisition. We reasoned that to understand
classroom and testing language problems we needed
basic knowledge about how children understand language.
We needed to establish a base line with which to compare problems in classroom performance.

306

We utilized a procedure in which pairs of children 'acted out' sentences read to them by an adult. The sentences were in both active and passive voice, with direct and indirect object constructions. This procedure followed earlier work by Sybillyn H. M. Jennings (Jennings, 1968). Modifications of this previous work involved the use of video recording equipment to monitor the children's non-verbal activities while responding to the stimulus sentences. Examples of the sentences used are: *The boy gives the ball to the girl; The ball is given to the girl by the boy.*

Here I wish to point out the theoretical importance of our method for subsequent work in the classroom. The central issue in the acting out study was not merely psycholinguistic: asking children to act out the stimulus sentences given to them verbally, noting if they carried out the expected action, and then making a judgment about their internalization of a grammatical rule. The study had to concern itself with the constraints of the stimulus—response experimental paradigm. We wanted to explore how this kind of format affects both the child's interpretation and reasoning, and how it affects the researcher's inferences about the child's underlying linguistic competence from his performance. As sociolinguists interested in the role of cognitive processes in social interactional settings, we wanted to see if the experimental framework captured, explicated or obscured the socially organized cognitive complexities of the day-to-day interactional scene within which routine testing of children and classroom teaching and evaluation take place.

The acting out procedure was video-taped and contrasts with standard psychological testing because we attempted to study (Jennings, 1972) the child's understanding of our instructions, the setting, and the task. The general format in psychological testing (and opinion or census surveys) is to provide subjects or respondents with a few instructions that are standard introductions to the task that lies ahead. The test (or survey) is then presented in the form of standardized

307

and presumably objective questions like *"point to the thing that can walk in this picture,"* that can be answered by an open (oral remark or pointing gesture) or a closed response like *"circle the thing that is most like what is in the box on the left."* The assumed connection between the stimulus questions and the expected responses are based on prior work with some pretest group that enabled the researcher to claim that his test (or survey questionnaire) has been normalized with respect to some sample of a larger population. The normalizing process is designed to eliminate problems in the test or questionnaire and to insure that 'appropriate' items are included — items that subjects or respondents seem to find answerable and that, when collected, will give some kind of distribution to their aggregated responses.

Once the test is standardized, the child's responses are the basic source of information as to the child's underlying intelligence or knowledge about some subject matter, and provide information about the success of the particular teaching programs the child has experienced, as discussed in Chapter 3.

Little or no attention is given to the respondent's ability to express his reasoning in language that the test or survey presupposes. The instructions themselves and the ability to carry out the test or survey or classroom assignment assume considerable sophistication on the part of the subject or respondent. The t test is designed to evaluate the child's intellectual competence, yet his understanding of the instructions, and his possession of the required language abilities and presumed knowledge about a number of unstated objects and events are not examined.

It is difficult to question the above paradigm or framework despite many advances in our understanding of the child's cognitive growth and language development. The testing situation seems straightforward and clear; it seems to possess a relatively obvious set of procedures for administering the test items, and it also allows for an apparently unequivocal scoring method that is designed to locate easily each student

relative to others. It takes considerable work and
ingenuity to challenge the existing framework of
psychological testing.

Grounds for such a challenge are provided by
our examination of the moment-to-moment interactional
setting which the tester treats as irrelevant in
justifying inferences made from the test. Critics of
tests have not examined the test or the classroom in
terms of the display of abilities across a social
exchange. Instead critics have been led into broad
genetic and environmental issues and arguments. Our
thesis is that the complex interactional competence
required of tester and child to produce and attend
to the test cannot be reduced to nor captured by broad
and often misleading glosses like genetic or environmental influence. We know very little about the everyday reasoning ability of children and adults. We tend
to focus on the products of the thinking processes and
not on the ways in which the cognitive organization of
these processes may embed and display themselves in
social interactional settings. These settings are very
complex largely because they cannot be made to 'stand
still' for us to watch or examine carefully. These
interactional settings are thus difficult to bbjectify
and formalize. The theme of this chapter is that the
investigation of social interactional competence is
crucial and is facilitated by the use of technical
aids like video and audio tapes which extend our observational limitations in studying interactional
settings.

Our study of how children act out stimulus
sentences in active and passive voice with direct and
indirect object constructions was designed to focus
on the interactional features of the activity itself.
How the child decided who was the agent and recipient
of actions was generally pertinent to his understanding
of instructions in testing and classroom settings. The
use of these instructions and related language constructions is also relevant to the stereotypes or
typifications teachers invoke in screening children
for placement into kindergarten trakks or streams

(see Chapter 2).

How language is used in actual social settings and how it conflicts with other sources of information is seldom examined in psycholinguistic research. Whereas educational psychologists employ standardized tests under presumed controlled conditions (see Chapters 3, 4, and 5), and psycholinguists utilize single sentence units as the basis for understanding the child's ability to acquire language, little is said about the child's abilities to receive and produce utterances that are presumably linked to prior communicational exchanges. The role of the child's prior knowledge, and its articulation with a testing situation that produces stimulus conditions that are introduced by design or fortuitously, presumes the ability to impose context-restricted interpretations that can be seen as consistent with previous understandings. Social and psychological cognitive abilities are necessary features of these communicational exchanges, yet the educational psychologist ignores them, and the psycholinguist subsumes these interpretive abilities under the broad label of 'competence'.

The developmental psycholinguist employs a model that revolves around the notion of a bounded sentence defined as a string of lexical items or their presumed equivalents that conform to a subject-verb-object construction. This SVO construction is presumed to be self-contained; rules that can operate on the notion of an auditorially perceived sentence presumably can ignore information that is visual or kinesthetic or somesthetic. Blind adults, for example, seem to use oral language with the same facility as a seeing adult, but their ability to reference objects and events by their speech is not always clear because of the visual information presumed in all talk (Ima, 1971). Thus, although the psycholinguist may employ experimental designs which require responses based on cross-modal information for examining the child's knowledge of language, or make use of the complex home setting in studying the child's language development from approximately 15 months to 36 months, it is the perception

and organization of acoustical information that is
being analyzed. But the researcher's analysis also
relies on normally available nonacoustical information
that remains a tacit resource for subjects and researchers. This tacit use of information from visual
and other sources (including one's ability to interpret
utterance fragments and expand them into meaningful
"chunks" (Miller, 1956) based on cultural knowledge)
while employing a model that is primarily acoustically
based is not examined clearly by the psycholinguist.
Linguistic theory claims that the acoustical signals
are mediated by a formal system of rules said to underlie the acoustical information. But how are we to
explain the rules if sound patterns are organized by
immediate and underlying selective processes in their
reception and are subject to alterations by reflexive
thought? We cannot treat the issue as a simple pattern
recognition problem.

Recent work by Kolers (1972) illustrates the
general issue when he argues that adult subjects create
moving visual illusions from stationary stimuli. He
notes that the illusions cannot be explained by gestalt
principles or rules governing feature analysis extraction. This work suggests how cognitive abilities
are necessary to the interpretation of visual stimulus
conditions that seem to begin with a response to movement and are followed by the creation of recognizable
patterns. Thus the contour of the stimuli is not
primary. The visual system is said to supplement inputs to it through cognitive organization and re-
organization. The child's ability to recognize shapes
and movements considered normal by adults would have
to be understood in this context of definable stimulus
conditions. Thus the child must go beyond the information given to it if he is to create interpretations
that are contingent on the child's cognitive processing
of available socially organized memory storage. The
child's ability to use language to describe visual
appearances is presupposed by an adult's instructions
to the child and the adult's interpretation of a child's
response.

The teacher or tester's decision to expose children to verbal instructions should be based on the child's cognitive processes, his attentiveness to and organization of situated semantic and syntactic information. In teaching children to read it is important to recognize how the materials used can be distorted or altered by the child's attention, memory organization, and ability to express himself verbally. Can the child relate his own knowledge of language to the reading materials?

What is missing from the educational psychologist's model of intelligence is the psycholinguist's conception of the child's linguistic competence and how this competence is presupposed in the assessment of intelligence. But both the educational psychologist and the psycholinguist need a model of how attention and memory are integral to an interpretive ability necessary for learning and carrying out the tasks that comprise tests of intelligence and experiments in language. An understanding of basic theoretical issues and experimental results in attention and memory is helpful for recognizing the central role our study gives to the interactional context within which experiments, tests, classroom instruction, and evaluation take place.

ATTENTION, MEMORY, AND THE INTERACTIONAL SETTING

Psychological tests, traditional learning theory experiments, linguistic tests for grammaticality, questionnaire surveys, and some artificial intelligence programs for natural language all share basic normative elements in their conceptions of language use. In each of the above verbal information is transmitted through the bounded sentence as the basic unit of analysis. In some cases the use of bounded sentences is confined to instructions (psychological tests and learning theory experiments) while truncated sentences are permitted as responses. In other cases the use of bounded sentences by subjects is basic to the evaluation of the model being used, as in the case of recording the child's use of utterances to show a SVO construction in the study of developmental psycholinguistics.

312

Further, subjects or respondents are not explicitly expected nor encouraged to link different
experimental or test materials with prior, immediate
or subsequent items not defined by the stimulus conditions. While stimulus field and reflexive thought
processes making up the experimental setting or interview situation are actually enormously complex informational repositories that are central to an understanding of the experimental item, the presumed interaction is only between stimulus item and vaguely defined 'stored' information. A central assumption of
research using experimental or testing or interview
conditions is that the setting is essentially a
passive or controlled input to the presumed basic
interface between stimulus items and stored knowledge
of rules or general competence.

In this section I want to indicate a few of
the theoretical conceptions and experimental results
that are basic to an understanding of this interface
between stimulus items and stored information. In
the next section I will suggest a few changes in the
traditional, supposedly context-free model. I will
then examine a classroom setting where the teacher
was presenting a fairly routine lesson involving
verbal representations of physical space. A video
tape of the classroom lesson was used to examine
traditional models. Possible modifications of
traditional work will be presented in the next section.

A classical problem in studies of memory and
attention deals with the number of things anyone can
attend to at once. Whereas psychologists have been
preoccupied with this issue for many years, sociologists
interested in the educational process have never
attached any importance to the problem. The sociologist's
concern with social behavior has been more removed from
the actor's everyday experiences. He has usually been
concerned with more global concepts like status and
role, idealized norms, conformity to normative rules,
occupational mobility over generations, etc. The
microcosm of social interaction is seldom linked to
cognitive processes, nor are these events seen as

313

relevant to larger macro-issues like organizational
complexity and function. When we study the activities
of a classroom, it becomes necessary to pinpoint
organizational features of how lessons are presented to
children and evaluated vis-a-vis definitions of school
success. But we also need to examine aspects of the
children's verbal activities, nonverbal movements,
and the cognitive processes inherent in their perception of the teacher's presentation.

A basic issue in attention is the actor's
simultaneous execution of many disconnected conceptual
processes. The problem is presumed to depend on the
difficulty of the tasks involved (Norman, 1969a). If
two children are involved in a private game, it will
not be easy for them to follow the teacher's physical
and verbal activities. The immediate issue is how
limitations on the number of events we can attend
and follow influence our perception and interpretation
of events we do not attend. Deciding what objects
and events subjects are attending is difficult in a
classroom setting, nor is it obvious in experiments
or controlled interview settings. Therefore, examining classroom settings and regular psychological testing situations that have been videotaped are essential
first steps for indicating the problematic nature of
the child's attention.

An important complication of attention involves
switching our perception from one event to another,
for the switching can affect our recognition and
reception of information of the event and create confusion about our judgments of its temporal properties
(Norman, 1969a: 9). Norman suggests that if attention
is due to a serial device, then presumably there should
be difficulty in determining the details of events and
their time sequence when we are not attending them.
Another problem is that often we impose a desired sequence on our experiences and thus alter the time
structure as it occurred. Through our attention we
create temporal ordering and thus a coherent organization
of experience despite independent observation or reasoning that would claim a contradictory ordering which

314

could be demonstrated by independent observers or a
videotape of an event. The experimenter's, the
teacher's or the tester's conception of temporal order
and coherent organization cannot be equated to the
subject's creation of order. Children are particularly
notorious for creating conceptions not intended nor
deemed relevant by the experimenter's model. Norman
(1969a: 10) quotes William James to underscore the
importance of selective attention: "Suffice it mean-
while that each of us literally chooses, by his ways
of attending to things, what sort of a universe he
shall appear to himself to inhabit." The quote from
James has been available to us for some time, but it
is very difficult to change the experimenter's conception that 'objective' data can only be obtained by
using presumedly controlled stimulus conditions.

The sociologist or anthropologist would want
to add another dimension to the quotation from James:
an actor's selective attention to objects and events
is organized by cultural or normative constraints to
perceive, evaluate and account for his experiences.
Our present research traded on these cultural conceptions and also sought to make them problematic in
order to clarify our own dependence on cognitive
processes for creating research categories. The interpretation of a stimulus, or response, or a reward
is not culturally or normatively homogeneous in some
context-free sense, but constrained by the setting
during negotiated interactional exchanges. More
obvious claims could perhaps be made about cross-
cultural interpretations.

The material from James (1890) stresses how we
can make our attention accentuate some sounds or
colors or objects more than others, or how our
'confident expectation' of something enables us to
see or hear it better when it occurs, or how our con-
centration can almost create or make us believe some-
things that we actually imagine. Yet Norman stresses
the point that although we can be convinced that
attention alters the temporal order of our perceptions,
we know little of the mechanism or mechanisms involved

315

in producing such changes. An important factor in
selective attention is how different channels of information are selected or rejected and how they are
to be measured. Hearing and seeing subjects employ
physical, psychological, and social cues to select
and reject channels (Cherry, 1953; Norman, 1969a).
It is very difficult for the subject to describe the
rejected channels, and even the channels we presume
are selected require descriptions in the form of subjects' accounts or experimenter instructions, and
both are biased by the language employed and by the
information the language system presumably indexes.

In the classroom the child is continually exposed to simultaneous messages or information that
may be represented as spoken or written normative
language displays, acoustical paralinguistic signals,
or kinesthetic movements. I am using the term information to subsume sensory signals recognized or
attributed to objects or activities or settings, and
the idea of thought processes that are normatively
and privately organized. We can also imagine tactile
information when the texture of particular objects is
described or employed in a lesson. For example, in
our study, the teacher illustrated the use of preposition that indicate location by the use of sample
sentences spoken to the child and the use of felt
objects that would cling to a blackboard. The child
was to establish a correspondence between the spoken
sentences used by the teacher and the location of the
felt objects above and below a line on the blackboard. The relationship between the sentences and
the location of the felt pieces on the blackboard
could be quite confusing to the child. A further
complication stemmed from the different thoughts the
child could generate based on the interaction between
his memory and incoming information. Even when the
classroom was relatively quiet, the child was continuously exposed to competing sources of information
from the teacher and his classmates. The issue is
not simply what stimulus (or stimuli) was being
directed to the child by the teacher or experimenter

or tester and assumed to be under the adult's control,
but what forms of competence and skills were needed
if the child was to respond to competing sources of
information. The child's attention, memory, and
motivation restrict his ability to recognize, receive,
process and generate information in a particular
setting.

The teacher or tester or experimenter must continually make dubious assumptions about the stimulus
information directed to the subject. During social
interaction it is impossible to sustain inquiries
about the reception of intended stimulus information
because the normative constraints of social exchanges
preclude continually asking the subject to repeat
everything intended by the teacher or tester. Even
when these social constraints are not followed, as
in the case of children whose competence is a problematic feature of the exchange, receiving a response
from the child who states *"yes"* (I did receive your
message) does not guarantee that directed information
was received or processed by the subject as intended
by the researcher or teacher or tester. Real time
does not permit a continual check-out of subjects'
reception of the intended message. By observing the
subjects' response we retrospectively deduce the
reception of our intended message. But this retrospective inference is usually geared to evaluations
of the response under the assumption that the stimulus
was properly received and understood.

Discussions of what the child or adult subject
receives and processes in the way of information prior
to producing a response presume that we know something
about the subject's ability to deal with complex informational settings. The issue is this: what do
we know about the child's capabilities for recognizing,
receiving, processing, and generating information?
Are we often divising lessons, tests, and experiments
whose very implementation presupposes the conditions
we are presuming to study substantively? Thus in
some of the classroom lessons we observed the teacher's
use of language required the child to know about

grammatical constructions the lesson was designed to teach. In the case of children the issue becomes especially difficult because our knowledge of language acquisition is not always carefully articulated with the child's language development and perception of the setting. One recent study (Bloom, 1970) contains important information on the necessity of articulating the child's activities and the activities of others with his or her speech productions. This study represents a minimal but important advance in attempting to reveal how researchers must confront contextual problems in making claims about the acquisition of syntactic structures. The actor's cross-modeling processing and integration of diverse sources of information force us to ask questions about context-free theories of language acquisition and use, and their limitations when as researchers we attempt to assess the role of attention, memory, and motivation in learning situations. We have few studies of child language acquisition and memory to inform us about how information is exchanged and how children process information in classroom settings. We must utilize indirect materials based on child language acquisition and adult studies of memory and attention. This presents an awkward situation but we have little choice if we are to underscore the importance of the classroom as a place to study key problems in the exchange and processing of information.

The central issue, therefore, is how we are to understand how a researcher or teacher or tester claims a relationship between a stimulus item and the response which the adult uses to pass judgment on the child's learning performance or intellectual development. Any use of experimental procedures designed to 'purify' and simplify the stimulus must contend with the complexity of the learning situation faced by the child in the classroom or at home. Studies of language acquisition or syntactic theory and memory and attention (relevant to testing and classroom settings) may be only peripherally connected to normal learning situations in the classroom and at home because the conditions for

318

processing information presented to adult subjects
in the experimental studies may not be realistically
linked to the demands required of the child during
routine learning in complex interactional settings.

Early work by Cherry (1953) reveals the problems
of processing information received from one person
when others are speaking at the same time (called
the "cocktail party problem"). This problem has been
made more precise in studies of "shadowing" a message
and involves repeating a message while simultaneously
receiving other auditory or visual material. When
one message is given to one ear and another message
to the other ear it was found that subjects 'rejected'
one of the messages and could repeat the message
'accepted' without difficulty. The subjects found it
difficult to repeat anything heard by the ear receiving the 'rejected' message. Norman (1969a: 19)
points out that this problem of "shadowing" a message
can be made easy or difficult depending on the material
and how the task is performed according to the instructions given the subject. Thus grammatical material
is easier to process than randomly presented words and
nonsense words. Grammatical constraints provide information that may not be evident from an examination
of the message's content, and so when cliches are used
the task becomes more difficult because grammatical
constraints may not help clarify the content. Norman
notes that shadowing interferes with memory but not
with perception. He reports that when a message is
shadowed it is repeated accurately but when the subject
is asked to remember the content of the material this
proves to be quite difficult. Careful attention must
be given to the shadowed material if it is to be
sustained as a task. Norman (1969b) found that a
temporary memory exists for material we do not attend
but receive, but no long-term memory is developed for
this material.

It should be clear that if adults experience
difficulties shadowing under idealized experimental
conditions then we would expect children to experience
more difficulties. We would expect children to follow

319

the teacher's remarks occasionally, but it is an
empirical question whether children can handle multiple
sources of information directed to them in the classroom and in testing situations. If the child's ability
to process grammatical material is central to his
remembering and understanding the task at hand, and
linking it to previous knowledge, then selective
attention and memory would be especially constrained
if the messages received are not easily processed by
the child because of dialect differences or because
of unfamiliarity with standarized syntactic constructions. The lag between what is received and produced
is central to our understanding of the role of cognitive processes in responding to stimuli presented
by teachers, testers, or experimenters, as is the
interference that arises from other children, or
from general conditions in the classroom or testing
room. We cannot evaluate the child's performance
unless we examine these issues carefully in their
natural settings.

Pick and Pick (1970: 813) suggest that the s
successful accomplishment of different tasks may
require particular focus on certain parts of the
speech stimulus. But we still lack precise material
on which aspect of the input captures the child's
attention and on what we must know to claim that
short-term memory is relevant for performance in the
classroom or testing situations. Does the child's
'focus of attention' as decided by an observer or as
judged by an instrument provide the basis for short-
term memory activation, or is shadowing necessary?

McNeill (1965 as reported in McNeill, 1970)
repeated an experiment by Miller and Isard (1963) in
which the latter authors gave verbal strings to subjects through a masking noise. The strings given to
adults in the Miller and Isard experiment were either
grammatical, anomalous, or scrambled, and the subject
was asked to shadow them as heard. The subject's
problem was to fill in parts of the string as obliterated
by the masking noise. This situation is similar to what
children would be experiencing in a classroom. In the

Miller and Isard experiment the subjects's shadowing was most accurate for grammatical strings, decreased in accuracy for anomalous strings, and was least accurate for scrambled strings. McNeill's experiment repeated the Miller and Isard study with subjects aged 5, 6, 7, and 8 years, but the task deteriorated into an immediate recall procedure because the 5-year-olds took so long to respond when shadowing. The results revealed that 5-year-olds performed considerably poorer with grammatical sentences than 8-year-olds, with 6-year-olds doing only a little better than the 5-year-olds. McNeill notes that accuracy in the experiment depends on how well the guesser can use semantic principles such as knowledge of selection restrictions on dictionary entries — the semantic markers used for locating a word in some context. McNeill gives the example of the term "crane." The selection restrictions for the term "construction" would match a semantic marker for one of the senses of "crane," to then produce "construction crane," but the semantic markers of this last phrase do not match the selection restrictions of the predicate "laid an egg." Hence, McNeill concludes that we would avoid an anomalous construction phrase like the "construction crane laid an egg," but would accept the phrase "the crane laid an egg." The 5-year-olds (and the 6-year-olds) could not make use of the semantic consistency information, while the 7 and especially the 8-year-olds were more successful. There was no difference in the 5-8-year-olds' ability to make use of syntactic information in guessing the obliterated parts of anomalous and ungrammatical sentences, but this syntactic information appeared to be a limited resource. The performance of the 5-year-olds suggests that the acquisition of semantic principles proceeds slowly in comparison with the rapid development of syntactic principles in 5-8-year olds.

McNeill states that poor performance is presumably based on poor perception. According to McNeill's study we could conclude that 5 or 6-year-olds are not making use of semantic or syntactic

information. We can thus suggest that our classroom
and testing situations are not consistent with what
children may be attending when they are processing
information adults assume is relevant for doing
intellectual tasks. We can therefore question the
tacit assumption on the part of teachers and testers
that standardized conditions exist and that the children
being exposed to lessons and tests can be taught and
evaluated under the assumption that there is an identical
or 'standardized' presentation of concepts and stimulus
materials. Thus despite the possibility of establishing various levels of 'normal' competence by reference
to developmental psycholinguistic criteria and to the
processing of visual information, we cannot make exclusive use of syntactic, semantic, or visual criteria
to explain routine performance on standardized lessons
and tests.

The linguist's formal conception of language
cannot be usefully applied to the classroom and testing
situation unless we can locate its use in the context
of information processing activities — the cross-modal
integration of information as it occurs in inter-
actionally contingent and emergent settings. The social
organization of memory enables the child to produce
descriptions or utterances acceptable to adults. The
work cited by Pick and Pick, Kolers, and McNeill is
offered to suggest that the child's own conception and
control of his language production and comprehension
must be understood by school officials and researchers
if educators are to develop curricula and psychological
tests designed to teach children and to evaluate their
performances and abilities.

For present purposes the psychological literature
on attention revolves around what has been called the
"filter model" (Norman, 1969a: 23-26; Broadbent, 1958)
and around the notion of analysis-by-synthesis
(Neisser, 1967). The filter model attempts to explain
the limitations on our ability to perceive competing
messages by reference to perceptual factors. The idea
is that the brain possesses a kind of filter that is
oriented to accepting some messages while rejecting

others considered 'undesirable'. It is not clear why some signals are allowed through the filter for further processing, while other information available is not allowed to flow into the organism. Thus, while simultaneously being exposed to other channels the organism is only 'tuned' to one and only the information from the 'tuned' channel will be processed further, remembered and used as a basis for a response.

Challenges to Broadbent's theory (Moray, 1959; Triesman, 1960; Gray and Wedderburn, 1960) noted that there were psychological features involved in attention and not just phusical characteristics of the stimuli, and that the content of a rejected message does leave an impression on the subject depending on the rejected messages content and how it is presented to the subject. So material submitted to the wrong ear (the rejected message) produced a response from the subject. As Deutsch and Deutsch (1963: 83) note "...a message will reach the same perceptual and discriminatory mechanisms..." regardless of whether the subject pays attention to it or not, and the information involved will be grouped or separated by the perceptual and discriminatory mechanisms. Thus sensory cues alone were found to be inadequate to explain the kind of selection going on when subjects receive information from several channels. Incoming signals may be analyzed by the subject according to some kind of ordered sequence of operation (as Triesman suggests) whereby certain physical features of the message are attended first, then, if necessary, perhaps grammatical ones are attended. It is difficult to demonstrate the relevance of these claims of adult operations for understanding the child's performance. But notice that modern linguistic theory has virtually nothing to say about such problems. The linguistic theories assume that different channels of information, attended selectively or not, are irrelevant for the production and comprehension of utterances.

We might conclude that the adult does not select incoming signals from different channels according to a central mechanism that attempts to handle one problem at a time, but instead selects from different channels in a complex process whereby every incoming signal receives some kind of attention vis-a-vis its meaning by reference to memory storage and to the sensory features of the incoming signals (Norman, 1969a: 33) Deutsch and Deutsch, 1963). Thus our model of the child's ability to process information must apply the adult model. But both models must also incorporate contextual exigencies because of differences in social knowledge and language development across adults and children that are not considered in the psychological theories of adult processing addressed here.

Whether one argues that (a) selection occurs because of attenuation of some channels to reduce the load on a central analyzing process, thus allowing for movement from one channel to another, or that (b) selection occurs when the signals go through a stage of analysis done by early physiological processes (Norman, 1969a: 33) because of a kind of precognitive selection, what is important for our purposes is the idea that the general social context and the expectations based on the situation play important functions in attention. Additionally, the subject's attention can be cut off from all sensory channels and focused on his own thought processes (Neisser, 1967, 214) which in turn influences attention given to incoming signals and affects subsequent responding.

When the child (or any subject) is exposed to multiple channels of information while responding to a tester's or teacher's question, the description of processing (a) or (b) given above with its various possibilities comes into play. To the extent that this is a viable description, we must acknowledge that multiple sources of information processed by different modes can lead to considerable difficulty for a description of learning as it may occur in the classroom and as it is relevant to a child's performance on a classroom lesson or psychological test. If the child cannot select among competing channels any elements that can be identified as meaningful, then he can hardly be expected to respond adequately to the teacher's questions or request for information. In the case of

324

a testing situation the child's internal organization
of information may be more central in his attempt to
apply the classroom experiences to the stimulus conditions of a test. The reader will recognize that
several problems exist here. The children in one of
the classrooms we studied were considered to be very
slow learners with low IQs. Their conduct in class
could easily be equated with the behavior of 'learning
disabled" children who are felt to have high or normal
IQs but whose academic performance is deficient (Bryan
and Wheeler, in press) but similar to low-income groups
(see Chapter IV) being described in this report; considerable time is spent in 'fooling around' rather
than working on task-oriented activities designated
by the Teacher.

   The general problem of pattern recognition is a
central issue here because the child must possess the
ability to identify particular acoustical patterns
embedded in an interfering environment which the child
himself often creates (by his talking to classmates,
moving furniture, or by his own outbursts), and he
must simultaneously match the acoustical patterns with
possibly unintelligble phonemic representations on
the blackboard or tester's booklet. The child's
response to a question from the teacher or tester may
require him to integrate unfamiliar visual patterns
that represent objects he can be assumed to know, but
the phonemic representations of the objects or phonetic
distinctions may be strange to him. But this equivalence between different sensory inputs, and a verbal
description of an object or activity, is not based on
asking the child to acknowledge or create these equi-
valences. The classroom lesson or testing program
assumes that such issues are not problematic features
when evaluating the child's performance. The analysis
of the child's understanding of different visual and
verbal inputs should not be taken for granted, but
should be demonstrated empirically by teachers and
testers. Further, we are not clear about how continuous feed-back mechanisms operate so that contextual
information about sound patterns, their intonation and

intensity, knowledge of grammatical rules, visual
appearances, and stored information interact with
competing sources that may suggest other meanings to
the child, or that may interfere with the child's
performance in classroom or testing situations.

A central point is that the grammatical context
is important for the perception of spoken words, for
as the grammatical context deteriorates so does the
perception of speech. But our elementary school
curricula are not developed from a careful examination
of the range of language acquisition abilities acquired
by children in different or particular classrooms. To
complicate matters further our knowledge of these
abilities remains weak. If we are not clear at the
outset about the child's abilities, much less his
capacity to recognize and receive and then process or
generate linguistic information, then we cannot esti-
mate how much interference could occur because of
inputs from unattended channels of information. The
problems of pattern recognition and attention must
be linked with (1) the quality and availability of
sensory information about events that have just
occurred; (2) a notion of immediate or short-term
memory which would contain information based on what
we can extract from a sensory image that is presumed
to be decaying rapidly; and (3) the idea of a long-term
memory wherein we can retain considerable information
(Sperling, 1967). But we still have to worry about
the retention of visual information, non-verbal sounds
and socially defined action.

If we can distinguish between types of auditory
information storage and types of visual information
storage, then we must also worry about the inter-
dependence of these two systems and how they would
interact when classroom and testing procedures employ
verbal utterances to index auditory, visual and kinesthetic experiences. And when we attempt to instruct
children we must keep in mind that our presentation of
new material should be organized to coincide with
existing information we presume the child possesses.
When we seek to test the child's intelligence or

326

understanding of a prior classroom lesson we cannot ignore how humans recode or combine elements of information (Miller, 1956). We cannot assume that the child has found the most or minimally efficient way of regrouping new information or old information into new categories when we present him with classroom lessons or testing materials. Adults assume that an explicit verbal categorization system is being used that is understandable to children. But the materials and instructions cannot be linked directly to an un-examined model of the child's ability to decode and encode verbal and visual or other information obtain-able from the setting. If particular speaker-hearers develop idiosyncratic ways of recoding information (Miller, 1956) then children must be told explicitly about the kinds of chunking operations the teacher or tester expects the child to have learned or should learn. If some children, because of their cultural setting, learn to depict their thoughts or obser-vations or desires or knowledge by the use of visual, non-verbal acoustical, tactile, and physical infor-mation, and by the use of truncated verbal information, then specific training would be necessary to show them how classroom and testing situations demand particular forms of verbal expressions.

The classroom routine is filled with interruptions that vary from class to class, but the testing situation if often uniform in that everyone takes the test simul-taneously and thus can be monitored for outbursts, or there is a one-to-one relationship between tester and student. Testing is usually done under more ideal circumstances, while learning in classroom and other settings takes place in noisy surroundings that are exceedingly difficult to evaluate and control.

Learning experiments do not simulate everyday learning conditions, but instead create ideal circum-stances that are not realistically linked to actual events. The possible simulation of classroom situations can be approximated with some experiments on attention and short-term memory, but the socially relevant con-textual cues of the classroom and the teacher or tester's

327

perspective for evaluating the children's performances cannot be equated with the experimenter's intention in the laboratory.

CONSEQUENCES OF BASIC THEORY FOR DISADVANTAGED CHILDREN
The limitations of attention, memory, and types of recoding procedures apply to all children, but some children seem to be in a more extreme situation. If we can believe the importance of short-term memory in human information processing, then the consequences of a class-room lesson for learning by disadvantaged children are especially serious. If short-term memory is a viable notion then new information being received requires some sort of rehearsal, and the capacity of the memory becomes central because of the amount and complexity of incoming information and its possible displacement of other elements. A teacher or tester would have to be familiar with conditions (1) in which certain types of acoustical and visual memory deteriorate; (2) in which the conditions can influence the subject's ability to process information provided initially by standardized American English instructions that are acoustical and partially visual; and (3) in which the instructions require a translation of verbal material into visual operations or standardized verbal operations. A key problem is the subject's ability to recognize incoming information in standardized American English, to link the material to other material coded in his long-term memory and then to generate utterances that are also couched in standardized sentences. We would expect children and adults not accustomed routinely to hearing and speaking standardized or formal language to have difficulty processing such information because rehearsal would be more difficult if the material were not easily recognizable and so could not be linked immediately to long-term memory. I am assuming that if memory is organized according to storage of dialect-relevant information and storage of syntactic structures sensitive to their contextual usage, then relying on the perception of several sources of information would complicate the processing of

instructions whose organization and lexical items presumed standardized rules and meanings.

When we conduct experiments on visual and acoustical memory the complexity of language instructions is seldom a variable condition of the research. When we note the inability of children and adults to complete certain tasks involving presumably obvious instructions and tacit visual information necessary for understanding the settings, we do not conduct an independent study of the subjects' competence with the language employed in the experiment. At most we make an effort to ensure that the subjects 'understand' the required task in some minimal by operational way. A variety of lexical items and syntactic structures are employed as if they were clear and obvious features of the task.

Let us assume that all children can replace previously learned grammatical structures by new experiences and new linguistic forms, and that these new linguistic forms can be learned spontaneously. The conditions of an experiment, a classroom lesson, a formal psychological testing situation can lead to a restructuring of material previously learned in other settings, and suggest that an evaluation of a child's performance is contingent on the conditions of how the experiment or lesson or test is administered and scored (see also T. G. Bever and D. T. Langendoen, 1971). Or we can assume (with recent work in developmental psycholinguistics, Brown 1970; Bellugi, 1967; Slobin, 1971; McNeill, 1971; Bloom, 1970) that there are different points at which we can monitor the child's linguistic ability to utilize grammatical rules of a highly constrained form, and that during his years of language acquisition the child can produce slight grammatical restructurings depending on the preceding stage of development. After age 12 and into adulthood, the Bever and Langendoen paper suggests that the adult would not be able to change his grammar by serious restructurings, but it is not clear in this paper if adults can produce or absorb slight restructurings, whatever 'slight' might refer to. Bever and Langendoen stress the importance of the learning and evolution of grammatical structure, and the interaction of language development with the conditions under which speech behavior is perceived and produced. The learning of new utterances and their influence on restructuring existing grammatical rules are constrained by the child's ability to comprehend something of the new utterance, a desire to say it, and the ability and desire to assimilate it to the grammar he has already acquired. So, neologisms presented to children are most likely to survive if they are articulated appropriately with some stage of development of language, and presumable environment of usage.

A major problem in understanding how speech inputs are recognized, and hence made comprehensible, stems from the complexity of the channels carrying the information. The organism is not passive in its reception of verbal information. Presumably the child's recognition is dependent on his stage of language acquisition and dependent on the memory of experiences that he can subsume under implicitly known grammatical structures. If he relies on visual and acoustic information generated by the setting, however, and on what for the adult is presumed to be 'obvious' knowledge at hand in the context, then the stage of language development and the particular grammatical structures the child has mastered according to linguistic and psycholinguistic criteria may not be central for comprehension and communication. The terms and phrases or sentences employed by the teacher or tester may be partially contex-sensitive in that they only clarify or elaborate or provide redundant explanation of 'obvious' visual, acoustical, tactile, and assumed common knowledge information presumed to be available to all members of the setting. The information presented to a disadvantaged child may be detached from the child's everyday practices whereby he recognizes and processes information in familiar surroundings. This problem of detachment occurs in studies done by experimental psychologists, who have used nonsense syllables or dictionary entries for serial learning experiments, or when new visual forms, colors, and musical tones, or standardized and isolated sentences are used. The subject may be forced to create memory structures that are strange or which make processing the experimental inputs difficult and misleading vis-à-vis what is natural or routine. When the experiments on memory and language are conducted with children (particularly from disadvantaged homes), it is difficult to know what we can assume about the child's language development. We have to devise instructions and tasks that require the integration of visual, acoustical, tactile and linguistic structures. The problem is further complicated when we deal with bilingual children whose first and second languages have reached unknown stages of development.

We cannot rely on the child's outputs to decide retrospectively whether he is capable of producing utterances with the same or similar grammatical structure as the teacher's, tester's, or experimenter's. The context may permit the child to exceed his level of acquisition by simulating what appears to be expected, and thus to produce *"correct"* forms. Hence, every classroom lesson or testing situation or experiment requires some independent checks on the subject's ability to process the grammatical structures and lexical items central to the comprehension of a task and its implementation.

If subjects perceive stimulus questions in psychological tests, or classroom tests as confusing or threatening, the resulting difficulties in attention will reduce the information retained in immediate memory. If we add a noisy background such as a classroom, or if we use a strange testing setting or a test procedure not explained clearly, then we should expect lower performance.

I am suggesting that current social and behavioral science research places to much emphasis on the analysis of verbal materials detached from the setting and occasion of use and relies too much on restricted occasions such as formal tests. Research findings on language structure often assume that the

displacement of visible and imagined objects and
events indexed by the speech behavior of respondents
can be reconstructed by the observer if necessary,
and that the utterances called data can be handled as
more or less self-contained expressions whose meaning
can be revealed by recourse to abstract syntactic or
conversational rules. But problems of attention and
the cultural organization of memory necessary for
processing standardized speech, the learning that
goes on in the setting, and the use of linguistic
codes that place great emphasis on visual and tactile
and non-verbal acoustic information, are essential
issues for understanding the meaning of classroom
lessons and testing situations or for understanding
everyday speech and conversations. Unless these more
subtle and difficult-to-study issues of social interaction are examined carefully, researchers can easily
fall back on a social pathology or genetic explanation
of differential school performance, while students of
language, on the other hand, will invoke abstract
rule systems for explaining problems of meaning.

BILINGUAL ISSUES

In our study we encountered children from homes
where both fairly literate and somewhat illiterate
Spanish was spoken (Mehan, 1971). In a few cases the
parents spoke Spanish at home but the children did
not pick it up and did not wish to speak the language
when we attempted to test them at home. In one case
the parents spoke Spanish but the child seemed to
perform at a lower level of achievement when Spanish
was used. Although the bilingualism of particular
children may receive support from a larger community
that extends beyond the family and that might enjoy
social, political, and economic backing, children may
face peer problems and school difficulties in their
use or attempted use of Spanish (Fishman, 1967;
Kjolseth, 1970; Gumperz and Hernandez, 1971).

The use of different linguistic codes is often
associated with different social settings and the
characteristics of the speakers. One code might be

spoken at home and another used for commerical
activities and formal encounters with strangers or
at work. If some of the child's knowledge is mapped
into Spanish, while other information is mapped into
American English, and the information in Spanish is
based on a dialect of Mexican or Chicano Spanish,
then the child's ability to transfer from one
language (learned as a dialect) to another (American
English), that may also be learned as a dialect, may
be impaired if always presented in classroom and
testing settings in standardized form. Serious
problems can emerge during his performance on official
testing occasions or even during routine classroom
lessons. It may be safe to assume that the child's
knowledge is divided between illiterate reading and
writing in American English and Mexican or Chicano
Spanish. We do not know, however, if the children
in our study can switch codes as easily as in the case
presented by Gumperz and Hernandez where American
English phrases or sentences were inserted in Spanish
statements, and Spanish phrases or sentences were inserted in American English statements. Nor can we
evaluate precisely the sometimes hesitant but ostensive
ability of the Chicano child to decode standardized
American English sentences as presented by the teacher
in the classroom or by the psychological tester.

The general problem of information processing
transcends the often sharp differences among contend-
ing theories about Black and Chicano performance in
the classroom and in testing situations. We know very
little about how cognitive processes interact with
language acquisition and use in settings where information processing is made difficult because of
dialect or bilingual differences, and where the cultural
knowledge that the child brings to the classroom and
testing situation is not examined independently of the
materials used for teaching and testing the child. In
the section that follows, I provide an examination of
the classroom lesson independently analyzed by Mehan
(Chapter 3) to show how ideas on cognitive processes
and interactional competence can help us understand

333

the learning process in the classroom. The reader
may wish to compare my analysis with Mehan's analysis.
In earlier chapters (Chapters 3, 4, 5), comparisons
of classroom and testing materials were made across
children and teachers; this analysis conducted across
observers provides another perspective on the in-
finitely possible interpretations of the 'same'
scene.

A CLASSROOM LESSON

The reader will remember that the lesson was
on the use of locatives. The setting for the lesson
was a round table in a corner of the classroom.
Various kinds of background noise can be detected,
and there are other interruptions such as one child
coming up to the table to see what the others are
doing, and the teacher's aide coming up to ask for
advice about some issue. The present scene is somewhat better than the usual classroom situation
because there are only five students and the teacher
is able to monitor what is going on without the kinds
of background interruptions characteristic of a lesson
presented to the entire class. But in other ways the
lesson is typical because many classes are divided
into ability groups, and the teacher frequently
directs a lesson to a smaller subset of the class.

The initial questions we can ask are how we are
to decide what the stimulus field consists of, and
what we consider to be a response, assuming we can
locate the stimulus that seems to be capable of a
pairing with some response that can be isolated. A
conversational model of speaker turns, A then B, or
ABABABAB (Schegloff, 1968) dictates that a sequential
pattern of stimulus-response exchanges (or question-
answer format) organizes the setting for the participants and the observer. But our previous discussion emphasizes that the visual setting clearly
seems to be organized around multiple sources of information.

The lesson begins with the teacher telling the
children to make a green line at the bottom of the

334

paper (see Appendix, line 1). The stimulus command seems clear, but I had difficulty deciding what the children recognized as tacit or explicit information. This is also a serious issue when we have a one-to-one situation between a psychological tester and a subject. The tester must assume that his or her instructions are clear and obvious to the child despite the fact that the child's actions may produce an obverse inference. The basic issue is that stimulus control is difficult to guarantee because we cannot be clear about what the child recognizes as relevant information, nor can we be clear about what is processed and what is retrievable from previous information that the tester and child may deem relevant to the task at hand. For the teacher the problem is compounded; even when working with three to five children, there are continuous distractions created by the children's routine activities.

The lesson begins with the teacher's remark orienting the children to the first task.

> 1:1   T: *All right, let's take our green crayon and make a line at the bottom of our paper.*

The lesson begins with the teacher drawing a line on her sheet of paper as she produces Utterance 1. The circular table around which the children are seated has an open space directly opposite the teacher to allow the camera angle to focus on her appearance and actions. She has a sheet of paper in front of her and a few crayons. My remarks to the reader are based on viewing the scene on the video monitor from the angle of the camera noted above, but I have a vivid memory of the larger classroom that I rely on tacitly. This means that one child is occasionally obscured by a second child whose back faces my view. I cannot clearly see the children's papers but occasionally catch glimpses of the teacher's sheet as she generates movements with her crayons and right hand.

As I write this down, I find it difficult to

capture what I think I 'see' and 'understand' about the setting. Thus each child has a sheet of paper in front of him or her and some crayons. As the teacher produces her remark, no one seems to object to terms like *"take," "green crayon," "make a line," "bottom," "of your paper."* The children begin to draw something on their papers. To me it appears clear that the visual setting is central for the children's apparent understanding of the verbal instruction. I assume that the quick side glances at the teacher's sheet of paper provide considerable information for each child.

> 1:2 T: *Take a green crayon and make a line at the bottom.*

The teacher repeats herself as the children engage in the task of carrying out her request or command. Her second remark deletes *"of your paper,"* but the referent seems clear to the children because there has been prior visual monitoring by the teacher to ensure that everyone possesses a sheet of paper and some crayons.

The visual information available to all of the children seems to constitute a basic frame regardless of the verbal accounts, and provides a perspective for orienting activities as meaningful vis-à-vis the teacher's commands. The videotape is not too clear, however, and does not always reveal 'looks' of hesitancy on the children's faces that might contradict my claims. The teacher seems to presume that her actions thus far are clear and intelligible to the children.

> 1:3 Ci: *Like that?*

With her question, Ci looks up to the teacher and seems to expect a confirming statement or glance. This child is directly to the left of the teacher and has the best view of the teacher's paper.

My remarks provide interpretations of the visual information available to me by the camera angle which enable me to structure the events I claim to witness.

In doing this I create a particular imagery for my analysis by trading on my normative conceptions of what is 'perfunctory' about a 'glance', what seems to be an interrogatory statement, and a whole host of understandings I treat as 'obvious' and 'clear'.

    1:4 T: *Okay, yeah, all right, now...*

I think the teacher is telling the group that they are doing well as she glances around the table, but she also seems to be telling Ci that her line is fine *("yeah")*. Her visual scan is quick and seemingly perfunctory.

    1:5 Ri: *Now what are we going to do?*

This child has remained standing but he continues to move back and forth from the table.

It now appears that some of the children (at least two) are relying on verbal information for further instructions while completing the first task of drawing the line at the bottom of the page. Their attention to verbal inputs is compromised by the first task because the setting requires that considerable time be given to monitoring the visual inputs available.

    1:6 T: *Now take your orange crayon and make an orange worm under the green line. We'll pretend that that's grass.*

The teacher's remark does not say what an orange worm should look like, nor does she elaborate her statement about pretending *"that that's grass"* by connecting this latter utterance with the green line drawn earlier. No one seems to be doing much after this remark, but I cannot tell what (if anything) the teacher may have been thinking or picking up as information from her glances around the table when she said that or the next remark.

    1:7 T: *(Still looking at Ci) It's just a*

*little wiggle. Here, let me show you
on this one. An orange worm.*

The remark *"this one"* refers to a different
sheet of paper than the one before the teacher. The
teacher assumes this second sheet of paper is an
obvious reference available to the children visually.
She then draws the *"worm"* on this second sheet of
paper as she utters *"orange worm."* The two girls
next to her (Je and Ci) are leaning over to observe
the teacher's actions, but all of them can see the
sheet she is drawing on, though it is upside down
for them.

1:8 Di: *Hey, can you make it on yours?*

Di's remark must be understood by reference to
what I assume she observed the teacher doing: drawing
the *"orange worm"* on a different sheet of paper than
the one that she drew the green line on earlier. Di's
"yours" refers to a pointing action on her part to the
teacher's sheet with the green line. During this exchange Je has been moving about in her seat quite a
bit, continuously glancing at her paper and the
teacher's paper.

1:9   T: *No, I'm, watch... watch... you make
          it on,*
1:10 Je: *Over here, make it? (pause)*
1:11 Ci: *(tapping the teacher with her crayon)
          Under?*
1:12 T: *Listen! I'll only say it once. Make
          an orange worm under the green line.*

The teacher starts to respond to Je's *"make it
on yours"* and Je's pointing (*"over here?"*) Operation.
The teacher's *"I'm watch... watch..."* remark presumably is intended to tell Je that she doesn't want
to demonstrate each instruction on her own paper, but
wants to watch the children do it on their sheets of
paper. The teacher does not complete the explanation

338

to Je. When the teacher says *"listen!,"* her elbows
are on the table and she raises her two arms as if to
quiet Je and Ci who are on her right and left, respectively. Even as the teacher starts to explain to
Je why she did not place the *"orange worm"* on her
paper, Je interrupts with *"over here?"*

    1:13 Di: *Like that?*

It is difficult to see if Di is pointing to her
paper here because she is partially obscured by Do.

    1:14 T: *Beauutiful! Okay.*

The teacher looks over to Di but does not seem
to be looking at Di's paper when she says *"beautiful,"*
but is glancing around the entire room.

    1:15 Ri: *I made two orange worms (laughs).*

Ci is tapping the teacher again here with her
crayon and the teacher turns toward her and says:

    1:16 T: *We're going to pretend that that green
line is the grass, okay? Can you pre-
tend with me?*

When the teacher says, *"Can you pretend...,"*
she is looking at Ci. I think Ci gives her a nod in
acknowledgment and perhaps says *"yes,"* but there is
so much background noise, it is difficult for me to
feel certain.

    1:17 T: *All right. Where is the orange worm,
Do?*

The teacher looks across the table to Do.

    1:18 Do: *Right there.*

Both Do and Di seem to point to their papers as

Do says *"right there."*

    1:19   T: *Okay, tell me where he is.*

The teacher insists on a more elaborated response, but as Mehan (Chapter 3) notes in an earlier and independent analysis of this scene, the teacher does not explain that the child's response is presumably not a complete 'answer'. Instead the teacher asks for elaboration.

    1:20   Do: *Under the grass.*

The elaboration is provided by Do.

    1:21   T: *Okay...*

The teacher seems to approve of the elaborated answer, but to repeat Mehan's (Chapter 3) remark, this response does not meet the requirements of a complete, correct answer as the teacher has independently established and differentially insisted upon with other children. Mehan notes that Do is not told why her truncated response is presumably acceptable by the teacher. I note that Do is bilingual. We do not know to what extent this could have influenced the teacher in accepting Do's response as correct. The point is that the teacher always keeps such contingencies in mind when evaluating the performance of any child, including a child considered very bright but viewed as not performing well on an 'easy' lesson. Allowing truncated responses to 'pass' in the classroom can be a problem on a later occasion. If the testing situation does not include the tester's or teacher's making allowances for the child's bilingual difficulties or 'obvious' intelligence or the assumed 'obvious' informational context available to all in the classroom 'identically' as the teacher's remarks imply in this lesson, then the absence of this informality on official occasions of evaluation make the evaluations biased assessments of competence and performance.

> 1:22 T: *Okay. Now, would you please make um,*
> *a, a little brown seed under the*
> *grass.*

The teacher is looking around the table first
while producing this remark, and then down at the
table with occasional glances to the children.

The terms *"brown seed"* and *"under the grass"*
are presumed to be clear to the children.

> 1:23 Ci: *How do you make a little brown seed?*

The teacher does not respond to Ci's question.
She looks at Ci and then to another part of the room
as Ri provides an answer in the next round.

Notice that Ci's question does not ask what
"a little brown seed" is, but how to make it. Presumably seeing one made also satisfies what it 'is'
for present purposes. The child's response could also
be taken to mean that she 'knows' what a seed 'is',
but does not remember 'how to make it'. Teachers
and testers do not begin the lesson or test by clearly
identifying and defining each term to be used, and the
grammatical constructions necessary for this use, but
proceed as if particular normative information is
obviously known to the child.

> 1:24 Ri: *Easy. You see. You go like this.*
> *Simple. A little circle.*

Ri's response includes drawing something on a
sheet of paper that he and Ci can both see.

The language used by Ri displaces visual information until the last remark *"a little circle."*
If we were only dealing with the conversation, we
would assume that the last phrase *"a little circle"*
is adequate for instructing the child about the task.
But the children seem to have difficulty matching
visual information that seems obvious to an adult with

standardized verbal representations. The integration
of visual and auditory information and their representation verbally is what the task is all about,
yet carrying out the task presumes the integration
of information and its expressive verbal matching
that the teacher is trying to teach.

1:25 Ci: *Like that?*

Ci touches the object drawn by Ri as she says
"like that?"
Ci does not say *"oh, so a seed looks like a
little circle,"* but uses an indefinite verbal representation to index her use of visual information and
motor activities for comprehending what is going on.

1:26 T: *Oh, beautiful.*

The teacher's gaze returns to the table as she
says *"beautiful,"* but it is not clear what she is
responding to because she does not look at the object
drawn by Ri.
The videotape seems to show the teacher giving
off a perfunctory remark intended for the whole group,
yet she does not examine each of their drawn *"seeds,"*
and an observer with only a verbal transcription
would have to assume she is referring to the seed
drawn by Ri on the extra sheet of paper in front of
him, though the teacher appears to give a quick glance
at Ci's paper at the end of *"beautiful."* Now it is
the teacher's attention that has been disrupted and
this result in a rather diffuse kind of reward if we
can assume that the children attach the same significance to the teacher's remark as the present observer.
No acknowledgment is given to Ci's confusion about the
teacher's verbal instructions or the help she received
from Ri.
When Ci says *"like that"* (1:25), Do is pushing
off from the table continuously like a spring, and
the teacher looks at her as she says the first part
of *"beautiful."* Unless the observer has learned to

342

recognize the children's voices, it could appear that
Do is asking *"like that"* instead of Ci. I found it
impossible to decide between Do and Ci, but then I
retrospectively notice that Do seems to have made
her seed prior to Ci's *"like that,"* and as I go back
and forth between the transcript before me and the
videotape, I notice that Je's *"look at mine"* (1:27)
is followed by Ci's *"under what?"* (1:28), and I infer
that Ci is still drawing her *"seed"* because I can
catch occasional glimpses of her when Ri is not moving
(which is seldom). Thus I retrospectively decide that
Ci seems to be in the act of drawing her seed and could
be seen as asking for confirmation that she is drawing
the seed in the correct manner and location.

*In this lesson visual and tactile information
seem to be paramount, with the verbal representations
providing diffuse and indefinite markers for claiming
recognition and understanding of the information. The
verbal representations used by the children do not
organize the visual, tactile, and auditory information
according to categories or classes that are normatively
acceptable from the point of view of adult conceptions
of meaning, but instead serve to orient the children
to apparently "obvious" inputs based on other channels
of information.*

This brief dialogue was presented to show the
complexities of attention in interactional settings
where the teacher's lesson on locatives is implemented
against a background of classroom noise and interruptions from outside and within the group. The last
remark by Ci (*"under what?"*; 1:28) can be viewed as
illustrating how she seemed to experience difficulty
in remembering *"under the grass."* The dominant element
seemed to be the phrase *"a little brown seed"* which she
shadowed in (1:22). Although it would be difficult to
demonstrate clearly with this lesson, the possibility
should be explored that the child's shadowing is central
to carrying out the task asked by the teacher. Shadowing would be important if what is asked is not clear
and there is interference from other students' remarks,
and if the child tends to focus on one clause of a

sentence.

The teacher is attempting to teach the children to express verbally locations that an adult observer could claim to be obvious visual experiences for the children. The lesson is not introduced by remarks indicating what the children should easily recognize about the task and how to do it, but instead the children are being asked that they learn how to produce correct, standardized, American English sentences about visual and tactile information that is tacitly represented to them as 'obvious'. But we are not privy to the children's conceptions of the context. The linguist assumes that the child's responses, like the trained teacher's responses, follow options through syntactic structures available in the language. But it is precisely what is available to the child as 'language' or as socially understood options that is not clear, particularly when we are dealing with children (as in the case here) who are from low income families and whose parents have little or no formal education. The teacher's lessons must assume a certain level of language competence, but deciding this level is not an integral part of the teaching process, nor is this competence examined carefully when teachers are tracking or streaming children into ability groups. The tracking and streaming that is done is based on very crude evaluations of the child's linguistic performance. It is difficult to apply the results of developmental psycholinguistics to the present classroom group because the research of such psycholinguists as Brown and his associates (1970), Braine (1963), Ervin (1964), and Bloom (1970), to mention a few, are based on children from middle income families with educated parents. We often assume but do not possess data to show that middle income families encourage their children to verbalize their activities and intentions with standardized American English, using phrases and complete sentences. Yet children from middle income families seem to employ similar truncated expressions (particularly among themselves in play) as those quoted above by the low income children of the classroom we are discussing.

In the above dialogue the children do not clearly represent their thoughts about visual, tactile, and auditory sources of information and understanding with complete, standardized American English sentences. Je (1:10), for example, says *"over here"* when asked to draw an *"orange worm"* under the green line. Ci (1:11) does ask *"under"* in the same context. But after the teacher repeats the instruction, Di (1:13) says *"like that"* while looking at her sheet of paper as if presenting it to the teacher for examination. Then when the teacher (1:17) asks Do where the orange worm is, Do (1:18) says *"right there,"* again using taken-for-granted visual cues for her response. The teacher persists (1:19) and Do (1:20) responds with *"under the grass."* But the teacher does not follow through by asking Do to create a complete sentence. The teacher fills in from her earlier question *"where is the orange worm"* (1:17) and *"okay, tell me where he is"* (1:19) to complete the response by Do (1:20). The desired 'sentence' (see the underlined parts below) was presumably understood as follows:

1:17	T:	*"...where is the orange worm...?"*
1:18	Do:	*"Right there."*
1:19	T:	*"Okay, tell me where he <u>is</u>."*
1:20	Do:	*<u>"Under the grass</u>."*

In lines (1:23) and (1:24) when Ci asks for help in making a brown seed, it was noted above that Ri responds initially with verbally indefinite remarks (*"Easy. You see. You go like this"*) and then *"Simple. A little circle"* that carry visually relevant information and a presumed correspondence between the verbal *"a little circle"* and what is being drawn for Ci's visual understanding. Then Ci (1:28) later asks the teacher *"under what"* and receives (1:29) *"under the grass."* The sequence involved a considerable delay. The underlined material illustrates the time lag and what was shadowed initially. Do did not shadow *"under"* but remembers the term in 1:28.

345

1:22	T:	*Okay, now, would you please make um, a, a little brown seed under the grass.*
1:23	Ci:	*How do you make a little brown seed?*
1:24	Ri:	*Easy. You see. You go like this. Simple. A little circle.*
1:25	Ci:	*Like that?*
1:26	T:	*Oh, beautiful!*
1:27	Je:	*Look at mine.*
1:28	Ci:	*Under what?*
1:29	T:	*Under the grass.*

Some 22 seconds elapsed between the teacher's *"Okay, now..."* and the teacher's *"under the grass."* In addition to the considerable time that passes, there is interference during the lesson. The literature on selective attention seems most relevant to the classroom lesson described above, but in experiments the researcher assumes that the language usage is clear and obvious to the subjects. In the classroom, however, the teacher's goal of teaching the children how to form complete sentences using particular locatives to express relationships between objects is continually modified by contingencies of the action scene the teacher can only partially control. Her demands on the students vary and what is acceptable as correct answers varies. The following examples in this lesson (and throughout our materials) reveal how attention and memory are central features of the performances and evaluation conducted by the teacher.

The terms *"there"* and *"here"* and *"like that"* all signify location, and the visual information is presumed to be identically available and understood by all participants of the setting. But the teacher wanted the construction of locatives to be properly referenced in terms of implied relationships among a set of objects, and the objects and relationships are also assumed to be visually available to all in an (obvious and) identical way. The teacher wants *"proper"* standardized versions of the locatives in relationship to their referents. Consider the following

346

utterances.

I	II	III
"over here"	*"it's under the tree"*	*"yeah, the line"*
"like this"	*"under tree"*	*"a table"*
"right there"	*"off the grass"*	*"It's above"*
"under it"		

The utterances show an increasing use of more appropriate locatives vis-à-vis the referents which are
intended and increasingly prompted by the teacher as
part of the task. The child primarily relies on
tacit visual information and the use of diffuse verbal
expressions to index this information. As the teacher
supplied additional information or exemplary cues,
the child utilized particular lexical items to displace
his reliance on tacit visual information and thus
satisfy the teacher's concern with standardized grammatical constructions. The teacher's examples provide
more concrete guidelines for the child to follow if
the examples are couched in terms that make sense to
the child; the examples must reveal the desired representation between standardized grammatical expressions
and visually 'obvious' relationships from the child's
point of view. When one child picks up this central
principle, he can then monitor another child's performance and provide an additional model for the others.
But notice that the children are not motivated to
provide complete sentences unless pushed by the teacher
explicitly and given prompts that seem to suggest a
step-by-step clarification of the task. We could
speculate that perhaps this is consistent with the
home situation; the child is not expected to provide
complete sentences in low income families, and the
teacher routinely permits these truncated utterances
in the classroom most of the time. But we have no
clear evidence that would support such speculation.
The teacher does not use classroom conversations that
are routine features of the setting as examples of
what she is trying to get across in the lesson.

CONCLUSION

In the above lesson the teacher traded on truncated language usage to facilitate her instructions, but exercised differential evaluative procedures when deciding on the appropriateness of a response. The teacher assumed that the terms she used were clear and that the grammatical formulations she employed were understood by the children intuitively. The teacher did not dwell on her instructions and examples to the children by having each child shadow the instructions and examples first before proceeding with each lesson. Shadowing does not mean comprehension, but may insure the child's reception of the information to help eliminate some of the existing confusion noted above.

Throughout this chapter I have tried to stress the importance of studying the acquisition of interactional competence and its realization in everyday settings. When this theme is applied to the classroom setting and testing situations, we become aware of the complexities of information processing and how simplified our conception of learning has become in educational circles. I have tried to outline some of the elements and their combination that contribute to the acquisition of interactional competence and its implementation by focusing on the information processing activities required by classroom and testing situations.

I have tried to advance the idea that everyday social interaction is a creative activity that utilize several modalities and is tempered by selective attention and a memory system constrained by socially organized information. The ability to reflect on one's thinking is part of information processing. This reflection modifies any prior type of feature extraction that can be said to operate on sensory information inputs and outputs. We must recognize that the verbal constructions of the child or adult do not adequately index the kinds of information recognized, received, processed, and generated. We must also acknowledge that the nonverbal everyday

348

meanings expressed via different modalities and tempered by selective attention and a socially organized memory system can be distorted, poorly marked, or transformed when organized verbally. The verbal constructions may have variable use depending on the context and the way in which different participants trade on the use of other modalities, their thoughts about what is relevant, and the common knowledge attributed to others. Hence the child may comprehend standardized SVO sentences in American English but not be capable of generating similar utterances. Or the child may operate on fragments of standardized constructions while using interpretive abilities to fill in one or more possible meanings.

Throughout this book we have implied that the child may make use of what he presumes to be common knowledge of the setting and different objects and activities therein, while simultaneously producing truncated utterances to mark crudely various intentions and understandings. Classroom lessons and formal tests are adult-oriented and presuppose a knowledge and use of standardized American English in appropriate social settings for their implementation, yet knowledge and use are not clarified nor taught as a prerequisite for comprehending and completing the lessons or tests.

APPENDIX

1:1   T: *All right, let's take our green crayon and make a line at the bottom of our paper.*

1:2   T: *Take a green crayon and make a line at the bottom.*

1:3   Ci: *Like that?*

1:4   T: *Okay, yeah, all right, now*

1:5   Ri: *Now what are we going to do?*

1:6   T: *Now take your orange crayon and make an orange worm under the green line. We'll pretend that that's grass.*

1:7   T: *(Still looking at Ci) It's just a little wiggle. Here, let me show you on this one. An orange worm.*

1:8   Je: *Hey, can you make it on yours?*

1:9   T: *No, I'm watch... watch... you make it on,*

1:10   Je: *Over here? make it (pause)*

1:11   Ci: *(Tapping the teacher with her crayon) Under?*

1:12   T: *Listen! I'll only say it once. Make an orange worm under the green line.*

1:13   Di: *Like that?*

1:14   T: *Beauuutiful! Okay.*

1:15   Ri: *I made two orange worms (laughs).*

1:16   T: *We're going to pretend that that green line is the grass, okay? Can you pretend that with me?*

1:17   T: *All right. Where is the orange worm, Do?*

1:18   Do: *Right there.*

1:19   T: *Okay, tell me where he is?*

1:20   Do: *Under the grass.*

1:21   T: *Okay...*

1:22   T: *Okay. Now would you please make um, a, a little brown seed under the grass.*

1:23   Ci: *How do you make a little brown seed?*

1:24   Ri: *Easy. You see. You go like this. Simple. A little circle.*

1:25   Ci: *Like that?*

1:26   T: *Oh, beautiful.*
1:27   Je: *Look at mine.*
1:28   Ci: *Under what?*
1:29   T: *Under the grass.*

REFERENCES

ABRAHAMS, R. D.
1970a *Deep down in the jungle*. Chicago: Aldine.

1970b *Positively black*. Englewood Cliffs:
Prentice-Hall.

BANTOCK, G. H.
1961 Educational research: A criticism.
Harvard Educational Review, Summer, Republished
in *Problems and issues in contemporary education*,
an anthology from the Harvard Educational Review
and the Teachers College Record.

BARATZ, JOAN C.
1970 Teaching reading in an urban negro school
system. In *Language and poverty*, edited by
F. Williams. Boston: Markham.

BARATZ, S. S., and J. C. BARATZ
1970 Early childhood intervention: The social
science base of institutional racism. *Harvard
Educational Review* 40:29-50.

BAR-HILLEL, Y.
1954 Indexical expressions. *Mind* 63:359-379.

BECKER, H. S.
1970 *Sociological work: Substance and method*.
Chicago: Aldine.

BELLUGI, U.
1967 The acquisition of negation. Unpublished
doctoral dissertation, Graduate School of
Education, Harvard University.

BERKELEY: Educational Testing Service
1969 Cooperative primary reading test, *Manual*,
Form 12A.

BERNSTEIN, B.
  1964 Elaborated and restricted codes: Their
  social origins and some consequences. In
  Gumperz, J. J., and D. Hymes, *The enthnography
  of communication*. American Anthropologist,
  66, Part 2:55-69.

BEVER, T. G., and D. T. LANGENDEON
  1971 A dynamic model of evolution of language.
  Linguistic Inquiry, II, 433-463.

BLOOM, L.
  1970 *Language development: Form and function
  in emerging grammars*. Cambridge, Massachusetts:
  MIT Press.

BRAINE, M. D. S.
  1963 The ontogeny of English phrase structure:
  The first phase. *Language,* 39:1-13.

BROADBENT, D. E.
  1958 *Perception and communication*. London:
  Pergamon Press.

BROWN, R.
  1968 The development of Wh questions in child
  speech. *Journal of Verbal Learning and Verbal
  Behavior,* 7:279-290.

  1970 *Psycholinguistics*. New York: The Free
  Press.

BRUNER, J. S.
  1968 *Processes of cognitive growth: Infancy*.
  Worcester, Massachusetts: Clark University Press.

BRUNER, J. S., J. GOODNOW, and G. AUSTIN
  1965 *A study of thinking*. New York: Science
  Editions.

353

BRYAN, T. S., and R. WHEELER
In Press. Perception of learning disabled
children: The eye of the Observer. *Journal
of Learning Disabilities.*

CAZDEN, C. B.
1970 The neglected situation. In: *Language
and poverty,* edited by F. Williams. Boston:
Markham.

CHERRY, E. C.
1953 Some experiments on the recognition of
speech, with one and with two ears. *Journal
Acoustical Society of America,* 25:975-979.

CHOMSKY, N.
1957 *Syntactic structures.* The Hague: Mouton
& Co.

1965 *Aspects of the theory of syntax.* Cambridge,
Massachusetts: MIT Press.

CICOUREL, A. V.
1964 *Method and measurement in sociology.*
New York: The Free Press.

1968 *The social organization of juvenile
justice.* New York: Wiley.

1973 *Cognitive sociology.* London: Penguin.

1974. *Theory and Method in a Study of Argentine
Fertility.* New York: Wiley.

CICOUREL, A. V., and J. KITSUSE
1963 *The educational decision makers.*
Indianapolis: Bobbs-Merrill.

COLEMAN, J. S.
1958 Academic achievement and the structure of
competition. *Harvard Educational Review,* 29:330-351.

354

1969 Segregation in the public schools. In
The human encounter, edited by S. Stoff and
H. Schwartzberg. New York: Harper & Row.

COLEMAN, J. S., et al.
1966 *Equality of educational opportunity.*
Washington, D.C.: U.S. Government Printing
Office.

DAVIS, A.
1951 What are some of the basic issues in the
relation of intelligence tests to cultural
background? In *Intelligence and cultural
differences,* edited by K. Eells, et al. Chicago:
University of Chicago Press.

DEUTSCH, J. A., and D. DEUTSCH
1963 Attention: Some theoretical considerations.
Psychological Review, 70:80-90.

DEUTSCH, M. et. al.
1967 *The disadvantaged child.* New York: Basic
Books.

DOLLARD, J.
1937 *Caste and class in a southern town.*
New Haven: Yale University Press.

DUBOIS, W. E. B. (Editor)
1914 *Morals and manners among negro Americans.*
Atlanta: Atlanta University Press.

EELLS, K., et al.
1951 *Intelligence and cultural differences.*
Chicago: University of Chicago Press.

EKSTROM, R.
1959 *Experimental studies of homogeneous
grouping: A review of the literature.* Princeton:
Educational Testing Service.

ERICKSON, S. A.
1970 *Language and being: An analytic phenomenology.* New Haven and London: Yale University Press.

ERVIN, S. M.
1964 Imitation and structual change in children's language. In *New directions in the study of language,* edited by E. H. Lennesberg. Cambridge, Massachusetts: MIT Press.

FARNHARM-DIGGORY, S.
1972 *Cognitive processes in education.* New York: Harper & Row.

FISHMAN, J. A.
1967 Bilingualism with and without diglossia, diglossia with and without bilingualism. *Journal of Social Issues,* 23:29-38.

FLAVELL, J. H.
1971 Stage-related properties of cognitive development. *Cognitive Psychology,* October: 421-453.

FRASER, C., U. BELLUGI, and R. BROWN
1963 Control of grammar in imitation, comprehension, and production. *Journal of Verbal Learning and Verbal Behavior.*

FREIRE, P.
1970 *Pedagogy of the oppressed.* New York: Herder & Herder.

GARFINKEL, H.
1959 Aspects of the problem of common sense knowledge of social structures. Transactions of the Fourth World Congress of Sociology. Belgium: International Sociological Association.

1960 The rational properties of scientific and
common sense activities. *Behavioral Science,*
5:72-83.

1963 Experiments with and conceptions of 'trust'
as a condition of concerted stable action. In
Motivation and social interaction, edited by
O. J. Harvey. New York: Ronald Press.

1967 *Studies in ethnomethodology.* Englewood
Cliffs: Prentice-Hall.

GARFINKEL, H., and H. SACKS
1970 The formal properties of practical action.
In *Theoretical sociology,* dited by J. C.
McKinney and E. Tiryakian. New York: Appleton-
Century-Crofts.

GLASMAN, L. D.
1968 A social-class comparison of conceptual
processes in children's free recall. Unpublished Ph.D. dissertation. Berkeley:
University of California.

GOFFMAN, E.
1959 *The presentation of self in everyday life.*
New York: Doubleday-Anchor.

1961 *Encounters.* Indianapolis: Bobbs-Merrill.

1971 *Relations in public.* New York: Basic
Books.

GOSLIN, D. A.
1965 *The school in contemporary society.*
Glenview, Illinois: Scott, Foresman.

GRAY, J. A., and A. A. WEDDERBURN
1960 Grouping strategies with simultaneous
stimuli. *Quarterly Journal of Experimental
Psychology,* 12:180-184.

GUMPERZ, J. J.
    1964 Linguistic and social interaction in two
    communities. In *The ethnography of communi-
    cation*, edited by J. J. Gumperz and D. Hymes.
    American Anthropologist 66, Part 2:137-153.

    1971 *Language in social groups*. Stanford:
    Stanford University Press.

GUMPERZ, J. J., and E. HERNANDEZ
    1971 Bilingualism, bidialectalism, and class-
    room interaction. In J. J. Gumperz, *Language
    in social groups*. Stanford: Stanford University
    Press.

HANNERZ, U.
    1969 *Soulside inquiries into gheto children
    and community*. Stockholm: Almquist and Wiksele.

HAVIGHURST, R. J.
    1951 What are the cultural differences which
    may affect performance on intelligence tests?
    In Eells, et al., *Intelligence and cultural
    differences*. Chicago: University of Chicago
    Press.

HESS, R. D., and V. C. SHIPMAN
    1968 Maternal influences upon early learning:
    The cognitive environments of urban preschool
    children. In *Early Education*, edited by R. D.
    Hess and R. M. Bear. Chicago: Aldine.

HOLT, J.
    1964 *How children fail*. New York: Pitman.

    1967 *How children learn*. New York: Pitman.

HYMES, D.
    1964 Introduction: Toward enthnographies of
    communication. In *The ethnography of com-
    munication*, edited by J. J. Gumperz and D.
    Hymes. American Anthropologists 66, Part 2:1-34.

1968   The ethnography of speaking.   In *Readings in the sociology of language*, edited by A. Fishman.   The Hague: Mouton.

ILG, F., and L. B. AMES
1964   *School readiness: Behavioral tests used at the Gesell Institute*.   New York: Harper & Row.

IMA, K.
1971   Dittoed lectures.   Illinois Institute of Technology.

JAMES, W.
1890   *The principles of psychology*.   New York: Henry Holt & Co.

JENNINGS, K. H.
1972   Language acquisition: The Development and Assessment of Rational and Rationalizable Skills.   Unpublished Ph.D. dissertation.   University of California, Santa Barbara.

JENNINGS, S. H. M.
1968   Linguistic comprehension in nursery and kindergarten children.   Unpublished M. A. thesis.   San Jose State College, San Jose, California.

1969   Report of continuing research in linguistic comprehension.   Seminar paper, Psychology Department, University of California, Santa Barbara.

JENSEN, A.
1969   How much can we boost IQ and scholastic achievement?   *Harvard Educational Review*, 39:1-123.

KATZ, J. J., and P. M. POSTAL
1964   *An integrated theory of linguistic descriptions*.   Cambridge, Massachusetts: MIT Press.

KEDDIE, N.
1971 Classroom knowledge. In *Knowledge and control*, edited by M. F. D. Young. London: Collier-Macmillan.

KJOLSETH, R.
1970 Bilingual education programs in the United States: For assimilation or pluralism? Socio-linguistics Program, 7th World Congress of Sociology, Varna, Bulgaria.

KLAPP, O. E.
1962 *Heroes, villains, and fools.* Englewood Cliffs: Prentice-Hall.

KLINEBERG, O.
1944 *Characteristics of the American negro.* New York: Harper & Bros.

KOHL, H.
1967 *36 children.* New York: New American Library.

KOLERS, P.
1972 Public lectures. Salk Institute and University of California, San Diego. January.

KOLERS, P., and J. R. POMERANTZ
1971 Figural change in apparent motion. *Journal of Experimental Psychology*, 87 (1):99-108.

KOZOL, J.
1967 *Death at an early age: The destruction of the hearts and minds of Negro children in the Boston public schools.* New York: Houghton-Mifflin.

LABOV, W.
1969 The logic of non-standard English. In *Linguistics and language study*, edited by G. Alatis, monograph 22. Washington, D.C.: Georgetown University Press.

1970 The study of language in its social context. *Studium Generale,* 23:30-87.

Manuscript. Contraction, deletion, and inherent variability of the english copula.

MORAY, N.
1959 Attention in dichotic listening: Affective cues and the influence of instructions. *Quarterly Journal of Experimental Psychology,* 11:56-60.

NAGEL, E.
1961 *The structure of science.* New York.

NEISSER, U.
1967 *Cognitive psychology.* New York: Appleton-Century Crofts.

NORMAN, D. A.
1969a *Memory and attention.* New York: Wiley.

1969b Memory while shadowing. *Quarterly Journal of Experimental Psychology,* 21.

OLSON, J.
1967 Should we group by ability? *Journal of Teacher Education,* 18:201-205.

PARSONS, T.
1937 *The Structure of Social Action.* Glencoe: The Free Press.

1969 The school class as a social system: Some of its functions in American society. *Harvard Educational Review,* 29:297-318.

PETTIGREW, T. A.
1964 *A profile of the Negro American.* Princeton: Van Nostrand.

PIAGET, J., and B. INHELDER
1969 Intellectual operations and their development. In *Intelligence*, Vol. VII, trans. T. Surridge. Experimental psychology, its scope and method edited by P. Fraisse and J. Piaget. New York: Basic Books.

PICK, H. L., and A. D. PICK
1970 Sensory and perceptual development. In *Carmichael's manual of child psychology*, edited by P. H. Mussen. New York: Wiley.

RAINWATER, L.
1970 *Behind ghetto walls*. Chicago: Aldine.

REISSMAN, F.
1967 *The culturally disadvantaged child*. New York: Basic Books.

ROSENTHAL, R., and L. JACOBSON
1968 *Pygmalian in the classroom*. New York: Holt, Rinehart and Winston.

SACKS, H.
1967-1972 Unpublished lecture notes. UCLA and UC Irvine.

SCHEFF, T.
1967a Toward a sociological model of concensus. *American Sociological Review*, 32:32-46.

1967b A theory of social coordination. *Sociometry*, 30:215-234.

SCHEGLOFF, E. A.
1969 Sequencing in conversational openings. *American Anthropologist*, 70:1075-1095.

1971 Notes on a conversational practice: Formulating place. In *Studies in interaction*, edited by D. Sudnow. New York: The Free Press.

362

SCHELLING, T. A.
1960 *The strategy of conflict.* New York:
Oxford.

SCHUTZ, A.
1962 *Collected papers I: The problem of social
reality.* The Hague: Martinus Nijhoff.

1964 *Collected papers II.* The Hague: Martinus
Nijhoff.

1970 *Reflection on the problem of relevance.*
New Haven: Yale University Press.

SHIBUTANI, T.
1969 *Improvised news.* New York: Bobbs-Merrill.

SHULEY, A. M.
1966 *The testing of Negro intelligence.*
New York: Social Science Press.

SLOBIN, D. I.
1967 A field manual for cross-cultural study
of the acquisition of communicative competence.
Berkeley, California.

1971 *Psycholinguistics.* San Francisco: Freeman.

SPEARMAN, C.
1904 General intelligence objectively determined
and measured. *American Journal of Psychology,*
15:2051-293

SPERLING, G. A.
1967 Successive Approximations to a Model for
Short-Term Memory. In A. F. Sanders (ed.),
Attention and Performance. Amsterdam: North-Holland.

STEIN, A.
1971 Strategies of failure. *Harvard Educational
Review,* 41:158-204.

STEWART, W. A.
1969 Historical and structural bases for the recognition of Negro dialect. In Schools of languages and linguistics, edited by G. Alatis. Monograph series #22. Georgetown University.

1970 Toward a history of American Negro dialect. In *Language and poverty,* edited by F. Williams. Boston: Markham Press.

STRONG, S. M.
1943 Social types in a minority group: Formulation of a method. *American Journal of Sociology,* 48:563-573.

SZWED, J. F.
1970 *Black America.* New York: Basic Books.

THORNDIKE, R. L.
1968 Intelligence and intelligence testing. In *International encyclopedia of the social science,* edited by D. L. Stills. The Macmillan Company, The Free Press, vol. 7:421-429.

TRIESMAN, A. M.
1960 Contextual cues in selective listening. *Quarterly Journal of Experimental Psychology,* 12:242-248.

VALENTINE, C. A.
1971 Deficit, difference, and bicultural models of Afro-American behavior. *Harvard Educational Review,* 41:137-158.

WIEDER, D. L.
1969 Dittoed lecture notes.

WILSON, T. P.
1970 Conceptions of Interaction in Forms of Sociological Explanation. *American Sociological Review,* 35:697-710.

WOOD, H. L.
   1969   Zato coding as a model for ethnomethodology.
   Unpublished paper.   University of California,
   Santa Barbara.

ZIMMERMAN, D. H.
   1970   The practicalities of rule use.   In *Understanding everyday life,* edited by J. D. Douglas.
   Chicago: Aldine.

ZIMMERMAN, D. H., and M. POLLNER
   1970   The everyday world as a phenomenon.   In
   Understanding everyday life, edited by J. D.
   Douglas.   Chicago: Aldine.

SUBJECT INDEX

A 4
B 5
C 6
D 7
E 8
F 9
G 0
H 1
I 2
J 3